Italian Children's Literature and National Identity

"This is a timely, elegantly written, and very well researched study of the first fifty years of children's literature in united Italy, between this country's political unification (1861) and the beginning of fascism (1922). Truglio's book convincingly demonstrates the presence, throughout literary and cultural texts of this time period, of a pervasive analogy between the maturation of a child and the modernization of a nation. It is a must-read for all students and scholars seriously interested in the history of Italian and children's literature."

—*Cristina Mazzoni, University of Vermont, USA*

This book bridges the fields of Children's Literature and Italian Studies by examining how turn-of-the-century children's books forged a unified national identity for the new Italian State. Through contextualized close readings of a wide range of texts, Truglio shows how the nineteenth-century concept of recapitulation, which held that ontogeny (the individual's development) repeats phylogeny (the evolution of the species), underlies the strategies of this corpus. Italian fairy tales, novels, poems, and short stories imply that the personal development of the child corresponds to and hence naturalizes the modernizing development of the nation. In the context of Italy's uneven and ambivalent modernization, these narrative trajectories are enabled by a developmental melancholia. Using a psychoanalytic lens, and in dialogue with recent Anglophone Children's Literature criticism, this study proposes that national identity was constructed via a process of renouncing and incorporating paternal and maternal figures, rendered as compulsory steps into maturity and modernity. With chapters on the heroic figure of Garibaldi, the Orientalized depiction of the South, and the role of girls in formation narratives, this book discloses how melancholic itineraries produced gendered national subjects. This study engages both well-known Italian texts, such as Collodi's *The Adventures of Pinocchio* and De Amicis's *Heart*, and books that have fallen into obscurity by authors such as Baccini, Treves, Gianelli, and Nuccio. Its approach and corpus shed light on questions being examined by Italianists, Children's Literature scholars, and social and cultural historians with an interest in national identity formation.

Maria Truglio is Associate Professor of Italian and Women's Gender and Sexuality Studies at Pennsylvania State University, USA.

Children's Literature and Culture
Jack Zipes, *Founding Series Editor*
Philip Nel, *Current Series Editor*

For a full list of titles in this series, please visit www.routledge.com.

Italian Children's Literature and National Identity

Childhood, Melancholy, Modernity

Maria Truglio

Routledge
Taylor & Francis Group

NEW YORK AND LONDON

First published 2018
by Routledge
711 Third Avenue, New York, NY 10017

and by Routledge
2 Park Square, Milton Park, Abingdon, Oxon OX14 4RN

*Routledge is an imprint of the Taylor & Francis Group,
an informa business*

Library of Congress Cataloging-in-Publication Data
Names: Truglio, Maria, author.
Title: Italian children's literature and national identity:
childhood, melancholy, modernity / by Maria Truglio.
Description: New York: Routledge, 2016. | Series: Children's
literature and culture; 123 | Includes bibliographical references
and index.
Identifiers: LCCN 2017013896 (print) | LCCN 2017015826
(ebook)
Subjects: LCSH: Children's literature, Italian—History and
criticism. | National characteristics, Italian, in literature.
Classification: LCC PQ4199.5 (ebook) | LCC PQ4199.5 .T78
2016 (print) | DDC 850.9/9282—dc23
LC record available at https://lccn.loc.gov/2017013896

ISBN: 978-1-138-24340-8 (hbk)
ISBN: 978-1-315-27226-9 (ebk)

Typeset in Sabon
by codeMantra

for Jon

Contents

List of Figures

Acknowledgments

The words of gratitude that I can express here will surely fail to do justice to the generosity of the many colleagues, friends, and family members who have supported me during this project. Like Pipino, I will start at the end. I thank the editors from Routledge's Children's Literature and Culture Series: Philip Nel, Erin Little, and Elizabeth Levine, for their guidance and work on the manuscript. I am also grateful to the three peer evaluators for their careful reviews of the manuscript and insightful suggestions. The "leg work" for this project could not have been completed without the financial support that enabled research at the New York Public Library, Florence's Biblioteca Nazionale, the libraries at Yale and Harvard, and the Giunti Archives in Florence. I thank the Children's Literature Association for the Faculty Research Grant that got me started in the early stages of this project. I am also deeply grateful to Penn State's Institute for the Arts and Humanities (now the Humanities Institute) for two Individual Faculty Grants, which funded summer travel to Italy, and a Residency Fellowship, which enabled time for writing.

I am also indebted to the librarians and archivists with whom I worked for their expertise and generosity: Aldo Cecconi, Curator at the Giunti Archive in Florence; Sandra Stelts, Curator of Rare Books and Manuscripts at Penn State's Special Collections Library; and Manuel Ostos, Librarian for Romance Languages and Literatures at Penn State's Arts and Humanities Library.

This project has benefited from the helpful constructive criticism on drafts and from insightful feedback on conference presentations offered by colleagues at Penn State and elsewhere. I thank especially Paola Gambarota, Cristina Della Coletta, Jonathan Eburne, Johanna Rossi Wagner, Sherry Roush, Martina Kolb, Sarah Salter, John Ochoa, Carey Eckhardt, and the peer reviewers at *Children's Literature* who evaluated the article on Garibaldi that became the foundation of Chapter 1. My department heads who encouraged and supported this project at various stages—John Lipski, Bob Blue, Chip Gerfen, and Giuli Dussias—have my deep gratitude. I thank Children's Literature colleagues who provided a sense of community as well as feedback and mentorship: Daniel Hade, Laura Tosi, Lindsay Myers, Carl Miller, Marina Balina, and

Judith Plotz. I thank, too, all the Penn State students who have taken IT 430 "La letteratura infantile" and thus gave me a forum to share and refine the ideas that went into this book. I am deeply grateful to my colleague and "work husband" Nicolás Fernández-Medina, and my teacher, mentor, and friend Paolo Valesio.

I have been blessed with friends who have lent all manner of tangible and intangible support, especially during the dark period that coincided with this project, and I thank them *di vero cuore*: Jennifer Mittelstadt, Wes Franklin, Andrew Belmonte, Willa Silverman, Ernest Wachter, Rob Harper-Mangels, David Karp, Heather McCoy, Hilary Link, Rena Torres Cacoullos, Jennifer Monahan, and Gayle Grasso.

My parents Mario and Rose Truglio have spent a life time supporting my siblings and me, providing our education and encouraging us to pursue our goals. I am grateful for the foundations they laid and the support they continue to give. My sister Donna Haverty-Stacke has been a friend, hostess, sounding board, cheerleader, commiserater, confidant, and far more. My brother Joe(y) Truglio is my partner-in-crime, role model, and sanity-maintainer. I thank them both with the deepest love.

My sons Anthony Michael and Thomas Santino are my world. Among the best memories of my life are the times spent reading to and with them. They have my gratitude, admiration, and love always. This book is dedicated to Jon Bernhard, whose spirit is always with me and whose love has never left me.

Introduction
Two Grams of Melancholy

quel sentimento di italianità e di modernità che pure vogliamo insegnare.

[that feeling of Italian identity and of modernity that we also want to teach.]
—Scipio Sighele, *Eva moderna* 1910 p. 182

Pinocchio, as rendered by Disney's well-known film, eagerly strives to become a "real boy." What did becoming a proper boy (a more precise rendering of Carlo Collodi's "un ragazzo perbene") mean for the children reading Collodi's work and the hundreds of other books marketed for Italian youth at the turn of the last century? This study examines how the corpus of Italian children's literature construed the categories of "childhood" and "Italy" in the years between Italy's political unification (1861) and the rise of fascism (1922). I consider here approximately 40 such texts within the context of contemporary literacy rates, educational reform legislation, and the multiplicity of Italian dialects, with attention to how these issues varied according to class, gender, and region. I argue that these critically understudied books forged an analogy between Italy's modernization and a child's maturation, and made that analogy seem natural and necessary.

Informed by post-structuralist and psychoanalytic interpretive techniques and grounded by sociological and historical concerns, this study examines how books for children naturalized the link between modernization and maturation, and how they mobilized that link for Italy's national project. My aim in this study is to analyze how texts for children written after unification and before fascism, or during the early years of the unified state, simultaneously constituted that period as Italy's "childhood." I argue that these texts deploy a strategy of developmental melancholia: their narratives plot a course for Italy and for Italian children to grow up by abandoning and incorporating father figures (especially Garibaldi) and mother figures (especially the South, often described as feminine). One focus of my study is how the metaphor of the nation's infancy was disseminated. The novels, poems, fairy tales, and short stories of the post-unification era did not arise from or react to any actual status of Italy as child. Rather than serving as the "ground" for these children's books, the notion of Italy being in its infancy or childhood was instead the *effect* of this corpus of books. In other words, what has come to interest me is how the texts themselves constituted (rather than described) an image of a nation that must "grow up" with its children and that must modernize—economically, technologically, and politically—as its citizens matured cognitively, morally, and psychologically.

At times, children's books overtly formulated this overlay of child-as-nation and nation-as-child. One example comes from the very popular novel by Luigi Bertelli, who wrote under the pen name "Vamba." Gianni Stoppani, the young protagonist of Vamba's beloved *Il giornalino di Gian Burrasca* (1907–1908 in installments, 1912 as volume) [*Johnny Whirlwind's Notebook*] is born on September 20. Underscored in the illustration (see Figure I.1), Gianni's birthday falls on the same date on which Italian national troops entered Rome in 1870, marking the final phase of Italian unification. Thus, Gianni shares his birthday with Italy. In other texts, child protagonists share their proper names with the new nation. Carolina Invernizio tells the sentimental tale of a boy who was orphaned by the Messina earthquake. After much heartache and sacrifice, he is taken in by a wealthy Florentine merchant, and the narrator observes in conclusion that "[v]i è sempre una Provvidenza per i fanciulli buoni, che hanno il cuore generoso e devoto come quello del nostro Italo" [there is always a Providence for good children who have a generous and devout heart, like the one our Italo has] (*Cuori* 28).[1] The first name of the good-hearted boy and the author's use of "our" to describe him invite a double reading: Providence will watch over child and nation as they grow. Similarly, Sofia Bisi Albini names the most spontaneous and openhearted of the eight Darieni children "Itala" in her popular 1887 novel *Una nidiata* [*A Brood*]. A final, more humorous example of the association of Italy and child comes from Paolo Lorenzini, whose uncle was Carlo Lorenzini (Carlo Collodi), author of *Pinocchio*, and who wrote under the pen name "Collodi Nipote" [Collodi's nephew]. In his satiric *Sussi e Biribissi: Storia di un viaggio verso il centro della terra* (1902) [*Sussi and Biribissi: Story of a Voyage to the Center of the Earth*], the young protagonists Sussi and Biribissi undertake a (mis)adventure inspired by Jules Verne. At one point, Florence's police commissioner interrogates Sussi about his friends. Asked whether or not his comrades are adults, Sussi promptly replies, "no, sono italiani" [no, they are Italians] (165). Beyond these local identifications of children with Italy, and vice versa, a wide range of texts, as I argue, deploy this nation-as-child effect more broadly. The isomorphic construction and its use in "making Italians" emerge from the way in which these books leveraged two epistemological paradigms: recapitulation and melancholia.

Ecco fatto. Ho voluto ricopiare qui in questo mio giornalino il foglietto del calendario d'oggi che segna l'entrata delle truppe italiane in Roma e che è anche il giorno che son nato io come ci ho scritto sotto perché gli amici che vengono in casa si ricordino di farmi il regalo.

Figure I.1 Luigi Bertelli [Vamba], from *Il giornalino di Gian Burrasca*.

"In Search of a Nation"

In her study *The Pinocchio Effect: On Making Italians* (2008), Suzanne Stewart-Steinberg notes that "[t]he history of Italy between the founding of the unifying constitutional monarchy in 1861 and the rise of fascism in 1922 is the history of a state in search of a nation. It is the history of a fragile political structure in search of a national culture that would authenticate and legitimate it" (1). The present study addresses how turn-of-the-century children's books participated in this process. Specifically, I argue that the popular nineteenth-century evolutionary concept of recapitulation, which held that ontogeny, or the individual's development, repeats phylogeny, or the development of the species, undergirds the ideological agenda of this body of texts. As adumbrated most directly by Ernst Haeckel in his texts, which appeared in Italian translation in the late nineteenth century, this theory in the strict sense was a biological one: the individual human fetus in its physiological development during gestation goes through, in a rapid and telescoped fashion, stages that are morphologically parallel to those through which the human species developed over the course of history.[2] For children's literature, the outlines of this isomorphic construction took on a wide range of associations, enabled in part by the claims of contemporary science that moral character and behaviors had a biological grounding. Many of these children's books establish an implicit correspondence between the personal development of the child and the modernizing development of the nation. These narratives suggest that just as a human individual must grow from a naïve, untamed, and bestial imp into a mature, productive, and rational adult, so too the nation must progress from rural, feudal, and local relations to urban, capitalist, and national structures.

To preview one example here, Luigi Capuana's *Scurpiddu* (1898) [*Nimble-Legs*], which I analyze in more depth in Chapter 2, urges this double forward trajectory through its tale of a lost orphaned boy in rural Sicily. Scurpiddu's path to maturation includes learning the correct Italian rather than local dialect names for everyday objects, traveling to the city of Catania to be amazed by telegraphs and the railway, and eventually embracing a definable, regimented identity as a soldier in the national army. Along the way, the boy must also cut his unruly hair and forget the painful memories of his mother. Capuana's text establishes a set of oppositions: feminine, rural, local identities are associated with childhood and must give way to the masculine, urban, national values that define the adult. Such texts solder the analogy between national modernization and personal maturation, and have the effect of making modernization appear as inevitable as the human body's physiological growth and as necessary as an individual's moral and intellectual development.

Recapitulation in Italy

In his study of the intersections between psychoanalysis and the field of children's literature, Kenneth Kidd summarizes the nineteenth-century evolutionary concept of recapitulation and points to the range of applications to which it was put by practitioners of many disciplines. Kidd reminds us especially of the maneuver that Jacqueline Rose elucidated in her 1984 study of Peter Pan: that by which the supposedly "natural" association of children with fairy tales derives from a "metanarrative" that equates children with the folk. Kidd elaborates on how the notion that "ontogeny recapitulates phylogeny" was deployed to create hierarchies in many fields, including psychoanalysis. These hierarchies claimed that children, criminals, "primitive" cultures, and "young nations" could all be seen as immature (3–4).

In the Italian context, Cesare Lombroso (1835–1909) was the most influential voice in the scientific community in regard to disseminating the evolutionary-based concept of recapitulation, in this case through promoting the theory of atavism specifically and biologically determined understandings of behavior generally.[3] In her recent study of sexology in Italy, Chiara Beccalossi summarizes, "Lombroso's conception of evolution—like that of many Italian scientists of the time—was a synthesis of philosophical, biological, and anthropological theories drawn from authors such as Herbert Spencer, Jacob Moleschott, Ernst Haeckel," and others (119). In a departure from the then-dominant school of classical penology, which understood criminal acts as the result of an individual's free will, Lombroso sought to understand criminal behavior as grounded in a person's nature. This new understanding of criminality was based on the concept of atavism or "the reappearance in a modern context of elements typical of earlier stages of the development of the human species" (120). Lombroso's mobilization of atavism to account for deviance derived from recapitulation and implied that the criminal belonged to an "underdeveloped stage of human development" (121).[4] Similarly, Lombroso relied on recapitulation as the epistemological mechanism through which to account not only for criminals and deviants but also for women: "Haeckel's law of recapitulation also helped Lombroso to explain the position of women in the evolutionary process: they were in an infantile and inferior state because their process of development in thousands of years of evolution had been halted at an earlier stage than men" (Beccalossi 136). The notion that women are atavistically attached to earlier stages of human development informs my analysis of the representation of girls in this corpus of children's books, and in Chapter 3, I examine a broad range of articulations that this gendered use of recapitulation enabled.

In the period I am examining, several specific intersections between Cesare Lombroso and his followers on the one hand and children's authors on the other demonstrate that these notions of recapitulation were not simply "in the air" at the time but rather were disseminated through various networks of the cultural and intellectual elite. The Sicilian writer Luigi Capuana, for example, who penned multiple collections of some of the most popular fairy tales and several novels for children, dedicated a volume of two short stories, *Un vampiro* [*A Vampire*], to Cesare Lombroso in 1907, prefacing that volume with a letter to the criminal anthropologist hailing him as an "illustrious friend."[5] Edmondo De Amicis, author of the highly influential *Cuore* (1886) [*Heart*], collaborated with Lombroso and 11 other "friends" at a scholarly conference in Turin in 1880, in which various perspectives were offered in the examination of the effects of wine.[6] In the preface to his 1881 publication on this topic, De Amicis in fact somewhat jokingly notes that his own intervention aims to describe the effects of wine in the early inebriating phases, before excess drinking leads men to fall into Prof. Lombroso's hands—that is, before it leads to criminality (*Gli effetti psicologici* 3).[7] Cesare Lombroso's own daughter, Paola Lombroso Carraro (1871–1954), not only actively participated in scientific endeavors alongside her father and her husband as author of several psychological and sociological studies, but also wrote numerous books and fairy tales for children. She contributed to the journal *Corriere dei Piccoli* [*The Little People's Courier*] and penned such works as *Un reporter nel mondo degli uccelli* (1911) [*A Reporter in the Bird World*] and *Storia di una bambina e di una bambola* (1914) [*The Story of a Girl and Her Doll*].[8] Finally among these examples, Antonio Fogazzaro (1842–1911), well-known novelist and also a major voice in Catholic modernism and promoter of Christian evolutionism, wrote a laudatory preface to the 1903 edition of Sofia Bisi Albini's children's novel *Donnina forte* (1879) [*Strong Little Woman*].[9] The most popular children's writers and the leading figures in the evolutionary-based scientific community, then, had concrete encounters and exchanges. Rather than arguing, however, that these fiction writers took from Lombroso or from his followers' specific concepts about atavism, recapitulation, or gender, I suggest that cross-fertilization between the sciences and literary texts mutually supported these paradigms. We can recall, for example, that Lombroso cites local proverbs, literature, and anecdotes along with his photographs of criminals and tables of anatomical measurements in arguing for a corporeal legibility of deviance. Scipio Sighele, too, in *Eva moderna* (1910) [*Modern Eve*] draws not only on Lombroso and Otto Weininger but also culls material from Émile Zola, Honoré de Balzac, Sibilla Aleramo, Gabriele D'Annunzio, and other fiction writers to mount his arguments.

The pervasiveness of this paradigm and its broad use as an epistemological framework can be detected not only in the general structure of many narratives—the itineraries of their plots and protagonists—but also in brief descriptions in which the presupposition of recapitulation is not the effect but the invisible mechanism that enables the effects. For example, in *Il trionfo dei piccoli* (1915) [*The Little Ones' Triumph*], author Arpalice Cuman Pertile creates a sense of the endearing innocence and naiveté of her very young protagonists, the twins Franco and Luisa.[10] At about three months old, they take their first trip in an electric tram (*tranvai*). When he is a few years older, Franco narrates his memories of that day, describing it as "il nostro primo giretto per la città nel gran carrozzone che va senza cavalli" [our first little outing in the city in the big carriage that runs without horses] (55). The voice of the child describing a tram in this manner clearly renders that voice precious and "innocent." Franco here attempts to assimilate new experiences or stimuli by relating them to earlier and more familiar images to which they are similar. This process dramatizes the individual's cognitive developmental process and also, echoing Giovanni Pascoli's romantic poetics of the *fanciullino* [little child], captures the childlike vision of marvel and wonder before the world, allowing us as readers to see the familiar in a poetically defamiliarized way.[11] However, a child born into an already modern world, and one who, like Pertile's Franco, is already zipping through the city in an electric tram at three months old and who has not elsewhere in the book been described as interacting with horses, would not necessarily have to assimilate the novelty of the tram into a preexisting schema of horse and carriage, because for that individual child, the tram *is* the initial impression. Indeed, it is perhaps more likely that such a child would eventually, upon seeing a horse and carriage, have the impression that it was an odd kind of nonelectric tram. In other words, Pertile here is collapsing a historical development (in this case, of the technologies of transportation) into the biological development of the individual, as if each child, in his or her attempts to understand the world, had to replay the progression of the species in the same chronological order. Such a maneuver also has the effect of making the progression from horse-drawn carriage to tram seem as natural as the biological and cognitive development of an individual child. The sentence and its charming effects simultaneously rely on and disseminate the recapitulation theory. I argue in the present study that this kind of maneuver subtends not only specific narrative moments like this one from Pertile's novel, but also the plot structure of a substantial corpus of texts, and that it allowed writers to map modernity and maturity together.

Modernity all'italiana

The Italian experience of modernity, as has been well documented, was fraught with ambivalence, and Italy's modernization process, often described as "belated," generated anxieties that are refracted through the books written for and marketed to Italian children. For Italy, "modernity" in the decades between unification and fascism included a range of specific transformations that affected different areas of the peninsula unevenly and at different rates, and that indeed were often hotly contested and debated.[12] Of particular relevance in the lives of children, the Casati (1859), Coppino (1877), Orlando (1904), and Daneo-Credaro (1911) education laws sought to combat high rates of illiteracy and to promote the national standard idiom rather than local dialects. Family life underwent a change in the post-unification era, as the dominant model transitioned from the traditional extended structure to the modern nuclear family (Myers, *Making* 20–21). The extremely limited franchise that had been established with the birth of the nation was gradually expanded: the 1882 electoral reform gave the right to vote to all men who could prove literacy, and the 1913 elections were the first held under universal manhood suffrage (Lyttelton 243, 258). Technological developments in various fields included notably the founding of FIAT in Turin in 1899, with 71 car firms in Italy by 1907 (Clark 125), and the first military use of the airplane in Italy's colonial war against Turkey in Libya (1911–1912). Writers and activists such as Sibilla Aleramo (1876–1960), Anna Maria Mozzoni (1837–1920), and Anna Kuliscioff (1857–1925) gave growing visibility to the feminist movement. Indeed, the field of children's literature itself can be seen as an effect of modernity, in that the social changes enabled by industrialization and capitalism led to the creation of a market of middle-class children whose families had enough money to purchase books for pleasure and enough time and education to read them.[13] The perception of these changes as both deeply threatening and yet urgently necessary emerges in the texts I will discuss throughout this study: texts that themselves were products and instruments of modernity, or as Spinazzola calls them, a "prodotto tipico della modernità" [a quintessential product of modernity] (9). Passages from two books of the period that include the word "modern" in their titles illustrate and nuance these broader points.

Ida Baccini's *Memorie di un pulcino* (1875) [*Memoirs of a Little Chick*], which I discuss in more detail in Chapter 2, was one of the most popular children's texts of the period. Already established as a major voice in children's literature because of that success, Baccini includes a preface that expresses a particularly fraught experience of "modernity" in a later book she wrote for older readers, entitled *Libro moderno, ossia nuove letture per la gioventù* (1887) [*A Modern Book, or, New Readings for Young People*]. In the form of an imaginary dialogue between the author and a reader, Baccini's alter ego expresses her desire to write "un romanzo educativo" [an edifying novel] but laments that no one nowadays wants to publish such a text (v). Instead, "è necessario fabbricare i soliti mosaici, le solite enciclopedie da una lira e cinquanta, dove si passa bruscamente da un soggetto all'altro, dove si sfiora tutto, senza approfondir nulla" [one must construct the usual mosaics, the usual encyclopedias that go for a buck fifty, the kind of book that moves abruptly from one topic to the next, skimming over everything without ever going into any depth] (vi). What the author acquiesces to produce in light of these market demands, and what she gives to her readers under the "appropriate" title "Modern Book," is a collection of short chapters on topics as diverse as George Washington's mother, the Italian writer Ugo Foscolo, and the advantages of poverty. The prefatory dialogue, then, depicts the modern world as one that is suffering from a range of *losses*: loss of depth, loss of coherence, and loss of value. Such losses result in reading, writing, and publishing practices—and, implicitly, lived experience—that were rushed, superficial, and cheap. The "author" here poses as a valiant and yet doomed quixotic hero, fighting back the tidal wave of time, reluctantly agreeing to produce a disjointed "mosaic" with the promise that it will, at least, be the best mosaic possible. Of course, the work she produced leveraged in its very title the commercial appeal of the "modern" and the "new." The dialogue form itself, in which the reader/consumer is given a voice, dramatizes the condition of writing in response to market demands. Written in correct Italian, the volume contributed to the modernizing agenda of promoting literacy in the standard Italian to Italy's "youth," thus feeding that market. Indeed, the more traditionally minded authors who overtly bemoaned the transitions wrought by modernization often ran up against this conundrum: the conditions of possibility for their own texts and their very readership were in fact products of this lamented modernity.

Although not a writer for children, Scipio Sighele (1868–1913) produced several sociological and criminological studies that disseminated in Italy evolutionary-based concepts such as recapitulation and atavism, as well as notions of sexual difference that built on the influential works of Cesare Lombroso and Otto Weininger, all of which found various articulations in the children's literature of the period.[14] In his 1910 study *Eva moderna*, Sighele expresses a common reaction to the effects of modernity, here specifically framed in the context of proposing the proper form that public primary education should take for girls:

> Se vogliamo che le generazioni future siano fisicamente più sane e quindi moralmente più equilibrate di questa nostra generazione ove i nervi sono i terribili despoti del nostro organismo, e la nevrastenia è, più che un'eccezione morbosa, la triste regola generale, bisognerà pure che noi pensiamo ad educare la donna in modo ch'essa possa trasmettere ai suoi figli un sangue purificato dall'ossigeno dell'aria libera. (188–189)

> [If we want future generations to be physically healthier and thus morally more sound than this current generation of ours, for whom the nerves are terrible despots of our organism, and neurasthenia is, more than a morbid exception, the sad general rule, we will need to educate women in such a way that they will be able to transmit to their children a blood purified by the oxygen of fresh air.]

Throughout his study, Sighele vigorously promotes the modern agendas of granting women the right to vote, legalizing divorce, and expanding compulsory, secular, public education for boys and girls. Yet here and elsewhere—he had previously lamented "la nostra vita affrettata e febbrile" [our frantic and febrile life] (152), for example—he also evinces a sense of modernity as inherently diseased, as making nervous ailments the norm rather than the exception, and, implicitly, as feminizing all Italians by producing a whole generation of hysterics. The remedy he proposes relies on nature, on taking girls out of the diseased urban areas, out of the "fumose e assordanti città" [smoky and deafening cities] (187), in order to send them to school in the healthy country, so that they can transmit their rehabilitated strength and vibrancy to their offspring via their cleansed "blood." Paradoxically, and symptomatic of the ambiguous experience of modernity I am indexing here, Sighele proposes that the solution to the feminizing effects of the modern city is to send girls to the country to become "stronger" (187), more robust, and indeed more masculine. Sighele here not only claims a biological basis for moral behavior (as I noted above), but also discloses the fundamental implication of gender in the discourses that sought to lay hold of and diagnose modernity.

While Sighele's text typifies many of the contemporary reactions to social and economic changes, he tellingly puts into focus how these clusters of anxieties about modernization were tied specifically to the question of Italian identity.[15] In his discussion of educational reform, he asserts that he himself would never judge anyone else's personal religious beliefs. However, in terms of national policy, he insists that the Church cannot be expected to promulgate "quel sentimento di italianità e di modernità che pure vogliamo insegnare" [that feeling of Italian identity and of modernity that we also want to teach] (182). Secularism, modernization, and Italianness are here mobilized as of a piece, as all mutually implying and depending on each other.[16] If, then, modernity was being experienced as a loss—loss of depth, of nature, of coherence, of religion, of health, of gender stability—and as a fractured superficiality, like the flat tesserae of a mosaic, then what does this link imply about "Italianness"? I argue in this study that, in the domain of children's literature, evolutionary recapitulation was the mechanism by which Italianness-as-modernization was naturalized, while melancholia was the structure through which the experience of modernity as loss could be made meaningful and effectively constitute Italian subjectivity.

"The Poetry of Sad Things": Melancholy

In his preface to a collection of six short stories for children, published in 1890, the Neapolitan intellectual Michele Ricciardi remarked, "se ne potrebbe dare facilmente una ricetta: prendi dieci grammi di eroico, due di malinconico e fa' un libro per fanciulli" [one could easily write up a recipe for children's literature in our culture: take ten grams of heroism, add two grams of melancholy, and you've got a children's book] (9).[17] Ricciardi goes on to extoll the collected stories, written by the young author Giuseppe Errico, by claiming that they will break out of this formulaic, predictable mold and offer a more complete vision of children and their lives. Alas, even Errico seems to be following the same "recipe": many of his stories tell sentimental tales of children who have suffered the loss of loved ones. Ricciardi here perceives, though he does not analyze, the "dominant notes" resonating through the late-nineteenth-century corpus of children's books, somber notes that would in fact echo into the twentieth.[18]

The ingredient of melancholy so necessary to cooking up a children's book was perhaps best defined by Edmondo De Amicis himself.[19] In his discussion of the effects of wine, De Amicis had included "melancholy" among his list of reactions experienced by some people after too much drinking. His definition aptly describes the tone generated by his own novel *Cuore* and by so many other books that imitated or were influenced by that novel. Wine, De Amicis claims, can often elicit in the drinker "the sentiment of sad things, or rather, the sentiment of the poetry of sad things" (*Il vino* 22).[20] Rather than defining melancholy as a direct apprehension of or response to an event ("sad things"), De Amicis adds a clarification that insists on the mediation of "poetry" in the experience of melancholy. This textualization of melancholy, which endows it with a certain pleasure, operates throughout the children's books I analyze, books that deploy melancholy as a developmental itinerary.[21]

The "sad things" that trigger the melancholic tones of Italian children's literature often include death. Indeed, deaths are not only virtually omnipresent in the corpus, but often serve as the precipitating event that enables the subsequent narrative. In Virginia Treves's *Piccoli eroi* (1892) [*Little Heroes*], the protagonist Maria must take charge of her younger siblings because her mother had died. In Ida Baccini's *I piccoli viaggiatori: Viaggio in China* (1878) [*The Little Travelers: Trip to China*], young Carlino is sent on a sea voyage because, since his father's death, his mother has been unable to discipline him properly. Sofia Bisi Albini dedicates her novel *Una nidiata* to Maria, who, having died, will never be able to read it.[22] Bisi Albini thus conjures the specter of this dead girl at the very opening of her narrative, casting a shadow over the story of the Darieni clan. The novel focuses particularly on the withdrawn and discontented oldest siblings, Silvio and Sandra, who are described several times as melancholic (4, 49, 86) while they navigate their way into adulthood. The counterpoint provided by their more carefree younger siblings suggests that the death of youth has elicited this torpor. Errico's collection opens with a tale called "La morte della nonna" ["Grandma's death"], and the title story is triggered by the narrator's memory of his dear childhood companions: a lamb named Michele, who had to be sold, and his dog Mily, who died soon after.[23] Carolina Invernizio's *Cuori dei bimbi* (1915) [*Kids' Hearts*] begins with a description of the Messina earthquake, which buried almost an entire family under the rubble.

The surviving boy must travel north to Florence, his experiences giving rise to the story. Similarly, Invernizio's *I sette capelli d'oro della Fata Gusmara* (1909) [*The Seven Golden Hairs of the Fairy Gusmara*] opens with the blunt declaration that the young protagonist's mother had died when he was three years old.[24] Since that moment, his father has fallen into a mute torpor with all the hallmark symptoms of a deep depression, remaining "chiuso nel suo mutismo, senza curarsi del bimbo" [enclosed in his silence, unable to care for the boy] (3), and young Falco seems fated to grow up with a "sorriso melanconico, triste" [sad and melancholy smile] (3).[25]

We can discern more specifically how Italian children's books mobilized losses as the enabling condition for melancholic narratives by looking at the opening of an extremely popular early text: Ida Baccini's *Memorie di un pulcino*.[26] This best-selling text, which enlivens its heavy-handed didacticism through the use of charming animal characters and engaging language,[27] opens with a traumatic loss—the death of the chick's father:

> Nacqui a Vespignano, nel Mugello, in Toscana, l'anno 1874.
> Il babbo non l'ho conosciuto, e tutte le volte che ne domandavo alla mamma, era una scena da far intenerire anche i sassi. Si metteva a schiammazzare in modo compassionevole, e fra quei suoi gridi raccapezzavo a stento qualche cosa, come per esempio, girarrosto, fuoco, tirare il collo e altre piacevolezze dello stesso genere.
> Io, come potete immaginarvi, ero in quel tempo troppo piccino per capire come fosse andata la faccenda; ma fin d'allora cominciai a non poter più soffrir gli spiedi, e quando per cercar la mamma ero costretto a far capolino nella cucina della massaia, mi sentivo venire i bordoni. (29)

> [I was born in Vespignano, in the Mugello region of Tuscany (north of Florence) in 1874. I never knew my dad. Anytime I tried to ask my mom about him, it stirred up a scene that would make even stones cry. She would start making such a pitiful fuss, and between those cries of hers I would scrape together bit by bit a few things, like, for example "spit," "fire," "wring his neck" and other pleasantries of this sort. As you can well imagine, at that time I was too little to understand how the whole thing had happened. But ever since then, I was no longer to stand the sight of a spit, and whenever I had to peek into the farmer's kitchen to look for my mom, I would get goose bumps.]

The violence evoked by the passage is mitigated to a degree by displacing the narrative from the human to the animal world, using a chick rather than a child as the protagonist. Nevertheless, the direct address to the readers forges a link, eliciting a relationship of empathy between reader and protagonist who share the condition of being "too little." Indeed, while shifting the developmental itinerary meant as a model for human children onto the chick helps soften the blows of this violence, at the same time, this gesture also legitimates the use of such disciplining techniques. Children, like animals, must be tamed, and indeed, the domesticating virtues of obedience, forgiveness, and patience are the fundamental lessons the chick learns in this text.[28] Furthermore, the way in which the chick must retroactively construe the traumatic loss through the mother's narration of it replicates the reader's position: both chick and child reader learn about the father's death through words rather than as witnesses, and both must "piece together" the story by putting together the verbal fragments, as if assembling a mosaic from so many tesserae.

In Chapter 1, I analyze in more depth the theme of lost father figures and how children's books offered the image of Giuseppe Garibaldi within that context. I want to underscore how the story of the loss of the father initiates the chick's developmental journey, one that will force him to abandon "liberty" and his mother as he moves from country to city (87). At the same time, this opening memory creates fractures and gaps, as indicated by the list of disconnected words punctuated by sobs. Like these verbal gaps, the psychological wounds from that initiating loss do not heal, as the chick continues to suffer painful emotional reactions "since then."[29] Indeed, it is in the question of healing that Freud initially locates a distinction between mourning and melancholia. While the mourning process is "extraordinarily painful," Freud underscores that "when the work of mourning is completed the ego becomes free and uninhibited again" (Mourning 245). In contrast, "[t]he complex of melancholia behaves like an open wound" (252), and its unconscious mechanisms make it impossible to discern how exactly it comes to an end (257).

Sigmund Freud's initial analysis of melancholy ("Mourning and Melancholia" from 1915, published in 1917) led him to describe this depressive state as a pathological form of mourning. Unlike mourning, with which it shares many visible features, melancholy does not end with the freeing of the ego's cathexis to a lost love-object; it does not always have an identifiable precipitating cause in empirical reality (such as the death of a loved one); and it manifests itself not only in the kind of emotional withdrawal and pain typical of "profound mourning," but especially in "self-reproach." Melancholy, he goes on to postulate, entails an identification with, rather than a letting go of, the lost object, and is marked by a "regression of libido into the ego" (258). The deep ambivalence attached to that object now is taken into the ego, which can in turn "treat itself as an object" (252). The "conflict due to ambivalence" drives this struggle into the unconscious (256). Later, Freud speculated that what he had initially diagnosed as a pathological process was actually a normal and indeed formative mechanism. In *The Ego and the Id* (1923), he suggests that such "regressive identifications" ("Mourning" 242) and incorporation of lost love-objects enable the constitution of the ego's "character" (*Ego and Id* 18).

Judith Butler engages Freud's work on melancholia in developing her postulation that gender is radically performative and that the sexed body itself is an effect of such performativity rather than its ground or cause. In *Gender Trouble*, she takes Freud to task for his recourse to so-called "dispositions" as temporally prior to the identifications and incorporations that constitute gender identity (73–84). She presents the case that rather than being "pre-discursive" givens, these masculine and feminine dispositions were posited by Freud as a necessary starting point for his narrative of the Oedipal drama. Instead, she insists that such dispositions are in fact produced by the melancholic process, rendering gender "identity" itself a melancholic effect of "a law imposed by culture" (81).

Dominick LaCapra reconsiders Butler's engagement with melancholy. He points specifically to what he considers a slippage or lack of distinction between "absence or structural trauma" on the one hand and "constitutive or originary loss" on the other. Such an "unexamined" equation can universalize melancholy as constitutive of subjectivity generally. He claims that "absence not conflated with loss would not entail the postulation of melancholy as the source of subjectivity; by contrast, it would allow for various modes of subjectivity (of course including melancholy, which may indeed be especially pronounced in modernity). In any event, if a special status were to be claimed for melancholy as a mode of subjectivity, this claim would be sociocultural and would have to be investigated and substantiated not in seemingly universalistic but in differentiated historical terms" (73–74).

My study seeks to argue—precisely, to "investigate and substantiate"— how children's literature in Italy between unification and fascism enacted the construction of melancholy as a definitive mode of subjectivity for Italians. Deeper than a mere description of how Italians may have been feeling at the time or of the emotional tone of narratives, but delimited by specific "differentiated historical terms," this melancholic subjectivity was profoundly implicated in the forces of modernization, with an inflection defined by Italy's troubled experience of melancholic. The psychoanalytic understanding of melancholy summarized here frames my readings of the formative work carried out by texts that remember nostalgically and ambivalently all that was felt to have been lost in the necessary process of modernization, and that construct a national identity on the ground (or better, groundlessness) of this loss.

Eric Tribunella's study of American children's literature serves as a methodologic model. Specific points of contact between the texts that I study and those he examines help elucidate the different contours that were forged by the projects of subject formation in turn-of-the-century

Italian society and in later twentieth-century American culture. One point of contrast concerns the disciplinary mobilization of what Tribunella calls "contrived traumas." He notes that the rise in literary representations of hurt children's bodies correlates with declining support in American public opinion for corporeal punishment, particularly after Benjamin Spock's famous 1946 condemnation of this disciplinary practice (*Melancholia* 129). This displacement of physical trauma from the corporeal to the fictional realm enabled the "formation of social subjects along culturally legitimated [esp. heteronormative] lines" (134) even while real children's bodies could be "sheltered" and "protected" (129). In contrast, young Italians at the turn of the century for the most part did not enjoy the legal and cultural privileges of being considered "fragile objects" (Tribunella, *Melancholia* 129), as evidenced by legislation regarding labor practices and education.[30] Furthermore, with a death rate in turn-of-the-century Italy roughly three times higher than that in the early-twenty-first-century United States, occasions for children to be directly affected by uncontrived traumas were ample.[31] Literary representations of painful losses, then, do not seem to have been necessary as a compensation for a lack of actual painful experiences.[32] Rather, these narrations became the instruments through which experienced traumas, deaths, and other losses (to emigration, for example) could be endowed with specific meanings and mobilized for the project of promoting national identity and personal maturation.

Speaking about the "invention" of Italy beyond the field of children's literature, Nicholas Doumanis notes that "[f]in-de-siècle Italians, at least the minority who had any ardour for 'Italia,' were also melancholic about it," in part because in spite of various "symbolic manifestations of progress, Italy was still a predominantly backward nation" (108). I argue here that through the intervention of children's literature, the "melancholia" that Doumanis perceives does not merely designate a pervasive attitude or a mood, but is rather the textual mechanism that navigates the tensions between "progress" and "backwardness." When I claim that these texts constructed a melancholic Italian identity, I do not mean to imply that Italians are by "nature" sentimental, nostalgic, or resigned, but rather that modern Italian subjectivity was organized around the story of a loss. Modernization is identified in these children's texts both as the cause and as the telos of a developmental melancholia.

Real Boys

As will become evident throughout this study, the touching book *Cuore* by Edmondo De Amicis serves very often as a paradigm in the field of children's literature. Set in a boys' elementary classroom, *Cuore* depicts a masculine world in which young Enrico Bottini (like Pinocchio) and his ensemble of classmates must develop into "proper *boys*." In her study of major sociological, pedagogical, and literary texts of the period, Stewart-Steinberg trains her lens on the "gendered language by which Italians were to be made," arguing that "gender constructions played a constitutive role in how national discourses were to be made effective" (3). Lucia Re has shown that the gendering of its national subjects was a central strategy launched by the moderate leaders of the Italian State in their struggle for hegemony and attempts to modernize the nation (162–163). Thus, I analyze gender constructions throughout my study because this discourse permeates and indeed grounds the Italianization project. Specifically, I look at how heroism was adumbrated melancholically as an experience of lost father figures, while the South often figures maternally or in other feminized fashions. I also examine books written for and about girls and those written by female authors in Chapter 3. This examination shows that the boy's path to maturity is constructed as the paradigm for the national subject. Girls, in fact, seem always already adults, whose role is to activate the maturation of their male companions. In all of these itineraries, the modern, adult Italian subject emerges as a melancholy one—the recapitulation model posits not only an isomorphic relation between individual and society, in this account, but also a melancholic trajectory of abandoning attachments from time past and from childhood. These attachments are rendered specifically as the paternal figure of Giuseppe Garibaldi and the maternal figure of the South.

Chapter 1, "Garibaldi's Shadows: Heroism and Melancholia," interrogates how children's books present the past and stage an emotional relationship to the past.[33] This section analyzes how the dominant posture of sentimentality offered the idea of loss as constitutive of Italian identity. Specifically, I examine the representation of unification hero Giuseppe Garibaldi in about a dozen popular children's books from the 1880s to the First World War. It is not surprising that these books should adopt patriotic heroism with such great frequency as a theme or that they should oversimplify the complex history of Italy's nineteenth-century unification, deploying this history as heroic mythology for young readers. What is surprising, and what I show in this chapter, is how these stories perform not so much an advocacy of heroism as a mourning of it. The melancholic depiction of heroism in these books announces an ambivalent relationship to modernity. Children's literature constructed a narrative in which growing up meant revering but leaving behind epic heroism embodied in the famous figure of the liberation warrior. These texts contributed to the project of "making Italians" by providing a heroic fetish through which a melancholy modern subjectivity could emerge. In this section, I analyze such well-known texts as Giuseppe Abba's *Da Quarto al Volturno: Noterelle di uno dei Mille* (1891) [*The Diary of One of Garibaldi's Thousand*], Edmondo De Amicis's *Cuore*, and Virginia Treves's *Piccoli eroi* and lesser-known works such as

Giuseppe Nuccio's novel *Picciotti e garibaldini* (1913) [*Young Fighters and Garibaldi Followers*] as well as the special issue of Vamba's *Il giornalino della Domenica* [*The Little Sunday Paper*] that celebrated the centenary of Garibaldi's birth. Here, stirring passages about the Christlike warrior hero's manly courage stand side by side with advertisements for products to cure bed-wetting and anemia.

Chapter 2, "Geographic Expressions: Mapping Modernity," reveals how children's books used geography as a justifying metaphor and a supposedly natural grounding through which to link more tightly the association between personal and national maturations. Children's books operated along with actual post-unification maps as a "means for making Italy imaginable," since indeed "[c]artography provided the crucial means for visualizing the nation" (Doumanis 94). In Chapter 2, I analyze how cartographic imagery, narrative accounts of journeys, and geography books plotted the convergence of growing up, going north, and modernizing for Italy and for Italians. In books that include visual images of Italy's landscape, such as those of Lake Como that adorn Lino Ferriani's *bildungsroman*, and in those that describe geography, as in Carlo Collodi's *Il viaggio per l'Italia di Giannettino* (1886) [*Giannettino's Trip through Italy*], the recourse to Italy's *terra*, to the land or ground itself, fosters the illusion that the project of making Italians was, precisely, grounded: based in some core facticity that pre-dated convention and culture. Often these texts claim merely to provide their readers with knowledge of the truth that is already there, obscuring to some extent their role in discursively generating that truth. Texts such as Collodi's *Il viaggio per l'Italia di Giannettino* and Augusto Vecchi's *Al lago degli elefanti: Avventure di un italiano in Africa* (1897) [*At Elephant Lake: the Adventures of an Italian Boy in Africa*] map personal and national development as progressive journeys. Like childhood itself, the South and the qualities these books associated with it must be given up. Instead, the maturing child and the modernizing Italy must embrace the values embodied in the urban north. The texts code these itineraries as renunciations. They depict the South—at times within the new national borders, and at times beyond it—with deeply nostalgic tones but as a necessary sacrifice in order to yield modern national subjects.

Chapter 3, "A Beatrice for Modernity: Girls in Italian Children's Literature," examines the construction of gender in this corpus. The children's books of this time period insist that the trajectories described in the first two chapters be forged by a *male* subject. More precisely, I argue that the modern Italian subject is in fact produced and simultaneously gendered by these itineraries. Girls, instead, do not develop or modernize. Rather, the girl is imagined as atavistically attached to origins, paradoxically a permanent child and always already a (maternal) adult. The books I examine show how the notion of "Italianness" that was then being promulgated was predicated on an image of the girl as embedded within history. While boys were offered developmental models that encouraged them to grow up and to take Italy into modernity, girls instead remained fundamentally outside that process both individually and as ciphers for national "development." On the thematic level, for example, girls are often tied to rural images of innocence, and on the formal level, poems at times use verb tenses indicating motion for boys but stasis for girls. While playing the role of a modern-day bourgeois "Beatrice" (Dante's grace-giving and beloved spiritual guide) by inspiring the passage of boys into men, the girl also embodies all that is abjected in the constitution of a melancholy adult citizen.

Chapter 3 will analyze a range of texts written for girls by women. Indeed, children's literature was one of the few domains in which women of the time in Italy could operate without censure, and several women authors not only penned books for pleasure reading and for the school curricula, but also edited children's periodicals. The increasing literacy of girls and women was a significant effect of Italian modernity, giving rise to deeply ambivalent responses. An advocate of education for women, Sighele laments in his 1910 study that illiteracy was so much higher in Italy than elsewhere in Europe, ironically noting that Italians hold "il triste record delle barbarie" [the sad record for barbarism] in this regard (162). He notes too that the rates were higher for women than for men. Using civil marriage licenses as an index, he points out that 35.50% of men and 47.95% of women could not sign their own name to the document (162). He celebrates the fact, however, that school enrollment for girls in Italy was catching up to that for boys. Using the 1901–1902 academic year, he records that 1,434,844 boys and 1,298,505 girls were attending school (public and private combined) (172). Carolina Invernizio movingly dramatizes this statistic in her 1912 novel *Spazzacamino* [*The Chimneysweep*]. Widowed and living in a small mountain village, Mamma Cabel agrees to have her 12-year-old son work for the *padrone* Pietro in Turin, although she knows the risks of this venture. Her disempowerment is underscored as she must sign the grim contract with a "hieroglyphic," marking her illiteracy (13). Broadly charting the slow but significant increase in literacy for women, Katherine Mitchell summarizes census data and notes that in 1861 "female illiteracy was on average 86 per cent in rural areas and 77 per cent in town and cities." Forty years later, that figure had decreased notably, with a female illiteracy rate of 62% in 1901 (9).[34] In the context of these demographic changes, Chapter 3 analyzes several texts from various genres by Ida Baccini, Virginia Treves, Carola Prosperi, Carolina Invernizio, and Arpalice Cuman Pertile. However, I also here discuss books by men, such as Lino Ferriani's *Un piccolo eroe* (1905) [*A Little Hero*] and Luigi Bertelli's *Il giornalino di Gian Burrasca*, since the gendering that operates across the board subtends the formation of national subjects generally, as Stewart-Steinberg and Lucia Re have argued.

In selecting books from the hundreds that were published in the period under consideration, one criterion I used was a desire to include a broad variety of genres. Thus, my chapters submit to analysis examples of fairy tales, poetry, short stories, and novels, including diary-structure novels, travel accounts, and *bildungsromane*. This generic breadth enables me to discern the strategies of recapitulation and melancholy at play broadly, rather than as an effect limited to a specific genre. I also include both male and female authors (as far as such identities are discernible), and books that appeared to be marketed both for boys and for girls, since the deployment of gendering strategies is of crucial concern to my inquiry into the construction of national identity. Because I am not so much interested, in this project, in making claims for unacknowledged literary merit or underappreciated authorial genius, I neither evaluate aesthetic quality nor use that as a criterion for inclusion. Rather, with an eye to interrogating modes of constructing identity, I sought mostly to examine texts that achieved a high level of popularity, while acknowledging that this term is relative to the limited reading public for which they were produced. I used as evidence of popularity markers such as: publication in multiple editions; translation into other languages; contemporary name recognition of the author or illustrator (at times because they were also journal editors); or inclusion in bibliographies of recommended books, such as those by Vincenzina Battistelli or Olindo Giacobbe.[35] While I strove for a broadly representative body of works, I could not include all of the many fascinating texts produced in this period. The wealth of such material invites continued scholarship in this field.

Mapping the Field

This book, the first study in English or Italian to engage the corpus of post-unification Italian children's literature through the lens of recapitulation and melancholy, offers a new perspective on the much-debated question of precisely how Italians were "made"—in other words, on the fictional bases of national identities. My study builds on and makes connections between the scholarship in Italian Studies and in Children's Literature. In particular, I draw on the foundational studies of Pino Boero, Carmine De Luca, Antonio Faeti, and Patrizia Mencarani, whose work has contributed to delineating the corpus and to articulating the pedagogical aims and aesthetic merits of hundreds of children's books in Italy since the unification.[36] Powerful theoretical paradigms in Children's Literature Studies have been developed primarily from analyses of American and British texts.[37] I draw particularly on the way Perry Nodelman has connected strategies of "Orientalizing" to the field of children's literature, on psychoanalytically informed methodological models proposed by Jacqueline Rose and Karen Coats, and on Kenneth Kidd's account of the history of intersections and adjacencies between psychoanalytic discourse and children's literature. Most directly, my work is in dialogue with Eric Tribunella's *Melancholia and Maturation* (2010), which interrogates uses of contrived trauma in American texts in the service of heteronormativity, and with Lindsay Myers' account of how the fantasy genre in Italy intervened in specific political and social debates.

Through investigating the unique inflections that such strategies as the home-away-home structure, the mechanism of melancholy, and forms of mirroring take in the Italian context, this study advances the dialogue between the fields of Italian Studies and Children's Literature. In this way, I implicitly respond to the call issued by Emer O'Sullivan for a more globalized perspective in the study of children's literature. O'Sullivan has underscored how a comparative approach can question the romanticized and enduring image of "the world republic of childhood," as Paul Hazard put it, and unmask the potentially oppressive notion that "children throughout the world are all the same" ("Comparative" 195). More broadly, this book will shed light on a central question of the humanities, that is, in Judith Butler's words, "the way in which regulative strategies produce the subjects they come to subjugate" (125). My examination of these critically neglected texts illuminates how, in the liberal period between the end of old monarchical regimes of Bourbons, Hapsburgs, and Papacy (1861) and the rise of the modern totalitarian regime of Mussolini's fascism (1922), Italy's new citizens were constituted as proper national subjects.

Notes

1 Unless otherwise indicated, all translations from Italian throughout are my own.
2 German zoologist Ernst Haeckel (1834–1919) provided a particularly forceful exposition of the recapitulation model in his 1874 *The Evolution of Man*. Italian translations of Haeckel's works on evolution were published in Turin in 1892, 1895, and 1908.
3 Lombroso's major works include *L'uomo delinquente* [*Criminal Man*] (1876, with revisions in 1878, 1884, 1889, and 196–97), *L'uomo di genio* [*Man of Genius*] (1888), and *La donna delinquente, la prostituta e la donna normale* [*Criminal Woman, the Prostitute, and the Normal Woman*] (1893). Beccalossi points out that Lombroso's ideas circulated not only through his major texts but also through his conference participation and through his roles as editor and contributor to the international, multidisciplinary journal *Archivio di psichiatria* (founded in 1880) (131). On Lombroso, see especially Beccalossi 117–146 (for his role in developing theories of female same-sex desire), Stewart-Steinberg 184–288 (for his interventions in the infanticide debates, and how his works on tattoos and Spiritism participated in the project of "making Italians"), Pancaldi (for his role in promulgating Darwin's ideas in Italy), Hiller (for intersections between Lombroso and Italian literature and opera), and Harrowitz (on misogyny and anti-Semitism). Stewart-Steinberg pays particular attention to the way in which Lombroso's

self-declared founding moment of the atavism theory—his analysis of the skull of the Calabrian "brigand" Giuseppe Villella—is grounded specifically in an absence. The supposedly primitive feature in Villella's cranium was precisely the lack of the "occipital median spine" (230), the void that became "Villella's now famous occipital fossa" (231). Stewart-Steinberg goes on to argue that from this "nothing comes excess ... Villella's skull—which Lombroso preserved on his desk until his death—functioned, he himself stated, as his totem, his fetish, a filling of the void that he named 'criminal anthropology'" (231). I see a similar excessive filling of a perceived void operating in the corpus of children's literature I discuss.

4 Beccalossi continues, "the normal civilized man potentially had in himself the germs of atavism. Lombroso supported this idea by adopting Haeckel's evolution theory: if the biological development of an individual's organism (ontogeny) parallels and summarizes its species' entire evolutionary development (phylogeny), then every individual organism carries traces of criminality that for the most part remain latent, because criminality is a typical feature of the first stages of human evolution" (121).

5 Capuana had already drawn on Lombroso's work in his 1884 essay *Spiritismo?* On Capuana and Lombroso, see especially Hiller 167–217.

6 See the editors' preface to the illustrated volume, De Amicis, *Il vino* (no pg). The editors explain that the participants discussed wine from the points of view of legend and literature, pathology and physiology, chemistry, botany, natural history, economics, and crime. One other participant, the writer Giuseppe Giacosa, was the brother of scientist Piero Giacosa, whom I will discuss in Chapter 2 in connection with the children's author Giulio Gianelli.

7 The major Milanese publishing house "Treves" issued another edition of De Amicis's discussion of wine in 1890. This publisher, to which popular children's author Virginia Tedeschi Treves was professionally and personally connected, also issued several texts by Lombroso and by his pupils, including Lombroso's *Il caso Amerling* (1896) and *Cronache criminali italiane* by Guglielmo Ferrero and Scipio Sighele (1896). De Amicis, too, had a personal friendship with Treves (Boero and De Luca 57).

8 Other of her works, under her pen name "Aunt Mary," include *Le fiabe di zia Mariù* (1914) [*Aunt Mary's Fairy Tales*] and later *I giocattoli di zia Mariù* (1922) [*Aunt Mary's Toys*]. On Paola Lombroso, see Boero and De Luca 136, and Fava 273–274. For an insightful analysis of *A reporter* as a "Microcosmic fantasy," see Myers, *Making* 65–83.

9 He is best known for *Piccolo mondo antico* (1896) [*The Little World of the Past*].

10 It should be noted that Franco and Luisa are also the names of the protagonists in Fogazzaro's *Piccolo mondo antico*.

11 On Pascoli's *Il fanciullino*, see Myers, *Making* 66–68 and LaValva.

12 Especially useful for this overview are Lyttelton's chapter in the *Oxford Illustrated History of Italy*, "Politics and Society, 1870–1915" 235–263, and Myers, *Making* 19–24, 43–47, 63–67.

13 See Spinazzola's excellent discussion in his introduction. In charting the growth of the field of children's literature in Italy, which truly emerges only after the unification, he suggests that many of these texts described in detail the disadvantages and suffering endured by the lower classes, while the books themselves would clearly be "acquired" primarily by middle-class readers. Thus, such privileged young readers could gain a "miglior consapevolezza del loro ruolo nella vita nazionale" [deeper understanding of their role in national life] (13).

14 See also Stewart-Steinberg's chapter on Sighele's studies in mass psychology and hypnotism, "The Secret Power of Suggestion: Scipio Sighele's Succabal Subject" (64–96).

15 Elena Coda usefully synthesizes this nexus of issues as adumbrated by thinkers such as Simmel, Mantegazza, Lombroso, Nordau, and Weininger (80–84). In particular, Coda explains that the latter three "identify the city as the major cause of the propagation of neurasthenia—traditionally linked with the feminine—which is seen as the primal cause of degeneration ... life in the city suffocates one's individuality... The modern city becomes for these writers the indisputable site of everything that is considered negative and sick: weakness, femininity, decadence" (82).

16 Spinazzola claims that "il laicismo rappresenta il denominator comune più sicuro fra i nostri narratori per l'infanzia" [secularism represents the most certain common denominator among our writers for children] (14). In this study, I will also consider how several Catholic writers operated within the paradigms of recapitulation and melancholy.

17 In Giuseppe Errico's *Mily e Michele: Storielle per fanciulli* [*Mily and Michael: Little Stories for Children*]. I will return to this quotation, from which I have taken the Introduction's title, in Chapter 1.

18 Ricciardi employs both gustatory ("a recipe") and auditory ("musical notes") metaphors in claiming that heroism and melancholy have dominated children's literature. His multisensory language bespeaks, perhaps, the adult desire that children fully incorporate the lessons promoted in these books.

19 Errico dedicates the eponymous "little story" of his collection ("Mily e Michele") to De Amicis.

20 "Un'altra varietà frequentissima dell'ebbrezza, è quella della malinconia. Ci sono molti in cui il vino non eccita che il sentimento delle cose tristi, o piuttosto della poesia delle cose tristi [Another very common variety of drunkenness is melancholy. There are those in whom wine excites nothing but the sentiment of sad things, or rather the sentiment of the poetry of sad things] (22).

21 He adds, "c'è in fondo una compiacenza" [there is at bottom a satisfaction] (22).

22 The third edition (1907), which I consulted, attributes the dedication to the first edition (1887). It reads, "A Maria cara che non leggerà mai queste pagine che non tornerà più alla nostra nidiata" [To dear Maria who will never read these pages and will never return to our brood].

23 The level of detail in the description of the dog's death is remarkable: "Le membra incominciavano a irrigidirsi, le labbra tremavano convulse, i denti scricchiolavano, la lingua si affacciava arida fuori della bocca, e noi gliela umettavamo di latte. La povera bestia ci guardava ancora, ma stralunata, ma senza sorriderci più" [Her limbs began to stiffen, her lips trembled un-controllably, her teeth were grinding, her dry tongue hung from her mouth. We kept trying to moisten it for her with milk. The poor creature still looked at us, but was dazed, and no longer smiled at us] (66). The story makes clear that Mily (the dog) dies of depression triggered by the loss of Michele (the lamb). Mily's loss of Michele, coupled by the lengthy description of the dog's slow death, then, becomes an ominous model for the narrator's loss of Mily. Eric Tribunella has devoted a full chapter in his book on *Melancholia and Maturation* to American children's books about dogs (29–50). While the dog does not seem to figure nearly as prominently in Italian children's books, I return to Tribunella's analysis in my third chapter, where I discuss how the doll seems to play a role similar to the dog in the melancholic struc-ture of many Italian texts.

24 "Egli aveva perduto sua madre all'età di tre anni" [he had lost his mother at the age of three] (3).

25 Not only sentimental narratives and fairy tales, but also "swashbuckling" adventure stories are marked by this melancholic tone. I will discuss Emilio Salgari's famous pirate hero Sandokan in Chapter 1. His Black Corsair, too, has been described specifically as "melancholy." Galli Mastrodonato evokes this brooding figure from Salgari's 1898 best seller as "un uomo solo, pallido e assorto, ritto su un ponte della nave corsara, tutto vestito di nero e malinconicamente racchiuso nel suo spazio interiore" [a man alone, pale, and intent, standing rigidly on the bridge of his corsair ship, all dressed in black and melancholically engrossed in his private thoughts] (no pg). Galli Mastrodonato notes that the publisher issued 100,000 copies of the book with its brooding hero in its first printing.

26 The impact of this novel is attested to not only by Collodi's nod to it in Chapter XXVII of *Pinocchio*, but also by Bemporad's use of its popularity to promote other books. The cover of Cherubini's *Impresa Granchio, Bullettino e compagni* (1910) [*The Enterprise of Granchio, Bullettino and Friends*], issued as part of the "Blue Series," depicts Baccini's Chick along with Collodi's Pinocchio and Vamba's Ant (from his *Ciondolino*) climbing on a pile of books in front of a young boy and girl. The image clearly canonizes these three figures and the books that narrate their adventures. Lindsay Myers notes that *Memorie* "had some sixty-five editions between 1875 and 1895" (*Making* 22). Myers insightfully reveals how Baccini's "memoir fantasy" and similar books of the period replace human child protagonists with dolls or animals. This strategy allows the main character be passed from owner to owner and thus enables the book to provide the reader with descriptions of a variety of families at different socioeconomic levels (19–42). For a biography of Baccini and an account of the goals and influence of *Memorie*, see Nacci's preface.

27 On Baccini, see Boero and De Luca 29–31. They note in particular her successful use of lively turns of phrase.

28 Like feminizing, silencing, and ascribing qualities of inherent dangerousness, depicting the "other" (here, the child) as "not quite human" enables discourses of colonization (Nodelman, "The Other" 29).

29 In fact, once in the city the chick is subjected to a vicarious repetition of his own loss. He meets a rooster who tells the story of the night he witnessed his own mother's murder, seeing her strangled after having been fattened up for the humans' holiday meal. The rooster's story, which leaves him "sopraffatto da quelle memorie dolorose" [overcome by those painful memories], reactivates the opening scene of the chick's own traumatic loss (119–120).

30 For an in-depth study of the real and perceived dangers faced by children in Italy in the post-unification decades, see Ipsen, who argues that the economic, political, and demographic conditions of the decades leading up to World War I in Italy enabled "the discovery of working-class children by middle-class reformers" (11). He examines public responses to physical abandonment, emigration, labor, delinquency, and "moral abandonment" of children. He uses Pinocchio as an emblematic figure in his study, reading the puppet as "the image of the child who is at once endangered by the modernizing world in which he lives and himself is a danger produced by that world" (3).

31 The crude death rate (per 1000) in Italy from 1861 to 1870 was 30.9, improving in 1886–1890 to 27.0, and in 1906–1910 dropping to 21.1 (Kertzer and Barbagli xx). The infant mortality rate in 1900 was about 18% (Ipsen 35). By contrast, in 2015 in Italy, the crude death rate was 10.19, and in the same year in the United States, it was calculated at 8.15 (Central Intelligence Agency).

32 The passing of a boy's father in one of Baccini's novels is reported parenthetically, almost as a matter of course: "(il babbo gli era morto da un pezzo)" [(he had lost his dad a while back)] (*I piccoli* 15).

33 An abridged version of this chapter has been published as "Garibaldi's Shadows: Heroism and Melancholia in Italian Children's Literature" in *Children's Literature* 43 (2015): 51–83.

34 Mitchell also reminds us that on "3 October 1874, women were granted official permission by the government to enter the universities" (12).

35 On Battistelli and Giacobbe, who published their bibliographic guides at the dawn of the fascist regimes, see Fava 296–302.

36 Pino Boero and Carmine De Luca's *La letteratura per l'infanzia* (1995, 2009) [*Children's Literature*] is indispensable to scholars in this field. This text surveys hundreds of children's books from all genres from the Risorgimento to 2009. Proceeding chronologically, the authors evaluate and contextualize these children's texts with attention to aesthetic merit, pedagogical aims, and political relevance. Vittorio Spinazzola's trenchant *Pinocchio & C.: la grande narrativa italiana per ragazzi* (1997) [*Pinocchio & Company: Great Italian Narratives for Children*] analyses five texts from the turn of the century. His introduction provides a historically contextualized discussion of major generic features of Italian children's literature, including, for example, the creation of a narrative voice that is both "fraternal" and "paternal," a mixture of fictional entertainment and nonfictional instruction, the use of sentimentalism to forge ties with the community, and a conceptualization of childhood that digresses from the Northern European vision offered in *Alice* or *Peter Pan*. Lindsay Myers' recent study *Making the Italians: Poetics and Politics of Italian Children's Fantasy* (2012), one of the very few book-length studies in English on Italian children's literature, surveys the wide chronological span from the post-unification to the present day. She focuses on and indeed redefines the fantasy genre, examining through this approach how authors used specific generic strategies unique to the two-world structure of fantasy to engage very concrete political, social, and aesthetic questions. Patrizia Mencarani's *Piccoli italiani leggono* (2013) [*Little Italians Read*] focuses on the 30 years following the unification period (1860–1890). She argues that the books of these decades constructed an idealized bourgeois child, and she arranges her discussion thematically, harnessing quotations from a vast range of texts to summarize the morals and lessons that were overtly promoted by this body of didactic literature. First published in 1972, Antonio Faeti's *Guardare le figure* (2011) [*Looking at the Pictures*] is fundamental to any discussion of illustrations, providing detailed, historically contextualized analyses of over 75 artists and their works.

37 Jack Zipes has bridged Italian Studies and Children's Literature through his major contributions as both translator and critic, but his vast body of important work focuses primarily on folk and fairy tales, not on the novels, short stories, and poetry that I examine.

1 Garibaldi's Shadows

Heroism and Melancholia

Eroe: chi dà prova di straordinario coraggio e abnegazione, spec. in imprese guerresche;chi si sacrifica per affermare un ideale: *l'eroe dei due mondi*, per antonomasia, G. Garibaldi (1807–1882).

[Hero: one who demonstrates extraordinary courage and abnegation, especially in military undertakings; one who makes sacrifices in the name of an ideal: *the hero of the two worlds*, through antonomasia, Giuseppe Garibaldi.]

—*Garzanti Linguistica*

In his preface to a collection of Italian short stories for children published in 1890, the Neapolitan intellectual Michele Ricciardi remarked, "se ne potrebbe dare facilmente una ricetta: prendi dieci grammi di eroico, due di malinconico e fa' un libro per fanciulli" [one could easily write up a recipe for children's literature in our culture: take ten grams of heroism, add two grams of melancholy, and you've got a children's book] (Errico 9).[1] Ricciardi's recipe highlights the healthy doses of heroic imagery and sentimentality being doled out to Italian children in the late nineteenth century and into the twentieth. The memorable monthly stories that punctuate Edmondo De Amicis's *Cuore* (1886) [*Heart*] epitomize the potent mixture of heroism and sentimentality described by Ricciardi. In these tales from "the book that was best known and most read in schools" (Lollo 197), child protagonists from Italy's different regions offer models of courage and self-sacrifice to very powerful effect. In one such monthly story, a young boy from Padua, whose desperately poor parents sold him to a traveling circus, dramatically throws back the money offered to him by wealthy adults because they have insulted Italy.[2] In an escapist rather than openly didactic mode, Emilio Salgari's many late-nineteenth-century adventure novels offered extremely popular images of swashbuckling, daring Romantic heroes in exotic locales.[3] In *Le tigri di Mompracem* (1884) [*The Tigers of Mompracem*], for example, Sandokan the pirate with a small band of rebel followers takes on the colonial might of the British and Dutch. In yet another genre deploying this same theme, Lino Ferriani's 1905 *bildungsroman, Un piccolo eroe* [*A Little Hero*] charts the development of the earnest protagonist Pin. This "little hero" suffers a bloody nose while protecting a crippled classmate from a gang of other youths, saves a group of women and children from a rabid dog by beating it to death with a stick, and finally loses his own job by standing up to an exploitative London foreman in defense of a young Italian construction worker. Poetry of the period, too, more than sprinkled in the ingredient of heroism. Giuseppe Zucca's 1918 collection entitled *Vincere, vincere, vincere* [*Win, Win, Win*] gathers stirring poems written during the Great War to foster patriotic fervor. One poem paints the portrait of Giuseppe Lavezzari, a veteran of Garibaldi's 1860 campaign who volunteers to fight again in his old age. Rushing into the Austrian line crying "Viva l'Italia," he reveals his Garibaldian red shirt and dares the enemy to kill him (7–10). These and many other stories attest to the currency that martial exploits, courage, and patriotic self-sacrifice held in Italian children's literature in the decades preceding fascism.[4]

In this chapter, I explore the recurrent call to heroism that appears so often and so openly in children's books from *Cuore* through the First World War. As with many of the overt lessons promoted by books that state straightforwardly their agenda, the call to heroism is not masked, and its utility for the State is clear and rational: the need to inculcate in its youth a willingness to die for the Fatherland. It is not surprising that writers, even those who were penning books marketed as pleasure reading rather than as mandatory school curriculum, should encourage young Italians to be brave and selfless, and should offer heroic role models to their young readers to admire and imitate. As Lindsay Myers documents in her study of Italian children's fantasy books, such a strategy rose to particular prominence in the years 1915–1918 in support of Italy's belated and much debated entrance into the First World War. Myers points out that "[r]ealist novels generally proved more conducive to the dissemination of pro-war ideologies than did works of fantasy" (87), but even the fantasy genre, via allegorical strategies, served to justify and support Italy's intervention. According to Myers, works like Yambo's *Ciuffettino alla guerra* (1916) [*Ciuffettino Goes to War*] constituted a new "subgenre," which she terms the "Quest Fantasy." Even after the conclusion of the war, the agenda of inculcating patriotism persisted, as attested to by Olindo Giacobbe in the opening pages of his 1925 critical bibliography of children's books. In underscoring the care with which school teachers should select texts, he unabashedly lists the making of "valorous soldiers" as one of the goals of children's literature (Giacobbe, *Letteratura infantile* 4).

What I will examine here is the specific manner in which heroism is staged in many children's books of the period. It is not particularly surprising that these books should adopt heroism with such great frequency as a theme or even that they should simplify the complex history of Italy's nineteenth-century unification (traditionally referred to as the "Risorgimento"), consolidating and deploying this history as heroic mythology for young readers.[5] What is of interest in many of these Italian texts is that heroism seems to be staged neither as a present possibility nor as a future goal, but quite often as a memory. More precisely, what these stories appear to perform is not so much an advocacy of heroism as a mourning of it. Deployed in a melancholic structure, the mourning of heroism that I see operating in these books announces their ambivalent relationship to modernity.

The association between heroism and mourning emerges in Lino Ferriani's 1905 book *Un piccolo eroe* (mentioned above). Here, the call to heroism is staged in a scene of death: at 10 years old, the protagonist "Pin" listens to his dying father's exhortation to *"fa'l'uomo"* [become a man; italics in orig.] (105). Pin's father, an "honest blacksmith" (22), crushes his hand at work and suffers for a week from the subsequent infection. Finally, he utters his last word to his son, "Coraggio" [Courage] (108). Pin must assume the role of man of his own house and that of the neighboring widow and her daughter, as the narrator remarks, "ormai era considerato l'uomo delle due famiglie" [at this point he was considered the man of the two families] (115). The little hero emerges from the scene of death and goes on to display acts of selfless bravery. The readers are advised that Pin "ora sta per apparirci sotto una luce di vero eroe, di chi, cioè, inalzandosi al disopra degli uomini mediocri, e tanto più dei fanciulli, si rende noto e chiaro per un fatto grande, magnanimo, che gli frutta l'ammirazione, il plauso dei buoni, e la gioia interna della coscienza soddisfatta" [is now about to appear to us in the light of a real hero. A hero, in other words, is one who rises above mediocre men, and even more so above children, and who makes himself known for a great and magnanimous deed. A hero earns the admiration and applause of good men and the internal joy of a satisfied conscience] (116). This account of heroism includes the ingredients of manliness ("fa'l'uomo"), excessiveness ("al disopra"), and martial valor ("un fatto grande" that is enacted, as enumerated in the above list of Pin's deeds, as physical confrontation), which still constitute today the dictionary definition of heroism, evident in this chapter's epigram from Garzanti.[6] The texts I examine below, most of which were published in multiple editions and had wide circulation at the turn of the century, promote this traditional conception of heroism for their young readers. However, as a kind of shadow, they simultaneously mourn such heroism, coding it as an anachronism. In moving, so to speak, from an epic to a novelistic textuality of heroism, these children's books grapple with the question of the possibility of heroism in modern Italy. The conclusion to *Un piccolo eroe* exemplifies the dynamic I am describing. Ferriani's "little hero" takes to heart his dying father's command to become a man and after his more dramatic moments, emerges at the end of the novel as a productive and financially stable merchant with plans to open a delicatessen. Having read Giuseppe Mazzini's texts on the duties of man and having spent six years patiently working in England, he returns home ready to provide for his childhood sweetheart, Maria, as a stable husband.

The issue of defining a modern heroic mode goes beyond simply the challenge of finding new dragons to slay in a world of telegraphs and railroads, which Ferriani manages to do by having Pin bludgeon a rabid dog. In other words, it is not merely a matter of updating content. Instead, these texts structure modern Italian subjects on the very ground of this lost possibility. By extolling heroism, and specifically by fetishizing Giuseppe Garibaldi as the embodiment of this ideal, these texts both reveal and cover up anxieties about modern networks of social relations.[7] Ferriani rather eloquently articulates this very anxiety when he describes Pin's perception of modern London: "lo colpì la regolarità con cui questo movimento fantastico funzionava, come se tutti, uomini e cose, ubbidissero a un ordine superiore, a un direttore generale invisibile, ma onnipotente cui nulla sfuggiva e a tutto provvedeva" [he was struck by the regularity with which this fantastic movement functioned. It was as if everybody, men and things, were obeying a superior order, a general director who was invisible but omnipotent. Nothing escaped from this director who provided for everything] (187–188). The invisibility of the source of this omnipotent power disconcerts the protagonist, who initially reacts to the English city with "grave melanconia" [deep melancholy] (187) as he observes the trains and electric trams.[8] However, he cannot assume his role as a good Italian husband to Maria until he has spent time in the more modernized London. He must acclimate to the city and bring what he has learned, and earned, back into Italy. Pin's exposure to modernity in the North builds on, but also supersedes, what he had learned in school from his teacher Signor Stefano, who in his younger days had been a "garibaldino" (88). Ferriani describes the invisible capitalist-technological forces that regulate London through a rhetoric evoking theological concepts: providence, omnipotence, the superior order that commands absolute obedience, and the force that functions as the Prime Mover. Pin, then, attempts to understand new social relations, in which "men and things" are implicitly interchangeable, through a premodern epistemological grid. The use of this theological register to describe modern urban society, in effect, suggests that the latter has replaced the former. The fetishization of Garibaldi, who becomes a kind of "direttore generale *visibile*" as it were, compensates for this perceived loss.

A contemporary consideration of the image of the hero can help further elucidate these anxieties. In the same years in which these children's books were being written and circulated, Freud's colleague Otto Rank turned his critical attention to what he perceived as recurrent motifs in hero myths. He sought to strip these various myths down to the "ideal human skeleton" (65) that served as a common structure to stories from different times and places. In *The Myth of the Birth of the Hero* (1909), he argues that hero stories from Sargon and Perseus and from Moses to Jesus are ultimately grounded in memory. Specifically, he argues, a hero story is a coded elaboration of the subject's infantile perception of his parents, evoking a time when the parents seemed to him to be omnipotent kings and queens. The subject's repressed childhood hostility toward the father is projected and reimagined as the father's (king's) hostility toward the son, a structure that provides the psychological source of so many changeling stories. Rank ends the essay by connecting this family romance with contemporary anarchist attacks on political father figures. I turn to this important text not as an interpretive key through which to analyze the hero stories of Italian children's literature. Rather, this contemporary discussion of heroism sheds light on two major nexuses of issues that are bound up in and worked out through the books I will discuss, namely the perceived deterioration of paternal power and the epistemological paradigm of recapitulation.

As in Rank's analysis, the children's books that I will discuss here intimately link heroism to paternal figures. Pin, for example, is spurred to heroic deeds by his father's exhortation to "become a man." Similarly in *Cuore*, the monthly stories of heroism are dictated to Enrico and his classmates by the paternal teacher Signor Perboni, who, on the first day of school, begs his students to "essere i miei figliuoli" [be my dear little sons] (29), and it is Enrico's actual father who encourages him to study with the words "[c]oraggio, dunque, piccolo soldato dell'immenso esercito" [take courage, then, little soldier of the immense army] (37). In her novel *Piccoli eroi* (1892) [*Little Heroes*], Virginia Tedeschi Treves (who wrote under the name "Cordelia") shows how the protagonist Maria must heroically care for all her siblings in order to allow her widowed father to continue to work, and Lino Ferriani's brief contribution to the Garibaldi-themed issue of *Il giornalino della Domenica* (1907) [*The Little Sunday Paper*] discourages lying and calls for brave honesty among young readers by quoting Garibaldi's words to his own son Manlio, thus putting the "blond Hero" explicitly in the role of father figure (Bertelli 19).[9] Within the texts, then, father figures encourage heroism for the child protagonists and, by extension, their readers.

While the fictional fathers of all these "little heroes" were inspiring their children to acts of self-sacrifice and courage, the readers of these books and their families were witnessing significant renegotiations of patriarchal power in Italy on several fronts. In his study of "letteratura infantile" [children's literature], Vittorio Spinazzola reminds us that Italian children's literature came into its own in a period of post-Risorgimento anxieties—political, cultural, and "infine familiare per la difficoltà di reimpostare i rapporti fra i sessi e le generazioni in un'ottica più evoluta rispetto a quella dell'assolutismo patriarcale" [even familial because of the difficulty of redefining relationships between the sexes and between generations in a manner more evolved than that of patriarchal absolutism] (12). Changes in the modes of production were sending women out of the home and into the factories, particularly in northern Italy, where most of the writers and publishing houses of children's literature were located. These changes, as Silvana Andretta has noted in her study of contemporary literary depictions of childhood, were perceived as a threat to the family: "Il processo di trasformazione del sistema produttivo aveva provocata un indebolimento della famiglia, poiché anche le donne entravano nel mondo del lavoro" [The process of transforming the system of production had provoked a weakening of the family, since even women were entering the workforce] (8).

Along with industrialization and urbanization, however uneven and belated vis-à-vis other European nations, the decades at the turn of the century saw attempts to modernize the authoritarian civil code of 1865, specifically through agitation in favor of legalizing divorce. Between 1878 and 1902, eight different pro-divorce proposals were brought to parliament. In the same period, analyses such as Teresa Labriola's *Del divorzio: Discussione etica* (1901) [*On Divorce: An Ethical Discussion*] and literary works such as Anna Franchi's *Avanti il divorzio* (1902) [*Forward with Divorce*] and Sibilla Aleramo's *Una donna* (1906) [*A Woman*] aimed to sway public opinion.[10] Not surprisingly, none of the Garibaldian children's books that I have studied mention Garibaldi's own request to Rome's civil tribunal in 1879 for a state annulment of his nineteen-year marriage to Giuseppina Raimondi.[11] During these same decades, especially prompted by the 1897 scandal of the Neapolitan "Annunziata" foundling home, politicians debated various methods to combat the shockingly high mortality rates in the nation's institutions for abandoned children (Ipsen 15–49). Many reformers considered these death rates, and indeed the entire foundling home structure, to be an embarrassing sign of Italy's backwardness (36). Reformers proposed policies of providing government subsidies to unwed mothers to encourage them to keep their children, and of authorizing maternity searches. However, some politicians claimed that such "filiation subsidies" amounted to state-sponsored promiscuity (42). These foundling home reform debates, which continued into the first decade of the twentieth century, became another arena in which traditional Catholic family values could be perceived as being under attack by modernity (38).

In these same turbulent decades, Italy suffered a so-called hemorrhaging of citizens through emigration: an estimated five million Italians, mostly young men from the south, came to the United States between 1860 and 1920.[12] Emigration to the Americas of so many men, often including young fathers, left these generations of children to associate "father" quite literally with "absence." Giulio Gianelli, poet and author of a popular children's book that I will discuss in the next chapter, reflected in his *Pagine autobiografiche* [*Autobiographical Pages*] on the repercussions of his father's 1881 emigration to Argentina to seek work. Gianelli was 2 years old at the time, and his father never returned: "Quando mi ripenso bambino nella più remota infanzia se cerco di ri-vivere quella che era allora in me l'impressione circa la parola'babbo' non ricompongo che la più vaga idea. …Ancora ricordo che alla parola 'padre' si univa la parola 'America'" [When I think back to when I was a boy in my earliest childhood, if I try to revive what was then my im-pression of the word 'daddy' I can only manage to recreate a very vague idea. I do still remember that the word "father" was linked to the word "America"] (qtd. in Farinelli 150).

On the governmental level, the transition from absolute monarchies (Bourbons in the South, Hapsburgs in the North) to a parliamentary structure, as well as the significant loss of temporal power for the Pope in central Italy, represented a major shift away from the tradition of singu-lar, centralized, patriarchal power. Children's author Giuseppe Nuccio, in a novel that I will discuss below, succinctly articulates this tradition-ally vertical model of power. One of his characters is a clandestine lib-eral secretly plotting the overthrow of the oppressive Bourbon regime in Palermo and anxiously awaiting Garibaldi's arrival. This woman feigns agreement with the regime's soldiers, asserting that the king "è il vero padrone e signore che ci dà il pane dolce e ci fa vivere" [is the true fa-ther and lord who gives us sweet bread and allows us to live] (172–173). She pretends to endorse the clear vertical line of power: "Prima Dio e poi il Re e i nostri padroni, che lo rappresentano qui, in carne e ossa, dobbiamo ubbidire" [we must obey first God and then the King and our padroni, who represent him here in flesh and blood] (173). It was, of course, the unification's dismantling of such patriarchal absolutism that Nuccio's 1910 story celebrated. Although the constitution limited his authority, the Savoy monarch Umberto I, whose reign began in 1878, became a "father-figure" victim (when he was assassinated by anarchist Gaetano Bresci in 1900) of the same anarchist violence psychoanalyti-cally theorized by Otto Rank. In short, industrial modes of production, agitation for divorce and filiation subsidies in the name of enlightened thinking, the mass emigration of fathers, and a more liberal distribution of political power (that many felt was still not liberal enough) all contri-buted to the perception of threats to traditional paternal power in the de-cades preceding the First World War, while simultaneously constituting the very progress toward modernization (or, in the case of emigration, its unintended effects) that Italy needed to promote and embrace.

In addition to highlighting the link between heroism and paternal power, Rank's work points to a second key factor. Rank grounds his methodology in the recapitulation paradigm that held currency in this period in a range of fields. In developing his arguments, Rank relies on the premise that neurotics are like children and children are like primitives, so neurotic behaviors, children's fantasies, and primitive myths are generated by the same mental operations and thus may be used to interpret each other. In this maneuver, Rank is symptomatic of his time. In his study of the symbiotic relationship between psychoanalysis and fairy tales, children's literature scholar Kenneth Kidd has examined the recapitulation theory and the multiple kinds of hierarchies to which it was applied in turn-of-the-century thought. Drawing on Jacqueline Rose's seminal study, Kidd writes,

> Freud and his scientific predecessors were less interested in the fairy tale's literary status or in questions about its major audience [i.e., adult or child] than in what the fairy tale could reveal about 'primitive' man. The allegedly natural association of children with fairy tales, as Jacqueline Rose points out, emerges from a 'preoccupation with cultural infancy and national heritage,' a metanarrative in which children and the 'folk' are made equivalent (1984, 56). That metanarrative influenced and in turn was supported by popular adaptations of evolutionary theory in the nineteenth century. The evolutionary notion of recapitulation, first articulated by Ernst Haeckel (and popularly summed up as 'ontogeny recapitulates phylogeny'), found widespread application and adaptation from the nineteenth century forward, underwriting and overlapping with a broader theory of evolutionary social progress. Caucasian child and non-Caucasian primitive or savage (and sometimes the criminal) were said to be at the same developmental stage or level, and the theory was sometimes even extended to nations, with, say, the 'cultural infancy' of Western nations being ostensibly equivalent to the maturity of primitive cultures. ... Freud and his colleagues ... generally maintained the principle of recapitulation, seeing parallels among primitive people, children, and young nations. (3, 4)

Kidd here refers specifically to *The Evolution of Man: A Popular Exposition*, in which Haeckel energetically defends evolutionary theory against what he saw as the backwardness of the Roman Catholic Church. He insists upon the fundamental law of organic evolution, or the first principle of biogeny, claiming that "[t]he History of the Germ is an epitome of the History of the Descent; or, in other words: the Ontogeny is a recapitulation of Phylogeny; or, somewhat more explicitly: that the series of forms through which an individual organism passes during its progress from the egg cell to its fully developed state, is a brief, compressed reproduction of the long series of forms through which the animal ancestors of that organism (or the ancestral forms of its species) have passed from the earliest periods of so-called organic creation down to the present time" (6,7). Not only are these processes mirrors of each other, but indeed a causal relationship applies: phylogenesis is the mechanical cause of ontogenesis (7). This "law" allows the scientist to read phylogeny from ontogeny: by watching the individual human organism develop we can see the telescoped trajectory of the species' evolution. This powerful isomorphic construction—itself a product of modernity in its evolutionary basis—informs the structure of many children's narratives of the period. The forward trajectory of maturation for the child mirrors and naturalizes the modernization of the nation, both of which require the loss of epic heroism.

Rank's study of the hero myth, then, calls our attention to the ways in which paternity and recapitulation are linked to the motif of the hero. The construction of the myth of Giuseppe Garibaldi (1807–1882) in post-unification children's literature encoded Italian ambivalences about modernity and served as a strategy to guide and to fuse personal and national maturation. Beginning with Giuseppe Abba's 1880 *Noterelle di uno dei Mille* [*The Diary of One of Garibaldi's Thousand*] and echoed in at least a dozen texts before the First World War, the story of Garibaldi was put forth as a nationally unifying model of manly, epic, martial heroism. Indeed, Garibaldi remains, as it were, the textbook definition of the hero, as the Garzanti dictionary entry demonstrates. However, Garibaldi's story was simultaneously inscribed as a kind of epitaph: his *sui generis* heroism—utterly unique—was to be mourned rather than imitated. These narratives promote modernization and growing up as mutually confirming processes through the figure of Garibaldi. Variously encoded as classical epic, medieval romance, Christian hagiography, and primitive folklore, the General's story always already belonged to an admirable but inaccessible past. The figure of Garibaldi effectively idealizes the complicated history of Italian unification (which had resulted in a constitutional monarchy with a parliament elected by a very limited franchise). At the same time, as these stories suggest, his brand of heroism was no longer viable in the "grown up" world of a state with industrializing and even imperialist goals. It is in fact the *fusion* of Ricciardi's ingredients—heroism and melancholy—that could effectively promote a modern Italian identity by both celebrating and outgrowing its epic past and by mapping that national, historical trajectory onto the seemingly natural development of the individual child. These books did not merely cook up stories about courageous protagonists peppered with a touch of sentimentality. Rather, they postulate heroic melancholy as Italianness. Every proper boy (*ragazzo perbene*) is called upon (indeed, called into being) both to embody and to bury the Blond Christ in the Red Shirt as part of the process of growing up and of becoming Italian.[13]

Eric Tribunella's *Melancholia and Maturation* has mapped a similar trajectory operable in many classic works of American children's literature. Tribunella, who focuses on the construction of American adults through children's literature and its reception, illuminates a process he calls "melancholic maturation." Widely read children's books in the

United States that have been prized (literally and figuratively) and have also elicited controversy model the process of maturation through the use of contrived traumatic losses. Drawing on Freud as well as on trauma studies and queer theory, Tribunella reveals the ambivalent ways in which popular texts, like *A Separate Peace* and *Old Yeller*, discipline children through stories of painful loss. Through suffering such loss and incorporating the lost object's best qualities, the child achieves the melancholy, masculine, and heteronormative adulthood that is valued by American society. Lino Ferriani's novel follows this paradigm, from the young Pin's trauma of witnessing his father die from a festering, bloody wound to his assumption of the role as new responsible husband with the potential to become a father. I will show how a similar structure is at work in the texts I analyze, deployed within a specifically Italian context. Here, Garibaldi becomes the embodiment of the ideal of heroism, an ideal that is strongly cathected, necessarily lost, and ultimately introjected as part of the process of melancholic maturation. In the Italian context, this process is figured both as the growing up of each child and as the development of the nation as it moves into modernity.

Of the several Garibaldian texts penned by Giuseppe Cesare Abba (1838–1910), *Noterelle dei uno dei Mille* was the most popular. Italy's national poet Giosue Carducci, to whom Abba dedicated the work, facilitated its publication in 1880. The definitive edition was published in 1891 as *Da Quarto al Volturno*, and renowned poet Giovanni Pascoli composed the preface to the 1909 edition, inviting the "new generation of Italy" to read about Garibaldi's "far away heroic world" (Abba, *Edizione Nazionale* 99).[14] Abba's diary, which documents his firsthand experience on the famous expedition of the thousand red-shirts, continued through the twentieth century to be recommended to Italian youth as a stirring and patriotic text (Giacobbe, *Letteratura infantile* 67). Born in the northwestern region of Liguria, Abba was 22 when he participated in the 1860 campaign that ousted the Bourbon monarchy from southern Italy and enabled the South to join Victor Emanuel's northern kingdom. Abba went on to teach for many years in the public schools of northern Italy in Brescia, Lombardy.

Abba begins the diary on May 3, in Parma, summarizing the latest political events and pointing out that Garibaldi's native city of Nizza (Nice) has been ceded by the Kingdom of Piedmont to France. In spite of Piedmont's painful diplomatic move, Garibaldi will go to aid Sicily, and Abba will be among the "lucky ones" who will follow him (1).[15] Thus, the first image of Garibaldi in Abba's account is that of a leader dedicated to the cause even without personal benefit, an immediate model of selflessness. Here, too, Abba sets the stage for a narrative in which the hero appears more often indirectly (that is, people speaking about him) than directly. Abba sailed to Sicily from Genoa on the ship commanded by Nino Bizio (the *Lombardy*) rather than on Garibaldi's vessel (the *Piedmont*), and even in Sicily, Abba's company was rarely in sight of the general during the campaign. Thus, while the real cause of Garibaldi's physical absence in much of the text is historical, the narrative effect of such absence is mythical. Garibaldi emerges as a shadowy figure, punctuating the narrative with his rare and dramatic appearances. Abba, for example, concludes his entry of May 21 with the confident assertion: "Non si sa dove sia il Generale, ma Egli veglia per tutti" (80) [We don't know where Garibaldi is, but we know he watches over us all (53)]. Such an absent omnipresence turns the general into a paternal, providential god. Abba frequently contributes to the Christian rhetoric that cloaks Garibaldi in a messianic garb. He reports that the women in Rome called him "the Nazarene" (62) and imagines that the Neapolitan folk"dev'esso parso quello di Gerusalemme il dì delle Palme" (205) [must have looked like the people of Jerusalem on the first Palm Sunday (136)] as they greet Garibaldi entering their city. Through the Christological imagery (not unique to Abba, of course), this fortunate follower justifies the expedition as liberation and salvation rather than an annexation or colonization. In addition, the figuration of Garibaldi as Christ goes further, suggesting the hero's role not only as redeemer but also as sacrifice. Having modeled sacrifice in his decision to fight for Italy in spite of the loss of his native Nizza, his ubiquitous association with Christ announces that he must also become the sacrifice. As Tribunella has noted, the dynamics of sacrifice can be read as a rite of passage into "national membership" and "maturation" (*Melancholia* xiv–xv).

Furthermore, this Christianizing rhetoric joins the evolutionary paradigm that posits the imaginative islanders with their fantastical notions (and with their frightening ferocity) as primitive and childlike. Abba points out how the largely illiterate Sicilians' reliance on oral communication produced an endless series of corruptions of Garibaldi's name, remarking "il nome di Garibadli, che da Marsala intesi storpiato in mille guise, esse lo mutavano in quel di Sinibaldo, che fu il padre di Santa Rosalia" (160) [The name, that I have heard mispronounced in a thousand different ways ever since we landed in Marsala, has now changed to Sinibaldo, the father of Santa Rosalia (104, 105)]. Illiteracy and faith are linked to ignorance of historical development and of the forward movement of time: Abba suggests that the Sicilians believe that Garibaldi actually is the reborn father of their twelfth-century patron saint. As Abba narrates the native population's adoration of Garibaldi, he documents the general's greatness, while simultaneously establishing the inferiority of the southerners that the general has redeemed.

Abba himself, like the illiterate native population, sees Garibaldi as an incarnation of the past. He writes, "il Generale seduto a piè di un olivo, mangia anche lui pane e cacio, affettandone con un suo coltello, e discorrendo alla buona con quelli che ha intorno. Io lo guardo e ho il senso della grandezza antica" (39) [[t]he general, seated at the foot of an olive tree, eats his bread and cheese, slicing it with his own knife and chatting simply with those around. I look at him and have a feeling of the greatness of bygone days (26, 27)]. Like a reborn Sinibaldo, Garibaldi seems to have been transported into modernity from an earlier time. But Abba is at pains to distinguish the Sicilians' naïve and childlike *equation* of Garibaldi with Sinibaldo from his own erudite historical *analogies*. He does so through the heavy deployment of literary models. In one comparison, Garibaldi is a hero from Xenophon (196). The parallel not only associates Garibaldi with the grandeur of antiquity but also implies a civilization/barbarism dichotomy, in which southern Italy emerges as a modern-day Persia: Xenophon and his fellow Greeks on their "Expedition of the Ten Thousand" into Persia parallel Garibaldi leading his Thousand northern Italians into the South.[16] Continuing to cull models from ancient Greek history, Abba further claims that Garibaldi trusts his second-in-command Nino Bixio as his "Leonides" and that the Maddeloni Pass has become "our Thermopylae" (210, 225). The comparison calls forth the famous episode of Greek courage recorded in Herodotus, underscoring once again Garibaldi's bravery as well as the disparity in numbers between the small band of liberators and the far more numerous royal troops. In addition, for Abba's older readers, the image resonates with Giacomo Leopardi's famous 1818 poem "All'Italia." In this canonical patriotic text, the poet recalls the Greeks at Thermopylae in order to shame contemporary Italians who do not similarly defend their homeland. Through the association with Thermopylae, then, Abba suggests that Garibaldi has at last come to answer Leopardi's impassioned *"ubi sunt?"* call. Not only antiquity but also the Romantic period offers material for Abba's similes: Abba claims that Garibaldi is like Byron's Conrad, drawing on the 1814 *Corsair* of the British Romantic poet. The anachronism of Garibaldi—an epic and Romantic hero in a modern world—is rendered by Abba for his literate readers through a shared corpus of literary and historical texts (Herodotus, Xenophon, Byron, Leopardi). This strategy generates a self-consciously and historically aware nostalgic stance, set in stark opposition to the naïve enthusiasm of the primitive, illiterate Sicilians.

In this nostalgic vein, Garibaldi embodies simplicity and purity: "Così, con la semplicità di un Re pastore, con l'eleganza d'un eroe Senofonteo, meglio ancora! Così come egli stesso nelle foreste vergini Riograndesi de' suoi giovani anni, Garibaldi diede l'ora a segno di stella" (196) [So with the simplicity of a shepherd king, or shall we say with the elegance of a hero from the pages of Xenophon, or perhaps better still—like himself when young, in the virgin forests of Rio Grande, Garibaldi set the hour by a star (130)]. Ultimately, then, the range of similes and metaphors proves inadequate, as Garibaldi is comparable only to himself (another gesture of deification) and thus implicitly unrepeatable. For Abba, the general is a premodern hero, tied to nature (forests, shepherds, stars) and eschewing technology. Paradoxically, however, his exploits enable the modernization and growing up of the natives he liberates. In the entry of June 28, Abba with unabashed arrogance remarks that the inhabitants of Rocca Palumba "[p]arevano gente del medioevo rimasta viva proprio per aspettarci" (150) [looked like people from the Middle Ages preserved for this very purposes of greeting us (98)]. By following Garibaldi, the apparently frozen-in-time medieval Sicilians mature: as they march north, they move forward from local to national identity, from riotous insurgents to disciplined soldiers, from boys to men. Leveraging the term *picciotto*, which means both "youth/young man" and "Sicilian volunteers who joined Garibaldi's Red Shirts," and sounding almost like a proud father himself, Abba proclaims, "Che gloria di *picciotti* in quel momento! Due mesi fa erano riottosi a imbarcarsi pel continente: pareva che non avessero idea d'altra Italia, fuori del triangolo della loro isola: ma marciando per la Calabria trovarono i loro cuori, qui si son fatti ammirare. Caricarono come veterani!" (219) [This was the moment when the Picciotti covered themselves with glory. Two months before, they were riotous on embarking for the continent; it appeared they had no notion of any Italy beside their own three-cornered island. Marching through Calabria, however, they have become new men and they have won our respect here (146)].

By the end of the diary, the rhetoric of melancholy prevails, becoming acute at the conclusion in spite of the victorious outcome of the campaign. Abba recalls a "malinconia cupa" (243) [dark melancholy] pervading the surviving troops, and offering a rare direct description of the hero, he speculates, "[f]orse nella mente del Generale passava un pensiero mesto" (239) [Perhaps Garibaldi felt sad (160, 161)]. In the concluding pages, the model of heroism becomes a very monument to melancholy: "Così si andò verso il Palazzo reale, a sfilare dinanzi al Direttore piantato là sulla gran porta, come un momumento.... Il Generale, pallido come forse non fu visto mail, ci guardava. S'indovinava che il pianto gli si rivolgeva indietro e gli allagava il cuore.... Ora odo dire che il Generale parte, che se ne va a Caprera, a vivere come in un altro pianeta (244, 245) [We marched past Garibaldi, who stood at the great gate rigid as though carved in stone.... The General was paler than we had ever seen him before. He watched us go by. One could guess that tears were near and that his heart was sore.... Now I hear that the General is leaving for Caprera, to live as on another planet (165)]. Seemingly transported from antiquity to inspire the passage of the nation into modernity and the passage of Italian children into adulthood, Garibaldi is now transported away. Like a sacrificed Christ, he ascends to another realm ("to live as on another planet"). Indeed, the diary seems to narrate the very transition of the hero into his own monument ("as though carved in stone"). The gesture would become literalized in later children's books. The 1910 edition of Checchi's biography concludes with an appendix of 23 full-page images of statues commemorating Garibaldi from all over Italy and beyond, with Nizza's monument to its native son as the final image.

As popular as Abba's work was, Edmondo De Amicis's *Cuore*, published in 1886, boasted even wider appeal.[17] By 1904, the book stood alongside Collodi's *Le avventure di Pinocchio* at the top of the children's literature market. The influential and strongly patriotic novel is set in Turin (which had been Italy's first capital) and takes the form of the diary of a middle-class, primary schoolboy named Enrico. The diary structure parallels Abba's *Noterelle* and creates a similar effect of first-hand authenticity and immediacy. De Amicis echoes Abba, too, in depicting an exclusively male homosocial setting.[18] Young Enrico entrusts the day-to-day events of an academic year in a northern classroom rather than the exploits of a military campaign on a southern battlefield to his journal. Study, self-discipline, and devotion to education are the forms of "little" and "humble" heroism needed in the new Italy.

In addition to Enrico's daily entries, the novel includes letters that Enrico's parents write to him over the course of the year, often to inspire, praise, or censure him. The letter appearing as the first installment for the month of June serves as a brief but powerful biography of Garibaldi. The text enumerates the General's larger-than-life martial exploits in a series of staccato-like sentences in the remote past tense, evacuated of any historical explanation. Enrico and his readers learn that Garibaldi "salvò la vita a una donna ... combattè dieci anni in America ... difese Roma ... liberò Palermo ... lottò nel 1870 contro i tedeschi" [saved a woman's life ... fought for ten years in America ... defended Rome ... liberated Palermo ... fought against the Germans in 1870] (228) and so forth. This list culminates by promising Enrico that he "leggerai le sue gesta" [will read about his deeds] (228), using the word *gesta* and thus, in the context of all these heroic acts, evoking the medieval "*chanson de geste*" genre.

With the transition from past to future tense verbs, the letter moves into a hagiographic register: "quando non sarai più al mondo tu, ... ancora le generazioni vedranno in alto la sua testa luminosa di rendentore di popoli coronata dai nomi delle sue vittorie come da un cerchio di stelle ed ad ogni italiano risplenderà la fronte e l'anima pronunziando il suo nome" [When you (Enrico) will no longer walk the face of the earth, ... even still will those generations gaze on high to behold the luminous face of the people's redeemer, his head crowned with the names of his victories as if a circle of stars. The face and the soul of every Italian will glow at the sound of his name] (229). The apotheosis of Garibaldi here combines two specific biblical passages. First, the image of the crown of stars echoes St. John's famous vision recorded in Revelations (12:1): "A great sign appeared in the sky, a woman clothed with the sun, with the moon under her feet, and on her head a crown of twelve stars." At the same time, the ability of the hero's name to trigger spontaneous adoration evokes St. Paul's letter to the Philippians (2: 9–11): "Therefore God also has highly exalted Him and given Him the name which is above every name, that at the name of Jesus every knee should bow, of those in heaven, and of those on earth, and of those under the earth, And that every tongue should confess that Jesus Christ is Lord, to the glory of God the Father." This juxtaposition of biblical imagery creates a Garibaldi who is both Jesus and Mary, suggesting a kind of fantasy of original wholeness and sexual pre-difference. Through this rhetoric, De Amicis endows the modern, secular state with its religion. Through that religion, and through the acknowledgment of one maternal-paternal figure, the children of Padua, Lombardy, Florence, Sardinia, Naples, Romagna, Genoa, Calabria, and Sicily (about whom we read in the novel *Cuore* and who read the novel) become Italian.

Not only Garibaldi's heroic *gesta* or his secular divinity must be acknowledged, but also his death. The letter moves from past-tense verbs that narrate his heroic exploits to future-tense verbs that describe the unquestioning homage his name will inspire. We are left with an evacuated present, which is marked as a time of mourning. "Oggi è un lutto nazionale" [Today is a day of national mourning] and "il mondo intero lo piange" [the whole world weeps for him] (228) are almost the only instances of present-tense verbs in the passage. De Amicis in fact chose to set the novel four years previous to its publication, specifically in the year of Garibaldi's death. The letter of June 3 and, by synecdoche, *Cuore* as a whole, which remains notorious for heavy deployment of sentimentality, can announce the hero's death with the power of immediacy but also serve as a kind of epitaph. De Amicis marks Garibaldi's death and the mourning it generates as enabling the birth of the nation. By acknowledging Garibaldi as the mother/father of the nation, the children of each region become Italian, and in mourning that dead figure they become modern Italian adults.

Garibaldi's presence in *Cuore* is not limited to the obituary letter from Enrico's father. Rather, the effects of Garibaldi's 1860 expedition through the South inhabit the novel, embodied particularly in the character of the "Calabrian boy." Repeatedly described as "dark," which was a typical marker of southern Italians, this pupil joins Enrico's Turinese class where he is met with exuberant warmth from the paternal teacher, Signor Perboni.[19] In perhaps the best-known passage from the novel, Perboni uses the arrival of the Calabrian boy as an opportunity to remind the class (and the readers) that this very event—this union of south and north—exemplifies the marvelous fruit of the hard-fought unification movement: "Ricordatevi bene di quello che vi dico. Perchè questo fatto possa accadere, che un ragazzo calabrese fosse come in casa sua a Torino, e che un ragazzo di Torino fosse come a casa propria a Reggio di Calabria, il nostro paese lottò per cinquant'anni e trantamila italiani morirono" [Remember well what I am telling you. In order for this event to take place, for a Calabrian boy to feel at home in Turin, and for a boy from Turin to feel as if in his own home in Reggio Calabria, for this our country fought for fifty years and thirty thousand Italians died] (31).[20] While Perboni's stirring words imagine a kind of balance and reciprocity, the text itself dramatizes only the first scenario—that of the southern boy coming north. Piedmont absorbs Calabria, not the other way around, in spite of the rhetorical parallelism in Perboni's speech. This swarthy boy, who rarely speaks in the entire novel, becomes a shadow of his luminous blond liberator. In stark contrast to Giuseppe Garibaldi, whose *name* has the power to inspire awe, the dark student does not here receive a name, and throughout the novel he is called "il calabrese" [the Calabrian boy]. We learn later that the boy's name is Coraci, though this is revealed precisely in the moment of his being chosen to represent Calabria in a municipal award ceremony (139): that is, he is most "himself" (i.e., named) exactly when he is most literally assigned the role of *the* Calabrian in a kind of civic theater. Through its token southerner, and perhaps in spite of itself, the novel announces the effects of Garibaldi's campaign: the silencing of the "backward" South and its homogenization into the North. This shadowy Calabrian, whose presence in Piedmont was enabled by Garibaldi, must not aspire to his liberator's revolutionary heroics but rather, as his namelessness and silence attest, must quietly integrate himself into his Turinese schoolroom.

Signor Perboni's all-boy schoolroom was not the only one in which Garibaldi was conjured for nationalizing purposes. Collodi, like De Amicis, depicts a teacher who invokes Garibaldi, or rather his spectral image, in order to turn rambunctious rascals into proper Italian men. Collodi's 1890 *La laterna magica di Giannettino* [*Giannettino's Magic Lantern*] opens with the protagonist, now a fine young man, visiting his uncle Giampaolo and his class of boys who are 12 to 15 years old.[21] Poor Giampaolo is beside himself with frustration: this bunch of ne'er-do-wells, who do not believe that grammar or geography serves any purpose and who show "nessunissima voglia di studiare" [not even the slightest desire to study] (4), are sure to embarrass him when the school inspector arrives. Giannettino offers to serve as his uncle's teaching assistant for the 25 days that remain before the inspection. How will he manage where his uncle has failed? He uses the enchanting strategy of the magic lantern to instruct and delight the boys with images and stories of Italy's great men of the past. Ernico Mazzanti, already familiar to readers for having illustrated the first book edition of Collodi's *Le avventure di Pinocchio* and many other texts, provides the array of illustrations depicting such luminaries (indeed in a literal sense here) as Antonio Canova and Giuseppe Verdi, each positioned within a rounded frame that replicates the lantern's lens.[22] Thus, readers can assume the role of the schoolboys, seeing what they see. The image that opens Chapter 4 depicts Giannettino operating the lantern in front of the attentive class.

One pupil turns his head around to face the viewer and thus seems to invite us to join him in the classroom and to become one of the boys (see Figure 1.1).[23]

Not surprisingly, the models depicted for the boys to instruct them not only in history but also in the value of hard work are all men. The very last image in this visual parade of male role models is Giuseppe Garibaldi. Mazzanti portrays the Blond Hero *with* Victor Emmauel II, in an image that underscores Garibaldi's humility and dedication to the nation over his personal glory (see Figure 1.2). Similarly, when Giannettino provides the students with Garibaldi's birthdate (July 4, 1807), he adds the information that Cavour was born in that same year and Mazzini in the following year, clearly investing this historical accident with ideological meaning and leveraging it to create a unified version of the unification. However, at odds with such gestures that incorporate Garibaldi into a broader narrative about the birth of the nation and weave his story into a wider and unified effort are the gestures that insist on his uniqueness. Giannettino, first of all, recounts the biographies of the king and the warrior separately (even if their images are united) with Garibaldi's as the concluding and thus culminating story. In the sentence that opens his biography, the word "hero" appears three times (192). Giannettino goes on to highlight the fact that Garibaldi was a self-taught man, who

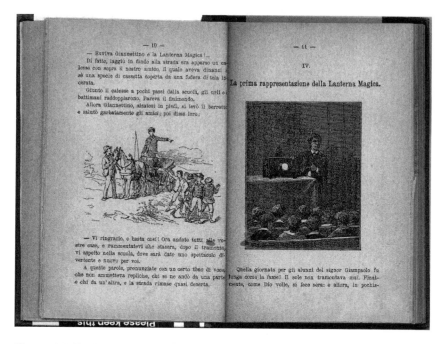

Figure 1.1 Enrico Mazzanti, from *La laterna magica di Giannettino* by Carlo Collodi.

did not need lessons in fencing or athletics because "imparò tutto da sè: fu maestro a sè stesso" [he learned everything by himself: he was his own master] (193). Such an assertion seems to work against the very *raison d'être* of Collodi's book itself and the pedagogical mission that gave it birth: we recall that the opening chapters dramatize precisely the urgent need for boys to respect their schoolteachers and submit to their lessons. Instead, this succinctly forceful insistence on his auto-didacticism, with the repeated use of "sè" [himself], serves to emphasize Garibaldi's uniqueness and echoes the familiar language of divinity— the one who creates himself rather than is created—that had already accrued around Garibaldi.

As the brief biography progresses, this tension—between the need to mobilize Garibaldi as part of a collective, national project and as a role model for obedient boys, in opposition to the need to insist on his inimitable uniqueness—begins to break the frames that seek to contain him. When asked about the hero's martial exploits, Giannettino lists the names of the major battles for which he is famous while the boys continue to gaze on his image. But rather than go into any detail about the various military campaigns he has named, Giannettino abruptly refers the students to a history book. The young teaching assistant, standing next to his modern (though, as Welle has pointed out, no longer completely novel) technological teaching prop, cannot adequately represent the hero: his deeds are in excess of what can be contained in this book or enclosed within the lantern's lens. And, it is with this gesture of Giannettino referring his students back to a history book that this book ends, suggesting that the narration can no longer move forward, but only turn backward:

— E queste campagne non ce le racconta?

— Non tocca a me a raccontarvele, perchè anderei troppo in lungo; tocca alla storia. Prendete dunque la storia d'Italia degli ultimi cinquant'anni; leggetela attentamente, e sono sicuro che dopo mi ringrazierete. E qui, miei cari amici, faccio punto e vi do la buona notte.

A queste parole tenne dietro uno scoppio battimenti e di *Viva Garibaldi*: e dopo pochi minuti le porte della Scuola erano già chiuse.

[And aren't you going to tell us about these campaigns?

It is not up to me to tell you about them, because I would go on and on: this is history's job. So go get the history of Italy of the last fifty years, and read it carefully. I am certain that once you have, you will thank me. And here, my good friends, I wrap it up and bid you a good night.

An eruption of applause and shouts of "Long Live Garibaldi" followed these words. After a few minutes, the doors to the school closed.] (196)

Thus school doors and the book (these are its last lines) close as the spectral image projected by the lantern goes dark and the voices keeping Garibaldi's name alive die away. Giannettino has fulfilled his promise to his uncle by revealing Garibaldi's "generous and noble heart" (193) to his students. At the culmination of this pedagogical project of turning uppity boys into Italian men, readers find flickering shadows, lingering echoes, and the injunction to turn back to history books.

Another text in which Garibaldi seems to be both necessary to and yet an uncomfortable fit for modern Italy is the novel *Piccoli eroi* by Virginia Tedeschi Treves under the pen name "Cordelia" (1849–1916). Cordelia had already established herself as the director of the children's periodical *Giornale dei fanciulli* [*Newspaper for Kids*] when she published *Piccoli eroi* in 1892 with Milan's Treves Brothers, the same house that had published *Cuore*. Cordelia openly announces her indebtedness

Vittorio Emanuele e Garibaldi.

Figure 1.2 Enrico Mazzanti, from *La laterna magica di Giannettino* by Carlo Collodi.

to *Cuore*. In her dedication of the novel to "children between nine and fourteen years old," she clearly echoes De Amicis's own dedication and calls De Amicis a "dear and illustrious teacher."[24] *Piccoli eroi* met with great success.

The protagonist, Maria Morandi, is the 17-year-old eldest sibling of a lower-middle-class family in Milan (one of the most industrialized cities in Italy at the time). We learn in the first sentence of the book that Maria's mother has died, leaving Signor Morandi, an office worker, with six children. The novel, then, unfolds in the space of heroic melancholy: as they mourn their mother, the Morandi children must learn to be "little heroes." The siblings, and the children reading about them, receive guidance through the stories that Maria narrates periodically as they spend the summer in their modest country cottage. These stories, with their brave and self-sacrificing child protagonists, mirror in content and function the nine famous "monthly stories" from De Amicis's *Cuore*. This deliberate echo allows us to chart another step in the elaboration of Italian heroism: from Abba's sprawling battlefields to De Amicis's and Collodi's public classrooms to Cordelia's private cottage, the spaces in which Italians are being made become smaller and smaller; the heroism being modeled ever more domestic. Such domestication does not, I think, derive solely from the fact that a woman wrote the novel or from the prominence of the female characters. Rather, the lessons here are intended for all Italian children, as the dedication explicitly states and as the central role of the male siblings implies. Indeed, the text is at pains both to celebrate the manly, martial heroism of the past and to disown and in a sense contain and domesticate that kind of revolutionary fervor.

To that end, the novel emphasizes the 1848 revolutions rather than the more recent wars for independence or Garibaldi's 1860 campaign, thus pushing those memories into a more distant past. Maria imparts the lesson of heroism to her vivacious and impatient brother Carlo, explaining that "al giorno d'oggi" [nowadays] a hero does not need to be a warrior but rather "eroe si può esserlo in tutti i luoghi, in tutte le professioni, alla scuola, all'officina, fra le pareti domestiche, purchè uno dimentichi sè stesso, rinunci al proprio piacere, alla propria volontà, per un alto ideale, per il bene del suo paese, della propria famiglia e dei suoi simili" [you can be a hero anywhere—in any profession, at school, in the office, at home—as long as you put your own needs aside, give up your own pleasures, and renounce your own will for an ideal, for the good of your country, your own family, and your fellow men] (11). Her words of wisdom to Carlo come in response to his agitated and impatient desire to become a swashbuckling military hero just like Garibaldi.[25] Maria must convince him that settling down to study for his Latin exams is the kind of heroism expected of him. Carlo's desire to imitate Garibaldi here is coded as childishness.

Maria is aided in her child-rearing duties by Don Vincenzo, an old friend of their deceased uncle. The children admire Don Vincenzo for having participated in the 1848 uprising against the Austrian Hapsburgs. He speaks nostalgically of the good old days of the 1848 liberal revolutions, idealizing the period as one of comradery, brotherhood, and unity.[26] Don Vincenzo's speeches consistently separate his youth from the present, speaking of "quel tempo" [back then], a time when "eravamo tutti eroi" [we were all heroes] (22). Don Vincenzo recalls the initial enthusiasm inspired by Pius IX, who appeared to embrace liberal ideas early in his papacy (21). The evocation of this Pope implicitly recalls Garibaldi, who had famously attempted to defend the short-lived Roman republic in 1849. The hero, however, remains safely buried in the nostalgic tales of bygone days.

Significantly, this old revolutionary explains the current economic and social structure in the Milanese province: he speaks glowingly of the rich industrialist family who lives in the villa on the hill and whose enormous factory provides employment for so many in the town. The generous Guerini family does not forget the poor or the church in its charity: in fact, the family has just purchased an organ for the local parish (10). Coming from the mouth of the old liberal insurgent, this paternalistic account of the modern industrial economic system is endorsed as the legitimate realization of Risorgimento goals.

The strike of the factory workers constitutes a dramatic climax in the novel. The workers become violent and spend their time getting drunk and letting their children run wild. For Cordelia, it is the working class, rather than the dangerous Sicilian natives, who occupy a bottom rung of the evolutionary ladder. At least twice, they are explicitly described as unruly and ungrateful children, as with the straightforward assertion, "[i]l popolo è come un fanciullino" [the folk are like little children] (32). Their status as children is aligned with their premodern primitive ignorance, as they embrace superstitious snake oil remedies rather than the antiseptic washes, which, as Maria patiently explains, are one of the many benefits of scientific progress. Signora Guerini, the wife of the factory *padrone*, is described as a suffering, "all-sorrowful" Madonna, and laments, "quello che mi rincresce di più è di vedere l'ingratitudine dei nostri operai, che abbiamo pur trattato sempre bene, come fossero nostri figli" [what hurts me the most is to see the ingratitude of our workers, whom we have always treated well, as if they were our own children] (61). In a mutually justifying analogy, Signora Guerini treats her upstart worker-children in a way that implicitly mirrors Maria, constantly at pains to educate and domesticate her energetic sibling-children. Factory workers—like the Sicilian *picciotti* in Abba's text—are perceived as threatening but necessary to the new Italy. The paternalistic discourse underwritten by a veneer of evolutionary theory works through the anxiety of class issues and is endorsed by the old revolutionary. The novel nostalgically conjures Garibaldi and his heroism but at the same time mournfully leaves him in the past so that the children and the nation may grow up.

Italian children who shared young Carlo's enthusiasm for Garibaldian heroics had ample material with which to stimulate and satisfy such fantasies. Emilio Salgari offered an imaginary space in which Garibaldian theatrics could be indulged, starting with *Le tigri di Mompracem* in 1883. Scholar Cristina della Coletta has convincingly shown how Salgari mined imagery from the cult of Garibaldi generally and, quite specifically, from Garibaldi's 1860 *Les Mèmoires de Garibaldi*, his autobiography, co-authored with Alexandre Dumas. Deploying the topoi of the adventure story, Salgari (as della Coletta shows) uses Garibaldi as the model for his fictional character Sandokan, a deposed prince-turned-pirate. Like Garibaldi, Sandokan is an underdog—we remember Abba's insistence on the disparity of numbers between the garibaldini and the Bourbons, for example. Just as Garibaldi faced the oppressive forces of empires and monarchies, Sandokan pits himself against the imperial might of the English. Salgari transposes Garibaldi's mid-century struggles against the Brazilian and Argentinian powers to the similarly exotic (from the Italian viewpoint) Malayan Islands. Della Coletta documents how Salgari imported specific lexical choices and broad discursive strategies from the Garibaldi/Dumas text almost whole cloth in order to mass produce a daring, larger-than-life avenging hero on the side of good in a clear-cut moral universe. However, della Coletta rightly notes that "Salgari's tone is more subdued and elegiac—if Garibaldi's world basks in a tropical dawn, that of Sandokan is fading into the sunset" (162). The melancholic tenor of Salgari's popular series of adventure novels, "[w]hile expressing nostalgia for the values of a heroic and idealized national past" (165) discloses that those values are no longer operable in the modern Italian state. Pino Boero and Carmine De Luca, too, underscore the melancholy tones of Salgari's work, which emerge most notably in the losses, separations, and departures with which the Sandokan novels tend to conclude: "Per quanto riguarda il primo ciclo, non sarebbe inopportuno rileggere le pagine famosissime e intense delle azioni, degli agguati, di una natura nemica, pronta a contribuire alle sofferenze dei protagonisti; ma altrettanto proficuamente si potrebbe riflettere sulla malinconia che tutto questo movimento sottintende, e per farlo basterà prendere le conclusioni dei volumi del 'ciclo di Sandokan'" [Regarding the first cycle, it would not be inopportune to re-read those famous pages that are so full of action and ambushes, pages that depict nature as an enemy, ready to inflict suffering on the protagonists; but just as usefully we could reflect on the melancholy that all this movement implies, and to do so it is enough to look at the conclusions of the Sandokan cycle] (67).[27] I would suggest that the melancholy that permeates the entire series, as perceived by Boero and De Luca, derives from plots that end in loss, but its effect is enabled by the genre. That is, the serialized, formulaic novels enable readers both to celebrate and to mourn the singular, *sui generis* epic hero whose stories they disseminate through the disjunction between the incomparable Garibaldi and the serialized Sandokan. The very form of the novels, in addition to their plots and tone, bespeak the misfit between the fetishized hero and the modern world in which his stories circulated and were consumed.

The contradiction between the larger-than-life, unique, and incomparable heroism embodied in Garibaldi (we recall the "over and above" of Ferriani, and the "comparable only to himself" of Abba) and the normalizing nature of the texts that offer his biography as a model for "making Italians" has already emerged in the novels considered above. The contradiction becomes even more jarring, almost comically so, in the popular children's periodical *Il giornalino della Domenica*.[28] Directed by Luigi Bertelli (an extremely well-known children's author himself, under the pen name Vamba), this Florentine journal commemorated the centenary of Garibaldi's birth in July 1907 with a Garibaldi-themed issue (anno 2, numero 27, July 7, 1907). Giuseppe Abba, Lino Ferriani, Augusto Vecchi ("Jack La Bolina"),[29] and other children's writers contributed pieces to the issue, which also included images of Garibaldi and even facsimiles of his handwritten notes. The short articles rehearse the by now familiar images. One piece alone, not even a full page in length, calls Garibaldi a "redentore di popoli ... paladino dei deboli ... San Giorgio di tutti gli oppressi" [redeemer of the people, paladin of the weak, Saint George of all the oppressed] (Bertelli, *Il giornalino* 7) and claims that he surpasses any hero from the pages of Virgil, Tasso, Livy, or Plutarch.[30] The rhetoric in this issue, in short, predictably resuscitates the luminaries of the classical world and of the medieval chivalric tradition in order to commemorate the birth of the hero.

However, these visual and verbal homages to Garibaldi are quite literally surrounded by reminders of the quotidian and decidedly non-heroic realities of modern-day Italy. Visually on the page, these essays, images, and facsimiles of the hero's own handwriting lie side by side with advertisements for all sorts of elixirs, medications, and nutritional supplements. For example, moms are advised that if their "little ones" wet the bed, they should not blame the children, rather, they should use Dr. Giutoli's infallible "anti-enuretic powder" right away (Bertelli xiii).[31] A youthful female face confesses "Io con Odol, per farmi più piacente mi risciacquo la bocca ogni mattina" [I rinse with Odol every morning so my breath is more pleasant] (v). Suitable for a July issue, the paper counsels nervous parents to turn to Fosfatina Falieres which "previene e arresta la diarrea così micidiale nei bambini sopratutto durante i calori estivi [prevents and cures diarrhea, so dangerous to children, especially in the summer heat] (viii). Even Nestlé makes an appearance, the Swiss company reminding readers that their formula "supplisce l'insufficienza del latte materno e facilita lo svezzamento" [supplements insufficient breast milk and facilitates weaning] (iv).

At points, the contradictions between the memories of Risorgimento martyrdom and the realities of twentieth-century marketing become acute, or perhaps better, "obtuse" in the Barthean sense. Beyond and indeed in spite of the informational content and even the symbolic meanings communicated by the advertisements or by the articles, another effect emerges from their juxtapositions. Two pairs of texts elucidate the "third meaning" that I am describing here. On page 24 in the right-hand-side column, new mothers are assured that "Iperbiotina Malesci" is a "[r]imedio naturale ... guarisce: Anemia, Scrofola, Linfatismo, ecc. ecc" [natural remedy that cures anemia, scrofula, lymphatism, etc. etc.] (see Figure 1.3). Above this, another advertisement for a shop in Florence boasts an excellent selection of baby carriages. The illustration shows a mother drawn with delicate lines, decked out in a fine cape and bonnet, and offering a balloon to her baby who is perched comfortably in the deluxe model carriage. Adjacent to these advertisements, in the left column, we are commanded to read ("leggete") Garibaldi's consoling letter to Mrs. Anna Poma, the mother of Carlo, fallen "martire alla patria italiana" [martyr for the Italian fatherland] (24). In his effort to comfort Mrs. Poma, Garibaldi remarks how the sacrifice of mothers is the greatest sacrifice of all ("il massimo dei sacrifici"). Under the letter to Mrs. Poma, we see a reproduction of a photograph of Garibaldi with consoling words in his own handwriting to another hero's mother. The text under the reproduced, autographed photograph reminds us that Garibaldi "fu buono come sanno esserlo soltanto i veri eroi" [was good, as only true heroes know how to be] (24). Thus, two rather incongruous discourses of maternity emerge side by side, each one issued as a sort of command: the first authorized by Garibaldi and couched in the religious rhetoric of sacrifice and martyrdom, implicitly casting Italian mothers as secular Madonnas who offer their sons to the fatherland; the other a call to shop for products that provide comfort and ease. In short, mothers are commanded to produce heroic sons on one side of the page and to accumulate and consume commodities on the other.

A similar relationship is created between the advertisement on page xiii and the illustration on page 19. An image of a contented and rotund mother pulling clothes from the laundry line and piling them on her son's shoulders accompanies the mother's joyful claim that she has been "spared so much work and effort by using Sunlight Soap" [Quanto lavoro e fatica risparmiati usando Sunlight Sapone!] (xiii). A few pages after the advertisement for this British product, another image appears as if in direct counterpoint: a mother stricken by a look of terror and panic grabs her two sons' hands and drags them away from an incoming cannon ball, under the title "I piccoli martiri della Repubblica Romana" [Little Martyrs of the Roman Republic] (19). The accompanying texts informs us that in 1849 these children fell dead at their mother's feet, smashed by

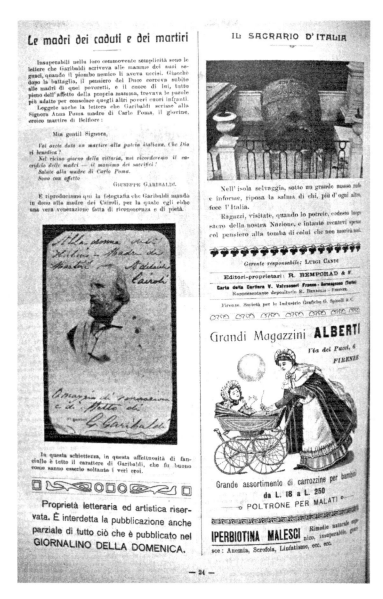

Figure 1.3 From *Il giornalino della Domenica*, edited by Luigi Bertelli.

a bomb that exploded two steps from her.[32] The advertisements, aimed at the parents (and specifically mothers) of the early-twentieth-century middle-class readers of the periodical, seem to comment ironically on the earnest, heroic narratives of sacrifice that they accompany. On the one hand, shopping is elevated to the level of patriotic duty: while the sword-carrying Garibaldi fights back tyrants in the name of liberty and independence, contemporary anemic readers do battle with bad breath, dirty laundry, and stomachaches, wielding the hygienic products of foreign corporations. On the other hand, commemoration is degraded to the level of consumerism. I am not suggesting that the journal editors intended this ironic structure. Rather, the parallelism—at times literal, in two columns of the same page—between the call to emulate past heroism and the call to consume modern products emerges as the effect of the mass-marketing of a fetishized Garibaldi. Indeed, recalling how many of the products advertised are in fact nutritional supplements, I would argue that the relationship that emerges is one of "supplementarity" in the Derridean sense: the advertisements both supplant the heroic discourse they accompany and reveal the lack, or "insufficiency" to quote Nestlé, within that discourse. The strategy of making Italians through the relentless purveying of a mourned Garibaldi becomes visible in the pages of the modern middle-class weekly. The supplementarity reveals that the "incorporation" of the lost loved object has become consumerism—the image of the hero himself has become a commodity—and that precisely *as such* the process is made effective.

The 1907 centenary of Garibaldi's birth was not the last occasion on which *Il giornalino* reminded its young readers of the nation's hero. Giuseppe Ernesto Nuccio (1874–1933), a regular contributor to the journal, dramatized the events of 1859–1860 in and around his father's native Palermo in his novel *Picciotti e garibaldini*, first published in 1910–1911 in installments in *Il giornalino* and then in 1913 as an illustrated volume by Bemporad.[33] Although by no means a classic on the scale of *Cuore*, the novel has had multiple reprintings.[34] Subtitled "Romanzo storico sulla Rivoluzione del 1859–1860," the novel as a whole exemplifies aspects of the realist tradition that had been forged by the great Sicilian *verismo* writers Giovanni Verga and Luigi Capuana. Nuccio's historical novel, which includes characters taken from real life such as Nino Bixio and Salvatore Maniscalco, immerses the reader in a wealth of geographic precision as it tracks the movements of the young revolutionaries by including the names of streets, piazzas, theaters, and churches in Palermo. The prose is rich in descriptive detail and transcriptions of his characters' Sicilian dialect, such as *"Oh matri, matruzza bedda!"* (170) pepper the narrative. However, embedded within this realist approach are a range of discursive strategies that mobilize premodern literary forms.

Over the course of the long novel (47 chapters), Nuccio builds a group of protagonists. The opening pages introduce us to the teenage shepherd, Fedele, who returns to Palermo from the countryside. In the city, Fedele encounters other boys, such as the 11-year-old orphan Pispisedda, the older boy Rocco who ends up imprisoned, and other boys whose nicknames exemplify various traits, like Centolingue ("Hundred-languages") and Cacciatore ("Hunter"), and thus an ensemble cast gradually forms. Because the boys are often separated—some secretly transporting weapons, some on messenger missions, some protecting the women—many scenes play out as reunions among subsets of the group. Readers are kept abreast of events throughout Palermo and its surrounding countryside as each boy brings his friends up to date on the events he has recently witnessed or deeds he has accomplished. This strategy allows Nuccio to limit the omniscient narrator's voice and instead offer multiple scenes of storytelling. The listeners in the text goad the speakers with demands of "tell us," as when Pispisedda urges young don Gaetanino to get to the point with "Contami, contami, fratuzzu" [tell me, tell me, brother] (180). The stories, coming from the mouths of the boys, are often interrupted with descriptions of the other boys' reactions. Empirical readers thus find a model in the desirous, eager fictional listeners, transported by patriotic fervor, elated by Garibaldi's victories and devastated by setbacks; thus, Nuccio constructs his ideal readers. Furthermore, the personalities of the different narrator-characters and the logistical demands of various settings allow Nuccio to draw on a range of genres. In this manner, Nuccio incorporates multiple discursive techniques into the realist frame.

The adult character known as "Indovino" [Fortune Teller], for example, recounts his memories of the 1848 revolutions and his predictions of a coming savior in biblical and prophetic rhetoric. It is he, in fact, who sets the stage in the novel's first chapter. As the boys gather around to hear his tales, he elides Sicilian history into Salvation history:

> Una volta—cominciò il vecchio con quella sua voce pacata che pareva venisse di lontano—una volta, un giovinetto—si chiamava Nicolò Garzilli, c'era il gelo e compiono ora nove anni—disse: 'Gli uomini non li deve comandare nessuno! Meglio morti che schiavi! E (come David che, piccolo quale era, se la prese col gigante Golia) il giovinetto se la prese col gigante Borbone. ...Santa Rosalia, la vergine palermitana che salvò Palermo dal colera, la salverà dalla schiavitù dei Borboni e manderà un guerriero fatato. E tutti quelli che lavorano la terra e quelli che vanno pei monti come siete voi, scenderanno alla pianura, e Palermo sarà libera per *secula et seculorum*. (2–4; Latin and italics in orig.)

> ["Once upon a time," began the old man with that peaceful voice of his that seemed to come from far away, "once upon a time, a young boy—he was named Nicolò Garzilli, it was winter, and nine years have gone by since then—said, 'Men must not be controlled by anybody! Better dead than a slave!' And (like David, who, little though he was, took on the giant Goliath) the boy took on the Bourbon

Giant. ... Saint Rosalia, the virgin from Palermo who saved her city from the cholera, will save it from the enslavement of the Bourbons and will send an enchanted warrior. And all those who work the land and those who come from the mountains, like you, will come down to the plain, and Palermo will be free for *secula et seculorum*.]

The direct reference to David and Goliath of course underscores the disparity in strength between tyrant and oppressed, the invocation of Saint Rosalia and her miracles typifies southern Italian spirituality which is marked by strong devotion to the local patron saint, and the biblical formula left in Latin evokes specifically the Vulgate's Book of Revelations, endowing the arrival of Garibaldi with the inevitable force of messianic prophecy. Taken together, this rhetoric inscribes the particular political history of Palermo into the realm of the sacred. At the same time, Indovino's opening phrase "once upon a time" (repeated twice), the image of the enchanted warrior, and (elsewhere in this passage) the phrase "cammina cammina cammina" (walk walk walk) all mobilize the standard rhetoric and imagery of fairy tales. Through the narrator-character, then, Nuccio is able to embed these premodern literary forms into his realist novel and to solder the association of Garibaldi with the premodern.

At other times, fairy tale codes are employed because, at the diegetic level, the presence of Bourbon troops requires allegorical strategies in order to avoid suspicion or punishment. In chapter 14, for example, young don Gaetanino enchants his friends with tales of "quanno magno" (dialect for Carlo Magno, Charlamagne). When Bourbon soldiers appear in the piazza, the boy "immaginò un *cuntu* tutto nuovo, mai detto o pensato" [came up with an entirely new tale, never before told or imagined] (54; italics in orig.). He goes on to weave the tale of the Mammo-drago, a creature with 100 heads and who commands 100,000 soldiers. These soldiers take all the food from the town to feed the ravenous Mammo-drago, leaving even the women and children to starve. Finally, one brave man decides to fight back, and a huge battle breaks out between the citizens and the soldiers. Don Gaetanino pauses in his narration and notes that the real soldiers in the piazza are clearly too dimwitted to understand the meaning of the story.[35] His intended audience, on the other hand—his fellow "rascals"—clearly know how grasp the true message of this fairy tale and see that the monster is a figure for the Bourbon oppressor.[36] With this gesture, Nuccio invites the children who read his novel to identify with the shrewd rascals in the piazza, helping them along in case they missed the hidden meaning. At the same time, he locates Garibaldi's story both within history (in the historical novel recounting realistically the events of 1859–1860) and outside of history, in the time of fairy tales. Garibaldi's rebellion, framed as a story that is entirely unique and unprecedented ("mai detto o pensato"), now unfolds in a space of total moral clarity and clear-cut good and evil: removed from historical complexity and ambiguity, the tale pits the courage of the good man against a monstrous, feminized (mammo resonating with mamma) and rapacious creature.

Like the biblical and fairy tale language used by Indovino and don Gaetanino, medieval images and topoi appear throughout the novel. At one point, for example, "Hundred-languages" directly evokes the *chanson des gestes* tradition with his reference to the Battle of Roncesvalles, and we are reminded how Garibaldi and his followers were outrageously outnumbered.[37] The accumulation of such references throughout the text suggests that a strictly modern, realist, positivist language could not contain the exploits of Garibaldi and his followers. A premodern language is necessary to describe him and his deeds. He belongs to the world of fairy tales, of medieval romance, and of prophecy—a world prior to and at odds with the reality of *Il giornalino*'s readership: bourgeois children who inhabit a society marked by the efforts of the anticlerical, secularizing, industrializing state to forge a modern nation. The fairy tale, biblical, and Romance traditions called upon to describe Garibaldi both extol and contain him within a bygone day. Indeed, Indovino himself, who functions as a kind of leader among the *picciotti* in the weeks preceding Garibaldi's arrival, ends up committing suicide once he has avenged himself on the Bourbon troops for having murdered his daughter years ago. As he plummets into a deep well, he buries his "far away" prophetic voice with him. Having witnessed the realization of his prophecies, he will not enter into the new, modern world created by his redeemer.[38]

The novel's illustrations echo the copresence of realist and non-realist discourses. In creating his images, Alberto Della Valle (Neopolitan, 1851–1925) employed the technique of staging and photographing *tableaux-vivants* and using the photograph as a model for his drawings. Della Valle was known for his long and fruitful collaboration with Emilio Salgari, for whom he completed 464 images between 1903 and 1922. In fact, Della Valle had illustrated over 30 of Salgari's books by the time he contributed his images to Nuccio's story (Pallottino 26, 58–60). The choice of this illustrator has two effects. First, his technique results in illustrations that are indeed photographic in their true-to-life detail, creating the sense that the images document the veracity of the narrative, thus contributing to the realism of the work and lending further weight to its calls for patriotism. At the same time, Della Valle's hand (his signature is visible in each illustration) links this historical novel to the popular swashbuckling adventure tales set in exotic locales for which Salgari had achieved fame (see Figure 1.4). This visual echo of Sandokan the Pirate and Salgari's other invented heroes fuses history and myth and thus makes the real Garibaldi assume the contours of a mythic, far-away, and inaccessible hero.[39]

— diceva Cristo : « Ricchi e po-
veri, sono figli di un solo Dio, dunque sono uguali e sono fratelli ». —
(*Pag. 88*).

Figure 1.4 Alberto Della Valle, from *Picciotti e garibaldini* by Giuseppe Ernesto
   Nuccio.

Indeed, the inaccessibility of Garibaldi is palpable throughout the novel.
As in Abba's diary, the general remains an elusive figure, as the Sicilians
hear and talk about him long before his actual arrival. The chiasmus
"Garibaldi viene, viene Garibaldi" [Garibaldi is coming, he is coming,
Garibaldi!]—at times also rendered in dialect, *"Piddu veni, veni Piddu"*
(183; italics in orig.)—echoes as a refrain many times by multiple characters through the first 200 pages of the book, becoming almost a pendulum
marking time until the coming of the savior. The effect of suspense and

anticipation were especially strong in the journal's original installment series. We do not read about the Marsala landing until Chapter 34, well into the novel, and the general does not appear in person until Chapter 40. Here, Nuccio describes Garibaldi as almost blindingly radiant and as rendering speechless those who behold him. The emphasis on his golden beard, long locks, and flaming blue eyes endow him with a fused masculine and feminine beauty (as we have seen in other texts), and the repeated imagery of a burning source of light links him to the sun.[40] Indeed, Garibaldi here becomes a sun god, the singular point of life-giving energy beyond language and upon which one cannot gaze directly. Nuccio thus builds anticipation culminating in the apotheosis of the sun god, the one who must be and at the same time cannot be imitated by the hundreds of dark-haired *picciotti* who adore him. Della Valle's illustration depicts him in a gesture that resembles a benediction, holding his hand over the head of one of the boys in a way that both deifies the general and suggests that the boys cannot fully "measure up" to him (see Figure 1.5).

While Garibaldi appears as a Helios figure, animal metaphors and similes abound in Nuccio's descriptions of the protagonists as well as the antagonists. The novel truly abounds with images of animals, which often appear multiple times per page. Heroes and villains alike are compared to puppies, monkeys, wolves, lambs, and rats, to name a few.[41] Della Valle's illustration (see Figure 1.4) includes an owl and a black cat along with the four children seated around the preaching Indovino. These particular animals contribute to the gothic-like quality of Indovino's home but also, given their apparent attentiveness to the speaking prophet, become metonymically figures for the boys to whom they are visually contiguous. The use of animals in similes and other figures of speech can serve various purposes in a children's book. Spinazzola, for examples, documents multiple such rhetorical moves in *Cuore*, showing how these comparisons, which, he asserts, are appropriate to the intellectual resources of young readers, at times underscore drama and at times soften or sweeten a situation (108, 109). Nuccio often deploys animal imagery to praise Sicilian courage and to celebrate the children's bravery. At other times, Nuccio's comparisons highlight the savagery, brutality, or stupidity of their oppressors. Serving to hyperbolize both good and evil, the pervasive zoological rhetoric coalesces to create a single effect. Populated with ferocious villains and with exuberant heroes, Sicily emerges as profoundly and thoroughly bestial, thus the abundant animal rhetoric justifies the arrival of the sun god and endorses his humanizing mission.

Extending further the suggestion that Garibaldi's arrival catalyzes the humanization of the South, Nuccio's text marks participation in the nationalist movement as a rite of initiation into adulthood generally and manhood specifically, a link that is enabled through the recourse to other literary genres. Early in the story, the tale of the mammo-drago fans the

— Turi, tu che conoscerai certo i monti dell'Inserra pezzo per pezzo....

Figure 1.5 Alberto Della Valle, from *Picciotti e garibaldini* by Giuseppe Ernesto
Nuccio.

flames of young Pispisedda's heroic fervor, and he is clearly impatient
to take up arms against the Bourbon "monster." The adult Giovanni
Riso, father to one of the boys of the group, tells Pispisedda that he must
be more patient. "Quandu u piru è maturu cadi sulu" [when the pear
is mature it will fall by itself] (56), Riso assures the youth in the pro-
verbial form for which southern dialects are known. In the context in

which Riso uses it, the proverb refers to the need to wait for the time to ripen before rushing into revolutionary action, but these words also open the general theme of maturity, linking it to patience and sobriety. The lesson takes on particular force as it comes from a respected father figure in the story and is offered to the restless orphan boy. In fact, the orphan Pispiseddu, the most developed and central character of the ensemble cast of *picciotti*, clearly finds a substitute family in his group of heroic revolutionaries—brothers among the other boys, fathers in the adults like Indovino, Riso, and ultimately Garibaldi himself, and indeed a mother in the imagined figure of "La Talia," who is lovingly invoked throughout the text. Nuccio deploys both animal metaphors and this substitute family structure to solder the processes of becoming human, becoming an adult, becoming a man, and becoming a modern Italian citizen, all of which are facilitated through Garibaldi. As Pispisedda pretends to be asleep in the corner, he listens to the adult men making plans against the Bourbons and preparing for the arrival of Garibaldi. The narrator reveals his thoughts, "Oh se egli avesse potuto trovarsi, piuttosto che accovacciato come un cane nel cortile, framezzo a quegli uomini che stavano per dire: 'Il tal giorno comincerà la guerra!'" [Oh if only, rather than curled up like a puppy in the courtyard, he could instead be among those men who were about to proclaim: "On this day the war will begin!"] (49).

Indeed, all the boys, early in the story, are described as possessing qualities in terms that underscore their premodern, juvenile, or bestial nature. Their energy, courage, and exuberance are certainly valuable and admirable, but in need of taming and maturation: "Cinque sono: Ferraù più forte di Orlando, Cacciatore più bravo di Davidde, don Gaetanino *puparo*, Centolingue che sa le voci di tutti gli animali e Sautampizzu che salta come un grillo" [There were five of them: Ferraù stronger than Orlando, Hunter with more heart than David, don Gaetanino the puppeteer, Hundred-languages who could imitate the voices of every animal, and Sautampizzu who could jump like a grasshopper] (38; italics in orig.). As these rambunctious *picciotti* prepare for the arrival of Garibaldi, the process of becoming adult men entails in particular protecting the local women, notably Fedele's mother and his sweetheart Giulia, thus their heroism is clearly marked as manliness. As a persistent theme throughout the text, and one that informs many of the most adventurous scenes, the necessity of safeguarding the women becomes quite clear when Pispisedda reminds Fedele that he and Ferraù must stand by the women at all costs.[42] In fact, many chapters later, the brave Ferraù does indeed sacrifice himself, throwing himself on a bomb and saving several of his comrades.

By the final chapters of the novel, the melancholy tone comes powerfully to the fore, as one after the other of the *picciotti* and *garibaldini* meet their ends, and Palermo is left in ruins. After Fedele dies in the arms of his beloved Giulia, the tally is taken: "Palermo stava per esser libera? Ma com'era ridotta! Pietra su pietra, tutta annerita dall'incendio e tutta arrossata dal sangue. E Fedele era morto senza veder la madre ...e la madre senza vedere il figlio! E Sautampizzu era morto e Ntinna e l'Indovino anch'essi" [Palermo was about to be free? But look what it has been reduced to! Stone upon stone, each one blackened by fire and reddened by blood. And Fedele dead without having seen his mother one last time ... and his mother without having seen her son! And Sautampizzu, too, was dead, and Ntinna and Indovino as well] (234; ellipsis in orig.). In addition to the death and the destruction, young don Gaetanino, overwhelmed by the trauma of the war, has become mute and catatonic.[43] In the midst of these climactic and traumatic final chapters, with their heavy emphasis on loss, Pispisedda and the surviving *picciotti* meet a new friend, a blond garibaldino from Trieste.

The Triestan boy inspires the *picciotti* who have not died to continue to follow Garibaldi north, rather than remain in Sicily to rebuild their devastated city. Indeed, with his far-reaching knowledge and broader perspective, the Triestan boy eclipses even Garibaldi in these concluding pages of the novel, as he takes the *picciotti* under his wing to broaden their horizons. He shows them a map of Italy, which they kiss with reverence as they solemnly commemorate the many who died for her (243). In these exchanges with the northern soldier, who speaks "italiano" (rather than dialect) in a sweet and beautiful voice, the *picciotti* receive not only more extensive geographic knowledge but indeed are corrected in their longstanding linguistic error, learning that they fight not for "La Talia" but for "l'Italia." Significantly, the scenes in which this northern boy corrects and educates the *picciotti* are profoundly melancholic, as Nuccio encodes the transition from local attachments to national affiliation in the language of loss. Just moments before Ferraù's noble death adds to the list of traumatic losses, the maturing and melancholy boys transfer their allegiance from *La Talia*—an almost anthropomorphized mother figure whose name had often been invoked alongside that of local patron Saint Rosalia—to *Italy*, an abstract concept figured on the Triestan boy's map:

> Pispisedda baciò l'Italia e poi la diede a baciare a Roccco, a Ferraù e a Turi mormorando, con gli occhi gonfi di lagrime: 'Ci fossero Fedele, Sautampizzu, Cacciatore. ...' e ripensò a quelle sere dell'ottobre dell'anno avanti e dell'aprile e del maggio, quando avevano gridato, tutti insieme: "Viva la Talia!'. Ora avrebbero gridato il nome giusto, tanto più dolce: L'Italia; ma le labbra dei morti non più. ... (243; ellipses in orig.)

> [Pispisedda kissed [the map of] Italy and then offered it to be kissed by Rocco, Ferraù, and Turi as he murmured, with his eyes full of tears, 'If only Fedele, Sautampizzu, Hunter were here ...' and he

thought back to those evenings in October of last year, and in April and May, when they had cried out, all together, 'Long live La Talia!' Now they would have cried out the correct name, a name so much sweeter: Italy. But the lips of his dead friends could no longer cry out. ...]

Depicted throughout most of the book as particularly energetic, daring, and almost capriciously audacious, by the conclusion, Pispisedda cannot help but almost obsessively and somberly return to the memory of all the friends who have died in the fight to liberate Palermo: "si morde le labbra a sangue ... Quanti morti!" [he bit his lips till they bled. So many dead!] (245). Vowing to commemorate them, Pispisedda and the now-recovered don Gaetanino will follow Garibaldi as he continues north. No longer under the spell of the prophetic and premodern Indovino, or inspired by the mother-goddess figure of La Talia, the boys instead follow the educated, articulate "garibaldino from Trieste." Here, at the novel's conclusion, the specific political agenda of Nuccio, consonant with that of Vamba and *Il giornalino* generally, becomes clear. Turning back to the heroic events of 1859–1860 becomes a strategy of promoting contemporary *irredentismo*—the movement in favor of bringing the so-called "unredeemed" Austrian-controlled territory of the northeast into Italy. As the blond garibaldino points out Trieste and Trento on the map, the early twentieth-century agenda of "unredeemed Italy" is authorized as the logical and necessary continuation of the unification and given Garibaldi's stamp of approval.[44] More broadly, however, the novel demonstrates how the protagonists must leave behind youth, native dialect, local allegiances, and the entire mythic, premodern world embodied in Garibaldi. While praising the courage and even the ferocity of the *picciotti*, Nuccio simultaneously marks the "South" as primitive, as immature, as that which must be mourned and left behind in the process of growing up for the protagonists and the nation as a whole.

Other adventure novels and biographies in the decades following Garibaldi's death reinscribed aspects of this myth. Giuseppe Fumagalli's 1892 *Vita di Giuseppe Garibaldi narrata ai giovinetti* [*Life of Giuseppe Garibaldi Narrated to Young People*]reiterates the image of Garibaldi as a fusion of masculine and feminine in its description of him as "Alto, forte, bellissimo nel volto, di maschia figura con la lunga chioma dorata spiovente sulle spalle" [tall, strong, with an extremely handsome face and masculine physique, and with long golden locks flowing down his shoulders] (42, 43) and underscores the martial aspects of his heroism through a chapter structure organized according to military campaigns (The War of 1848, The War of 1859, The War of 1860, The War of 1866, The War of 1870–1871). Eugenio Checchi's 1907 *Garibaldi: Vita narrata ai giovani*, published by Milan's Treves Brothers on the centenary of Garibaldi's birth, entitles its first chapter succinctly, "The Hero." Abba's 1904

text for children, *Storia dei Mille* [*History of the Thousand*], describes
Garibaldi selecting his crew in a manner reminiscent of Christ choosing
his apostles.[45] By the outbreak of the First World War, Garibaldi's image had become so pervasive in children's literature that his name could
be used as an adverb. Ubertis Gray ("Térésah") in her 1915 *Piccoli eroi
della grande guerra* [*Little Heroes of the Great War*], describes the missions that Belgian messenger boys undertook to serve their homeland as
"garibaldinamente rischioso" [garibaldinianly risky] (5).

The outbreak of the war, and Italy's entry in May of 1915 on the
side of the Entente Powers, prompted children's texts that celebrated
manly heroism in a more militant, forceful, and muscular manner, particularly by writers who promoted the war as a path to the "redemption" of territories under Austrian control and as the culmination of
Italian unification. The prefatory poem, first published in 1915, that
was reproduced as the frontispiece of Giuseppe Zucca's 1918 collection
Vincere, vincere, vincere: Liriche di guerra [*Win, Win, Win: War
Lyrics*], conveys this more aggressive posture. Opening with the imperative verb "Ammazza, ammazza" [kill, kill] the poem exhorts Italians not
to leave a single German on "our" soil, except as a "carogna/deforme"
[deformed carcass] (no pg). The enjambment that severs the adjective
from its noun linguistically enacts the physical violence being advocated
and adds emphasis to the gruesome image: the dramatic pause implies
that it is not enough for the enemy to be left as a mere carcass, but that
even more violence is demanded. This vigorous exhortation to militant
action reverberates through the collection. Zucca includes a poem of
26 five-line stanzas that celebrates the courage of Giuseppe Lavezzari
and is addressed specifically "ai bimbi d'Italia" [to the children of
Italy] (7). The narrator urges young readers to remember this hero, who,
as a good *garibaldino*, refused to die in bed and insisted on enrolling
even in his old age (8). He runs into the enemy lines revealing his red
shirt and becomes a model of the glory of those who die for liberty (10).
Other poems celebrate the Italian occupation of Gorizia in 1916 (11–13)
and the heroism of Enrico Toti, who, wounded three times, uses even
his crutch as a weapon against the Germans, hurling it at the retreating
enemy before he dies (14–16).

In surveying the children's literature of the war years, during which
time the war itself became the dominant topic in a range of genres,
Lindsay Myers has noted how writers sought to balance a "glorification
of war" with the "need to shelter child readers from the full horror of the
conflict"("Flying" 30). In the context of books that conveyed pro-war
messages by "naturalizing violence" or "engaging in jingoistic patriotism," she examines the subtleties of Arturo Rossato's illustrated fantasy
L'aeroplano di Girandolino (1916) [*Master Turnabout's Airplane*] (31).
She reveals how the words and images in this text encode a political
allegory within the more overt moral allegory that warns against greed,

sloth, and pride. Aimed at an audience of both child and adult read-ers, the fantasy manages to support Italy's intervention while remain-ing critical of the "scourge" and "inhumanity" of war (40). Similarly, Francesca Orestano has observed in this corpus how a simultaneous "[m]ilitarization of childhood and 'childification' of the war" (48) had to be managed: that is, children "were at once kept in ignorance of the horrors of the conflict, but also summoned by relentless propaganda to contribute to the war effort" (48). Térésah's 1915 *Piccoli eroi della grande guerra* clearly participates in the project of mobilizing coura-geous patriotism in a military context among young readers. I suggest that the melancholic evocation of Garibaldi in her text becomes one way in which she modulates this tension between glorification and sheltering, between militarization and "childification."

The author offers 10 chapters, each of which portrays a different form in which a child might enact, or indeed has enacted, heroic deeds in de-fense of the fatherland. We read tales of young people—mostly boys but some young girls as well—from Belgium, France, Trent, Milan, Alsace, England, and elsewhere who have endured extreme physical pain and even death performing patriotic acts as messengers, trail guides, and in actual combat. The author includes more "domestic" acts of courage as well, such as children who have saved their peers from fires or from drowning, because, she claims, "[l]a vita è tutta una guerra" [life itself is a war] (21) and because selfless courage displayed in youth can foretell future bravery on the battlefield. In one chapter, Térésah narrates the story of a young chimneysweep in Milan. Austrian soldiers attempt to force him to break the local anti-Austrian tobacco boycott by trying to shove a cigar into his mouth. After the boy refuses three times, with his teeth clenched shut, the soldiers bludgeon him to death with their bay-onets. The illustration of this brutal moment shows the boy as signifi-cantly smaller than the three soldiers surrounding him, emphasizing his courage (17). Meanwhile, the repetition of threes (three soldiers, three refusals) adds a fairy tale quality to this historical exemplum of heroism, and thus the author performs the balancing act identified by Myers and Orestano. In another chapter, we read about a French boy scout named Dieudonné Deliège, an expert cyclist who was captured by the Germans. Here, it is the tone of exhilarating adventure that packages and in a sense mitigates the violence. Deliège is forced to lead a group of enemy soldiers through the mountains along treacherous paths. He rides ahead at breakneck speed, fully aware that he is leading the group toward a hidden sharp turn. Flying off the path and into the abyss, he plummets to his death shouting "Long Live France," content in the knowledge that he is taking the German soldiers down with him (30).

Garibaldi makes a ghostly appearance in the chapter that follows the story of the self-sacrificing French cyclist. Térésah narrates the story of an unnamed 13-year-old boy in the Argonne region of France whose

house had been burned down by the Germans. When the Garibaldian
Regiment arrives, the boy secretly joins them in the fight, using the rifles
he takes from the bodies of the dead Italian soldiers. The troops later
find his mangled body lying in a pool of blood. Térésah follows this
historical narrative with a lyrical, speculative passage, musing on what
could have inspired this young boy to "wait for the Italians" and to join
them in the battle. She writes,

> O leggenda garibaldina, così grande, così pura, così bella, quali voci
> n'erano giunte a quel ragazzo nato di popolo che s'era messo ad
> un crocevia seduto ad aspettare, ad aspettare "gli italiani" come si
> aspettano nei racconti i prodi, i fieri, i gentili cavalieri dell'ideale?
> Forse gli avevano detto che, un giorno c'era stato nato un uomo
> d'Italia, guerriero e santo del popolo, che aveva dato il suo amore
> e la sua spada a tutte le cause e a tutte la patrie calpestate. E la
> sua spada era stata invincibile, e il suo cuore era stato una fiamma,
> e il suo sdegno era terribile, ma il suo sguardo faceva pensare al
> mite azzurro del cielo e nulla v'era di più dolce, di più paterno, del
> suo sorriso. Quest'uomo era stato chiamato il Liberatore. E forse
> il fanciullo francese che aspettava "gli italiani" aveva nel confuso
> della sua mente l'idea che, cogli italiani, dovesse raggiungere anche
> l'Eroe; l'Eroe che non è mai morto finchè il suo spirito comanda. Chi
> sa! Fore quel fanciullo aveva ragione di aspettare. Forse la Grande
> Ombra cavalcava realmente al fianco di quelli che andavano a
> morire. E domani verrà con noi, per la nostra vittoria. (32–33)

> [O Garibaldian Legend, so great, so pure, so beautiful. What were
> the stories that had reached this boy, born of common folk? He sat
> down at a crossroad to wait, to wait for "the Italians," just as, in ro-
> mances, one waits for the proud, valiant, noble knights of the ideal.
> Perhaps they had told him that, once upon a time, a man had been
> born in Italy, a warrior and a saint of the people. This man gave his
> love and his sword to every hopeless cause and trampled country.
> And his sword was invincible, and his heart was like a flame, and
> his scorn was terrible, but his gaze made one think of the mild blue
> of the heavens, and nothing was sweeter or more fatherly than his
> smile. This man had been called The Liberator. And perhaps the
> French boy who was waiting for "the Italians," in the confusion of
> his mind, had the notion that, along with the Italians, this hero too
> would arrive: the Hero who will never die as long as his spirit reigns.
> Who knows! Perhaps that child was right to wait. Perhaps the Great
> Shade was riding alongside those who were heading toward their
> deaths. And tomorrow he will come with us, toward our victory.]

In this stirring passage, the young boy's death is imbued with meaning
through the mediation of Garibaldi's ghost. The preceding historical

paragraphs praise and encourage the more aggressive, militant heroism typical of the books of the war era. But in this passage, the idealized images of a beautiful and pure medieval chivalry, seemingly so out place in the context of poison gas and the other modern military technologies that made the Great War so horrifying, elicit a kind of softening nostalgia. The same fusion of masculine and feminine qualities in the fatherly smile and heavenly gaze, the same religious imagery of saints and redemption, and the same recourse to a premodern discursive register that we have seen in earlier texts are all deployed, inspiring forward movement (toward tomorrow, toward victory, and indeed toward death) while marking the pastness of those inspiring ideals. The young French boy can remind us of the Sicilian peasants described in Abba's diary. Just as they, waiting for a savior, mistook Garibaldi for long-dead Sinibaldo, this boy (in the narrator's fantasy) confuses the modern regiment with the man whose name they bear. But like the primitive Sicilians, this boy in his confusion is portrayed as discerning a kind of deeper truth: "the Italians" in effect really are bearing within them, defined by, the ghost of the hero. The "Grande Ombra" [great shade or shadow] is effective in ushering children into the future, precisely because he is rendered melancholically.

In addition to penning his children's novel on the Little Hero Pin and his contributions on Garibaldi to the special issue of *Il giornalino*, Lino Ferriani, a lawyer and legal theorist, published detailed and impassioned studies focused in particular on the plight of underprivileged children in the new Italy.[46] In 1886, he examined the issue of infanticide in *La infaticida nel codice penale e nella vita sociale*, and in 1902, *I drammi dei fanciulli: Studi di psicologia sociale e criminale* examined child trafficking, suicide, and "school martyrdom" (the ways in which the contemporary public school system caused harm to many students, especially the poor and disabled). By marshalling and analyzing direct testimony and statistical data, Ferriani aimed to overcome the apathy of his fellow Italians and urged the formation of a new social conscience.[47] Without legal reforms and robust private initiative, he laments, and without a concept of social obligation toward marginalized and outcast children,

> Noi non avremo che sciupato il tempo in ciance rettoriche, in pappolate burocratiche, in disquisizioni mitigaie, e dovremmo finire con il melanconico ritornello di D'Azeglio: 'l'Italia è fatta, ma occorre fare gli italiani.' O non è tempo che si facciano? E per farsi, non c'è verso, debbano cominciare a rendersi finalmente *capaci* di risolvere il problema dell'infaniza in genere, e in particolare, quello più urgente, dell'infanzia infelice. (28; italics in orig.)

> [we will have done nothing but waste time in flowery chitchat, in bureaucratic rigmarole, in appeasing discourses, and we'll end with the melancholy refrain of D'Azeglio, "Italy is made, but we still have

to make Italians." Oh, isn't it about time that these Italians were made? And there is only one way to do it: they must begin to make themselves finally *capable* of resolving the problem of childhood in general, and in particular, most urgently, the problem of unhappy childhood.]

Already in 1902, Ferriani perceived the famous call to "make Italians" as a "melancholy refrain," an initiative rhetorically rehearsed but unrealized due to the many failures of the State to address real social and economic ills. While it is clear that Ferriani uses the adjective "melancholy" here in order to underscore the failure of the project of creating a national culture, I would submit that melancholia, as I have tried to show, constituted one of the very mechanisms through which that project was undertaken. In other words, D'Azeglio's "refrain" may be considered "melancholy" not (only) because in Ferriani's time it had not yet been completed, but because the project itself was structured through melancholia. As the shadow of Garibaldi fell upon the nation, children's literature constructed a narrative in which growing up meant revering but leaving behind epic heroism.[48] These texts contributed to the project of "making Italians" by providing a heroic fetish through which a melancholy modern subjectivity could emerge.

Notes

1 Ricciardi was a lawyer, editor of the Neapolitan journal *Pungolo Parlamentare*, and, with Benedetto Croce, member of the "Society of Nine Muses" (Carbognin et al.). In the preface to Errico's short stories, he laments that Italian children's literature has been limited by the two dominant "notes" of heroism and melancholy, and praises Errico's stories for their variety, clarity, and health.

2 In May 1904, *Cuore* sold its 301,000th copy, making it, alongside Collodi's *Le avventure di Pinocchio*, one of the top sellers in the Italian market for children's books (Manson 185).

3 Emilio Salgari (1862–1911) wrote 83 novels and approximately 150 short stories. See Boero and De Luca 65–72.

4 In his overview of the major threads in the tapestry of Italian children's literature, Ermanno Detti remarks, "much of Italian children's literature of the early twentieth century, even up to the 1960s, created little heroes who went off to die alongside soldiers to safeguard the Fatherland, or who helped their parents until their dying day, struggling against destitution and hunger" (148). I have elsewhere explored how Annie Vivanti's *Sua Altezza!* (1923) [*His Highness!*] and Dino Buzzati's *La famosa invasione degli orsi in Sicilia* (1945) [*The Bears' Famous Invasion of Sicily*], each in its own way, depart from this tradition. See Truglio, "Annie in Wonderland" and "Dino Buzzati."

5 Umberto Eco has remarked on this process in his provocative analysis of *Cuore*. He points out that the protagonist's father elaborates his patriotism "sempre senza la minima chiarezza ideologica, sì che a distanza di pochi giorni intese con il medesimo tono l'elogio di Cavour e di Garibaldi, dimostrando di non aver capito nulla delle forze profonde che divisero il nostro Risorgimento" [always without a minimum of ideological clarity, so much

so that within the space of just a few days [in the diary structure] he sings, in the same tone, the praises of Cavour and of Garibaldi, revealing that he has not understood a thing about the deep forces that divided our Risorgimento] (*Diario* 87).

6 In using "manliness" rather than "masculinity," I am following John Champagne's analysis, which charts how this gender distinction was historically linked to modes of production (33).

7 The remarkable proliferation of books dedicated to Garibaldi's life and exploits was already apparent in the period under discussion. In 1907, an advertisement for a new edition of Giuseppe Abba's *Storia dei Mille* [*History of the Thousand*] notes that "Garibaldian literature" is "far from scarce at this point," but that this "new and beautiful publication" would "enrich it" ("La letteratura garibaldina, non assolutamente scarsa ormai, s'è arricchita d'una nuova e bella pubblicazione" (Bertelli, *Il giornalino* 37). In the preface to the 1910 edition of Eugenio Checchi's *Garibaldi: Vita narrata ai giovani* [*Garibaldi: His Life Narrated to Youths*], the editors pose the question, "Perchè (diranno i lettori) un'altra vita di Garibaldi?" [Why (our readers will ask) another biography of Garibaldi?] (no pg).

8 Pinocchio, in Catani's sequel entitled *Pinocchio nella luna* (1911) [*Pinocchio on the Moon*], similarly expresses marvel at technologies such as Wilbur Wright's airplane (2) while decrying the afflictions suffered by Italians, such as poverty, worker strikes, slow trains, and earthquakes (23).

9 "L'allora piccolo Manlio per giustificare un lieve fallo disse una bugia, facilmente e tosto scoperta dal grande uomo che lo redarguì così: *Ricordati, piuttosto fatti bastonare, che mentire*" [When he was young, Manlio told a fib in order to excuse a minor transgression. The great man easily and quickly discovered this and scolded the boy, saying, "*Remember, it is better to face a beating than to tell a lie*"] (Bertelli, *Il giornalino* 19; italics in orig.).

10 See Frau and Gragnani 86–87 and Seymour 35–155. Divorce became legal in Italy in 1970 and was upheld by referendum in 1974.

11 The request was granted, on appeal, on the basis that the marriage had never been consummated. See Seymour 48–55.

12 See "Italian Americans." An estimated 1.5 million eventually returned.

13 Ricciardi's alimentary metaphor of a "recipe" for children's literature accords well with the notion of incorporating the lost object in Freud's account of mourning and melancholia: "The ego wants to incorporate this object into itself, and, in accordance with the oral or cannibalistic phase of libidinal development in which it is, it wants to do so by devouring it" (249–250).

14 "o fanciullo, o nuova generazione d'Italia, fermati! Sei nel lontano mondo eroico!" [oh child, oh new generation of Italy, stop! You are in the far away heroic world!] (Abba 1983, 99).

15 Unless otherwise indicated, Italian quotations come from Abba, 1961 and English from Vincent's translation.

16 Xenophon (c. 430 BCE–c. 355 BCE) was an Athenian citizen, historian, essayist, military expert, and associate of Socrates. His *Anabasis* (meaning "march toward the interior") recounts the expedition of 10,000 Greeks into Persia in support of Cyrus (Anderson).

17 While Isabel Hapgood's 1901 English translation is complete and reliable, I provide my own translations here to remain somewhat closer to the Italian, opting more for literalness than smoothness.

18 See Tribunella's insightful discussion of how *A Separate Peace* "[i]mplicitly likens school to the battlefields of war." As homosocial settings, both become "a place in which queer love can be expressed, albeit indirectly" (*Melancholia* 13). The possibility of queer love in these settings is opened but inevitably foreclosed as part of the process of establishing masculinity and

heteronormativity as requisite components of adulthood. Before the advent of queer theory, Umberto Eco discerned the implicit homoerotics in *Cuore*, describing Enrico's admiration for his beautiful, blond classmate Derossi as "a sort of homosexual attraction" (*Diario* 86). De Amicis's text itself openly establishes the "classroom as barracks" association as part of its inspirational rhetoric advocating unity. In his letter of October 28, Enrico's father writes, "[i] tuoi libri son le tue armi, la tua classe è la tua squadra, il campo di battaglia è la terra intera, e la vittoria è la civiltà umana. Non essere un soldato codardo, Enrico mio" [your books are your weapons, your classmates are your squadron, the battlefield is the whole earth, and victory is human civilization. Don't be a cowardly soldier, my Enrico] (37).

19 Adjectives for "brunette" (bruno), "dark" (scuro), and "black" (nero) appear five times in the first two sentences.

20 In his discussion of education and literacy in Italy between 1871 and 1887, historian Martin Clark quotes this passage from *Cuore*, a book that, he remarks, indicates "how schools purveyed a constant, relentless diet of patriotism" (38). He describes the Calabrian boy episode in particular as "nation-building, with a vengeance" (38).

21 See note 26 in Chapter 2 for a summary of John Welle's insightful analysis of book in light of its intermediality.

22 On Enrico Mazzanti (1852–1893), see Perella.

23 In analyzing the various illustrations from these books throughout my study, I have benefited from the work of Doonan on strategies of "close looking," Lewis on the dynamics of the "interanimation" of verbal and visual texts, and Nodelman's "Decoding the Images" on visual semiotics in children's books.

24 Cordelia's dedication reads, "Spero anch'io, per servirmi delle espressioni di un illustre e caro maestro, che esso possa interessare i giovani lettori e far loro un po' di bene" [I, too, hope—if I may make use of the words of a dear and illustrious teacher—that my book will interest its young readers and do them a bit of good]. Restieaux Hawkes claims bluntly "Cordelia is not a great artist. Yet this most popular of her books … has unquestionable educational value" (122). More specifically, Boero and De Luca rightly note that "Cordelia teme l'interclassismo, prova paura all'idea della perdita di privilegi e potere da parte della sua classe di appartenenza, perciò mette in opera tutte le possibili strategie per 'blindare' commozioni e pietà all'interno di gerarchie ben definite" [Cordelia fears the mixing of classes and is afraid of the idea that her own class may lose its privileges and power. Thus she deploys every possible strategy to mobilize sympathy and compassion for the established hierarchies] (73). My goal here is to analyze these "strategies" and contextualize them within the shared discourses of heroism. Cordelia's husband, Giuseppe Treves, was the brother of Emilio Treves, who had founded the Press.

25 "Il mio sogno è di diventar generale, vorrei fare come Garibaldi" [My dream is to become a general. I want to be like Garibaldi] (18).

26 "sono contento d'esser vissuto in quei giorni in cui eravamo tutti fratelli, e come si era stati compagni nelle lotte e nelle privazioni si ritornava ad esserlo nella gioia comune" [I am glad to have lived in those days when we were all brothers, and just as we were comrades in our struggles and privations, so we were in our shared joys] (22).

27 Quoting the conclusions of seven novels, the critics summarize: "C'è sempre, al fondo, una partenza, una separazione, un'inquieta incertezza" [There is always, at bottom, a departure, a separation, a troubling uncertainty] (67).

28 Katia Pizzi reports that 30,000 copies of the *Il giornalino* were printed weekly (208). The journal ran under Vamba from 1906 through 1911 then resumed publication in 1918. Editorship transferred to Giuseppe Fanciulli after Vamba's death in 1920 (204).

29 As his pen name Jack "the Bowline" implies, Vecchi (1842–1932) was a sailor and had participated in the 1866 naval battle of Lissa in Italy's Third War of Independence. By 1907, he had already penned several children's books on themes of maritime adventure, as well as his own biography of Garibaldi, *La vita e le gesta di Giuseppe Garibaldi* [*The Life and Deeds of Giuseppe Garibaldi*] (Bologna: Zanichelli, 1882). See also Boero and De Luca 354. In the next chapter, I will explore another of his novels, *Al lago degli elefanti* (1897) [*At Elephant Lake*].

30 Morradi, Giovanni. "Vera Gloria" [True Glory] *Il giornalino*, 7.

31 "Mamme! Se i vostri fanciulli soffrono di ENURESI, non ne fate loro una colpa, ma usate subito la infallibile POLVERE ANTIENURETICA del Cav. Dott. Luigi Giuntoli" (xiii).

32 "una madre vide cader morti ai suoi piedi i due piccoli suoi figli che, tremando, la seguivano, fracellati da una bomba che esplodeva a due passi da lei."

33 On Nuccio, see Boero and De Luca 87–93. See Fava 301 for a summary of how Battistelli's high praise of this novel in her 1923 bibliography seems to turn the novel's *Risorgimento* values into ideological brainwashing ("veri e propri condizionamenti ideologici") at the dawn of fascism.

34 Citations here are from the eighth edition (1956).

35 The soldiers, he notes, "avevano ancora sulle facce rosse il riso melenso di chi ride senza nulla comprendere" [still had on their rosy faces the slow-witted smile of one who laughs without understanding a thing] (54).

36 "I monelli avevano capito che Mammo-drago era re Borbone" [the rascals understood that Mammo-drago was the Bourbon king] (55).

37 "Ognuno torni alla sua squadra! Ora comincerà la battaglia di Roncisvalle—disse Centolingue ai due compagni" ['Everyone return to his own squadron! The battle of Roncesvalles is about to begin' said Centolingue to his two companions] (140). And, for example, the reader is told how the heroes were "assillati dal nemico cento volte più numeroso e armato di fucili e di cannoni" [assailed by an enemy a hundred times more numerous and armed with rifles and cannons] (97).

38 Indovino's home as well as his language mark him as non-rational and "primitive" and thus doomed to be barred from the new modern world that Garibaldi will inaugurate: "Quella era la casetta dell'Indovino. Come fu accesa una candela Pispisedda scorse un lettuccio, e sulle partei una folla di rozze immagini di santi, di amuleti e di rosari, e, sopra un tavolino, un teschio orrido che sbarrava le occhiaie fosche" [That was Indovino's little home. As a candle was lit, Pispisedda discerned a small bed, and on the walls a multitude of rough images of saints, amulets, and rosaries, and, on a small table, a hideous skull with its dark eye-sockets wide open] (42). Figure 1.4 shows Della Valle's image of Indovino speaking to the boys in his home, replete with the skull and other details from Nuccio's description.

39 Many of the images bear the date 1917 under the signature and thus were not part of the *Il giornalino* series but added to the later editions of the novel.

40 The terms "radioso," "luminoso," "rifulgeva," and "divampasse" [radiant, luminous, glowing, all ablaze] (198) accumulate on just one page.

41 Some examples include: "Ma Pispisedda si svincolò balzando addietro e scotendosi tutto come un cucciolo bagnato" [But Pispisedda broke free

(of Rocco's grasp) and jumping back he shook himself like a wet puppy] (176); "comparve il commissario Sferlazzo col birro Marotta, che gli si strascinava dietro come una vecchia scimmia accanto al domatore" [Commissioner Sferlazzo appeared with the policeman Marotta, who trudged along behind him like an old monkey next to his tamer] (176); "quei lupi di birri e soldati" [those wolflike Bourbon police and soldiers] (90); "Se non ci scannano come agnelli o non ci fanno la morte del sorcio nelle nostre case bruciate e distrutte, ci lasceranno morire di fame" [if they don't decapitate us like lambs or put us to death like rats in our burnt and destroyed home, they will let us starve to death] (91).

42 "Occore che tu ti tenga sempre vicino alle donne. Ferraù sa che deve stare sempre con te. Così potrà aiutarti, chi lo sa, in un modo qualunque. È un toro per forza, ma buono come il pane, e fedele come un cane mastino. Per le donne si butterà nel fuoco, se ce ne sarà bisogno" [You have to stand by the women at all times. Ferraù knows he has to stick with you, so he will be able to help you out doing anything you need. He is as strong as a bull, but as good as bread and as faithful as a dog. For the women, he would throw himself in the fire if he had to] (61).

43 I would relate the fate of poor don Gaetanino here to that of Leper from *A Separate Peace* according to Tribunella's analysis. For Tribunella, Leper, who suffers a mental break down in the army, plays the role of the witness who is neither the sacrificed object (Finny or Garibaldi) nor the maturing subject (Gene or Pispisedda) but who functions in the text as a warning to readers of the threat of not successfully navigating the melancholy process of maturation. Like Leper, don Gaetanino functions in the narrative "to present the potential risk of insanity" (*Melancholia* 16–17).

44 Pizzi demonstrates how the "*Giornalino* played a fundamental role in pursuing both vocally and relentlessly a patriotic program advocating that key portions of land at the northeastern borders, namely Trieste, Istria, and the Dalmatian coastline, be incorporated to Italy. ...both locally and more widely in Italy, these territories were largely perceived as Italian both culturally and linguistically" (203–204). See also Orestano, who summarizes the role of Bertelli's weekly paper in promoting "patriotic messages" about unredeemed Italy that were at times "tinged with militarism" (49).

45 A full-page advertisement in the special Garibaldi issue of *Il giornalino della Domenica* promotes an "elegantly bound" new edition of this text.

46 See Stewart-Steinberg's chapter on "An Unwritable Law of Maternal Love" for an analysis of Ferriani's contribution to the infanticide debates in turn-of-the-century Italy.

47 "la formazione di una nova coscienza sociale" (20).

48 I am echoing Freud's poetic "Thus the shadow of the object fell upon the ego" ("Mourning" 249).

2   Geographic Expressions
Mapping Modernity

Che bestia sono stata a non studiare meglio la Geografia! (124)

[What a brute I was for neglecting my studies of geography!]
—Pinocchio, from Cherubini, *Pinocchio in Affrica*, 1903

Fearful of the spread of liberalism at mid-century, Austrian Minister Prince Clemens von Metternich (1773–1859) famously deflated the revolutionary potential to which the name "Italy" might be put by using the phrase cited in this chapter's title. With increasing concern over what appeared to be a brewing storm, Metternich attempted to contain the term "Italy," insisting that it made sense only as a way to designate the peninsula itself, that is, as a geographical rather than a national or cultural expression.[1] Fewer than 20 years later, Italy would achieve political unification and become, as Stewart-Steinberg puts it, a "state in search of a nation" (1). In the decades that followed political unity, children's books leveraged Italy's geography as a way to buttress cultural unity. Furthermore, these books used geography as a justifying metaphor and as a supposedly natural grounding through which to solder more tightly the association between personal maturation and national modernization. In his historical analysis of "the notion of Italy," John Dickie has underscored that "human interaction with geographical space is always mediated by conceptions of geography," and that throughout time, "various 'imaginary Italies'" have had "historical force" (19).[2] It is precisely the "imaginary Italies" conjured by children's books through their specific "conceptions of geography" that I examine here. In this chapter, I analyze how cartographic imagery, narrative accounts of journeys, and geography books plotted the convergence of growing up, going North, and modernizing for Italy and for Italians.

The children's novel *Cuore* (1886) [*Heart*] by Edmondo De Amicis cogently dramatizes how children's literature participated in these processes. *Cuore* has remained one of Italy's most widely read books since its publication. Set in a Turin elementary school in 1882, the year in which the unification hero Giuseppe Garibaldi died, the book is dedicated to boys between 9 and 13 years old. De Amicis structured the text as the diary of 11-year-old Enrico Bottini, the son of an engineer. Early in the school year, Enrico recalls the arrival of a southern boy in his northern classroom:

> Allora il maestro gli prese una mano, e disse alla classe:—Voi dovete essere contenti. Oggi entra nella scuola un piccolo italiano nato a Reggio di Calabria, a più di cinquecento miglia di qua. Vogliate bene al vostro fratello venuto di lontano.... Detto questo s'alzò e segnò sulla carta murale d'Italia il punto dov'è Reggio di Calabria. ... —Perchè questo fatto potesse accadere, che un ragazzo calabrese fosse come in casa sua a Torni, e che un ragazzo di Torino fosse come a casa propria a Reggio di Calabria, il nostro paese lottò per cinquant'anni e trentamila italiani morirono. (31)
>
> [The master took him by the hand, and said to the class:—'You ought to be glad. To-day there enters our school a little Italian born in Reggio, in Calabria, more than five hundred miles from here. Love your brother who comes from so far away.' ... So saying, he rose and pointed out on the wall map of Italy the spot where lay Reggio, in Calabria. ... 'In order that this might occur, that a Calabrian boy should be as though in his own house at Turin, and that a boy from Turin should be at home in Calabria, our country fought for fifty years, and thirty thousand Italians died.' (9–11)]

This highly sentimental scene illustrates forcefully the social project that followed Italy's 1861 political unification, a project necessitated and challenged by the extreme linguistic, historical, and cultural diversity of the now "Italian" population. Here, the teacher's recourse to the wall map to show the Turinese children where their classmate was born, and to demonstrate Calabria's Italianness, dramatizes Benedict Anderson's assertion that "[a] map anticipated spatial reality, not vice versa. In other words, a map was a model for, rather than a model of, what it purported to represent" (173).[3] The image of Italy here, in a concrete sense, must generate rather than reflect the lived experience of it as a bordered, unified whole. The fictional children in the Turinese classroom—and the real children reading about them—must be exhorted to live up to, indeed to grow into, the unified image on the map. In fact, due to the significant regional economic and literacy disparities in Italy at the time, the children reading *Cuore* were mostly northern and middle or upper class, like Enrico. As the dark Calabrian is displayed before the rest of the students, the teacher insists that despite his apparent physical difference, the boy will become a mirror image of the children beholding him: the new political reality demands that they become interchangeable. Finally, the teacher's summary of the unification process offers the students a clear, teleological, and heroic narrative of Italy's recent past, a story that erases the historical complexities, conflicting agendas, and often fortuitous events that led to Italy's unification under Piedmont's Savoy monarchy, and a story that in fact emphasizes the losses that enabled the birth of the nation.

A few pages after the Calabrian boy episode, the map itself makes a visual appearance in an illustration by Arnaldo Ferraguti (see Figure 2.1).[4] This episode recounts the sacrifice made by noble Garrone (another classmate), who stands up and takes the blame for a misdeed that another boy had committed in order to protect that boy from punishment. In Ferraguti's image, the wall map of Italy appears prominently in the upper left corner, bigger than the window to its right. Garrone stands erect with his hand raised in the center of the image, while the seated classmates look on. As Garrone bravely declares "son io" [it's me], with his words from the narrative repeated in the caption, the map hovers over him as if to imply that the generous, sacrificial "sono io" is simultaneously a declaration of "sono italiano," and as such an appropriate fulfillment of the teacher's exhortation just a few days previously to behave in a way that honors the sacrifices of those who made Italy.[5] In short, these emotionally effective passages reveal how children's literature could function as a national map and as a personal mirror, forging a link between the two to chart a path of maturation and Italianization (Figure 2.1).

Signor Perboni's wall map functions much as do the maps that often accompany children's books and offer visual representations of fantasy spaces, such as The Hundred Acre Wood and Treasure Island. In analyzing these maps, Anthony Pavlik draws on Baudrillard's observation that it is "the map that precedes the territory ... that engenders the territory" (38). This claim pertains not only to fictional spaces in the strict sense, like Tolkien's Middle Earth, but also to "fictional" spaces (i.e., "made") like Italy itself, as I will argue in this chapter.[6] In the case of *Cuore*, the children in the northern classroom, called upon to accept and embrace the Calabrian boy as a brother, and more generally, to embrace national rather than local identities, must realize the "representation" in the image. This generative function is at work in G. E. Nuccio's *Picciotti e garibaldini* [*Young Fighters and Garibaldi Followers*]. When the blond soldier from the north shows the Sicilian revolutionaries a printed map, the young men transfer their allegiance from the mythical and maternal fantasy of "la Talia" to the unified, grounded space of "l'Italia." The image motivates them to continue fighting not just for Palermo's liberation but also for Italian unification. Kissing the map itself, the boys commit themselves to the cause of realizing the representation.[7] In short, the physical maps that these books contain, as in Ferraguti's illustration of the Italian map in *Cuore*, and maps that they verbally describe become synecdoches of the books themselves.[8]

Garrone si alzò di scatto, e disse: — Son io! (pag. 11).

Figure 2.1 Arnaldo Ferraguti, from *Cuore* by Edmondo De Amicis.

Map as Mirror

A wide range of texts for children from the late nineteenth century through the First World War deploy various kinds of mapping strategies. Some books reproduce visual images of maps as illustrations or frontispieces, others chart a protagonist's progress through various parts of Italy or beyond, and others employ cartographic vocabulary. These texts call on their child readers to orient themselves through such strategies. Whether as visual depictions, such as G.G. Bruno's illustration of the map of Africa draped over Pinocchio's desk in Eugenio Cherubini's 1903 *Pinocchio in Affrica* (see Figure 2.2), or as verbal representations

Figure 2.2 G.G. Bruno, from *Pinocchio in Affrica* by Eugenio Cherubini.

such as the description of Signor Perboni's classroom wall map cited above, maps provided a kind of national isomorph to the Lacanian mirror. The visible boundaries on display offer a coherent, distinct, and discreet national body through which Italy's new citizens were to recognize themselves. In fact, Corinna Teresa Ubertis Gray, in her rousing 1915 collection of heroic vignettes entitled *Piccoli eroi della grande guerra* [*Little Heroes of the Great War*], argues that children are, in fact, capable of understanding a seemingly abstract concept like "patriotism" precisely because of the concreteness of physical borders. A country's borders, the author claims, enable children to conceptualize a naturally grounded isomorphic link with their own body and with the walls of their own house. The interior space thus demarcated becomes a safe and protected one (8).[9]

Maps in these works function just as do the mirrors in which Ida Baccini's "Little Chick" comes to know himself in one of the most popular and influential early texts for children in the post-unification period.[10] Early in the tale, the chick-narrator (who functions as a stand-in for the child) recalls how his keeper, a young farm girl, used to take him into her room:

> Li si divertiva quasi tutti i giorni a mettermi davanti ad una certa lastra di vetro, nella quale vedevo un altro pulcino che mi somigliava tutto, e che, da quel grullerello ch'egli era, mi faceva sempre il verso. ...la Marietta rideva a più non posso, dicendomi che la

pigliavo con me medesimo, e che quell'altro pulcino ero io, proprio
io. Ci capite, voi nulla, bambini miei? Io, vi confesso, di no. (39–40)

[I would amuse myself there almost everyday by standing in front of
this plate of glass. In the glass I would see another chick who looked
exactly like me, and who, just like the silly little fool he was, would
always imitate me. ... Marietta would laugh and laugh. She would
tell me that I was really just getting annoyed with myself, and that
the other chick was actually me, really me. Do you understand any
of this, my readers? I must confess to you that I did not.]

Marietta, the orphaned chick's caretaker, must reveal to the chick who
he is in the mirror, just as Signor Perboni must point out Calabria on the
map to his students. The mirror described in the novel clearly works as
a synecdoche for the novel-as-mirror, as the chick himself makes clear
in his subsequent analogy between the image he sees in the mirror and
book illustrations.[11] The "memoir" in fact structures the split between
the chick-as-protagonist, who does not yet see the alienated image as
self, and the chick-as-narrator, who in the retrospective time of the narration has recognized himself. Having assumed the position of speaking
subject, the chick can now take up the role for his readers that Marietta
once played for him, as evidenced in his direct address to the reading
children. The scene, in short, works as an allegory of the book. It (mis)
presents its constitutive role as merely a reflection of a reality, a reality
that is so obviously already there that one can laugh, as Marietta does,
at those who don't see it. In so doing, the memoir offers the chick to the
reader as an ideal ego, as the reader's "me medesimo" and "io, proprio
io," even if (or indeed precisely because) the child initially perceives the
image as a foreign "altro" [other].

Later, while living with his new urban master Alberto, the chick encounters his reflection again in a goldfish pond. Still a subject in process,
the chick continues to believe that the image is his irritating nemesis
from Marietta's room. Trying to peck at this impertinent hanger-on, he
tumbles into the water (109). The moment reveals that the chick's formation and itinerary are still incomplete and that it is only retrospectively,
in writing his autobiography, that the chick can show (in his address to
his readers) the proper recognition of himself. Indeed the humor of the
scenario comes precisely from the reader's ability to assume the wiser position (that of the chick-as-narrator) and to perceive that the reflection is
"really" the protagonist. Karen Coats's Lacanian analysis of *Charlotte's
Web* can shed light on this dynamic. Marietta in the first mirror scene
functions much as the maternal Fern, while the chick, like Wilbur the
pig, embodies the developing child. Coats underscores the child's need
to conceptualize the play of "shifters ('I' and 'me') that will come to
stand for" the child, and the role of the mother or mother surrogate in

mediating the child's experience in mastering/being mastered by that process (19–20). The passage cited above plays on a range of first-person pronouns ("me medesimo," "io") as if the chick were "trying them on" through overuse and repetition. In Baccini's novel, Marietta (the mother surrogate) and her rural world must give way to Alberto and his urban home as the chick moves toward full subjectivity, thus the narrative itinerary links together the feminine, the rural, and the infantile and posits all three as preverbal stages to be passed through developmentally and geographically.

In fact, it is precisely through this isomorphic construction of child/nation that the "mapping" enacted by children's books engendered Italian subjects. These books offer maps *as* mirrors for their national subjects, and by means of this very conflation make the mapping effective. That is, by implicitly constituting "Italy" as a human subject that must "grow up," these books posit a simultaneous maturation narrative for the child and for the nation. Karen Coats's elegant synopsis of the Lacanian mirror, then, operates on the double level of personal and national subject. She writes,

> But unlike the traditional view of mirror images as passively accurate reflections of what is, Lacan's understanding of the mirror image is that it is an anticipation that structures a subject. The child looking into a mirror sees an idealized image of his potential. The image, in its specular completeness, is at odds with how he experiences his body. His trajectory of becoming is toward the image; he takes its completeness, fantasized as it is, as his goal. Though he may experience himself as fragmented and incomplete, he can imagine himself as whole, and it is toward this imaginary ideal that he moves. (6)

What I suggest is that these texts interchange "mirror" with "map" and "child" with "nation" in an apparently fluid and seamless way and cumulatively create an effect in which these substitutions seem natural and necessary. Thus deploying maps as if they were Lacanian mirrors, these texts seek to engender national subjects.

Cartographical Imaginations

In addition to establishing and naturalizing borders for the subject (as the reflections of Baccini's chick) and the nation (as the map in Perboni's classroom or the map that is kissed by Nuccio's young Sicilians), Italian texts plot a necessary and natural progression for their readers. The textual diegeses become prescriptive itineraries (Pavlik 35), melding the narrative and cartographic senses of the word "plot," as, for example, Baccini's chick must move from Marietta's rural world to

Alberto's urban home. These texts map personal and national development as "progressive" journeys. In these model itineraries, the South
and what it was made to represent must, like childhood, be given up,
incorporated, and superseded by the adult and modern values embodied
by the urban North. The texts code these journeys as renunciations,
depicting the rural, the southern, and the feminine with deeply nostalgic tones, but as necessary renunciations that yield melancholy, masculine, and modern subjects. While the "journey" in general, and the
home—adventure—home pattern specifically, can be seen as an almost
universal structure of children's literature, Italian children's books of
the period chart the journey in a particular way and code it with specific
relevance.[12] In varying ways, the children's books from *Cuore* to the
First World War that I examine in this chapter urge a northward and
urban-ward itinerary for their young protagonists. In Luigi Capuana's
Scurpiddu (1898) [*Nimble-Legs*], the title character begins the story
as an orphaned Sicilian boy. Scurpiddu's path to maturation includes
experiencing the city of Catania and its telegraphs, seismographs, and
railway. Along the way, the boy must also cut his unruly hair and forget the painful memories of his mother. Capuana's text establishes a
set of oppositions: feminine, rural, local identities are associated with
childhood and must give way, through a series of traumatic losses, to
the masculine, urban, national values that define the adult. In Ferriani's
Un piccolo eroe (1905) [*A Little Hero*], the Italian protagonist ("Pin")
goes North to work for several years in London in order to live up to
his dying father's exhortation to "fa l'uomo" ["become a man"] (105).
In Jack La Bolina's *Al lago degli elefanti* (1897) [*At Elephant Lake*], and
in Eugenio Cherubini's 1903 *Pinocchio in Affrica*, southward voyages
from Italy are undertaken only to underscore all the more vividly the
northern protagonists' intellectual and technical superiority vis-à-vis the
backwardness of the Africans. Giulio Gianelli's 1910 tale of "Pipino"
emerges from within and laments this tradition of stories that couple
going North with growing up, and that represent these itineraries as the
paths toward the idealized image of the map/mirror.

These and other books, which I will analyze in detail below, take
up and develop a longstanding "cartographical imagination" that had
been at work in Italian discursive spaces for several decades. As Nelson
Moe has shown through his analysis of politicians' letters from 1860,
these discourses created a "moral map" of the peninsula. Moe points
to the "ethical scale of values descending with mathematical regularity as one moves down the 'heel of the boot'" (134) and reveals how
"topographical adjectives" took on moral meanings (134). This rhetoric ultimately acquires a performative force, as "[t]he Piedmontese discourse on the south was an important enabling condition for ruling it"
(140). The children's books I will discuss build on this "Orientalizing"
and territorializing tradition. Indeed, the "Orientalizing" of the South

that Moe has analyzed in Italian political and scientific discourse is fused with the "colonization" of the child that Nodelman has analyzed in children's literature. This fusion, then, is enabled by and reinscribes the recapitulation paradigm. This cartographic imagination worked both within Italy itself and between Italy and other geographic and cultural spaces.

The performative force of this mapping can be detected in a brief vignette from Arpalice Cuman Pertile's 1915 *Il trionfo dei piccolo* [*The Little Ones' Triumph*], where the desire to assert cultural distance re-maps actual geographical distance. In a section entitled "I bambini lontani" ["Far away children"], the young (Italian) protagonists are taken to the cinema where they view a parade of children from around the world. The temporal sequence of the parade enacts the geographic distance between viewing subjects and viewed objects. First, children from various Italian cities march by on the screen. These Italian children are followed by those from other European countries, namely "francesi, spagnoli, tedeschi" [French, Spanish, German]. Already here we see the move from the specificity of city names to the more general listing of country names as an index of distance. Next in line come those from farther away: "Ed anche passarono bambini che vivono in paesi lontani da noi, tanto lontani che ci vorrebbero settimane e mesi di viaggio per andare a trovarli: giapponesi coi larchi abiti a fiori, cinesi col codino, americani vestiti in mille maniere" [And children also passed by who live in countries far away from us, so very far that it would take weeks, even months of traveling to go visit them: Japanese children with thier flower-patterned outfits, Chinese children with ponytails, American children dressed in all sorts of clothes] (207). The parade culminates, or logically should, in those who live farthest away of all from Italy, farther than America or Japan. Yet, the final image is of "piccoli selvaggi nudi e neri" [naked little black savages] (207). Here, "Africa"—even generalized as a continent, as opposed to the Italian cities or the European countries—remains unnamed, its namelessness functioning as an indicator of its obscurity (and recalling the nameless "Calabrian boy" of *Cuore*). The naked black children are positioned as last in line and hence farthest away, even if (and indeed to some extent because) Africa geographically is much closer to Italy than many of the other named places whose children are featured earlier in the parade. Thus, their "savagery" is made to contrast with the civilization of the Italian children who gaze upon them, and the modern cinematic technology that enables this gaze is implicitly offered as evidence of this contrast. The final scene of the film, described in the text, displays a white boy and a black boy embracing as "brothers" under the words "milk and chocolate." The image of the embracing boys appears not only in the ekphrasis describing the film but also twice as an illustration in the book, so the readers, like the young protagonists at the cinema, can see it. The touching humanistic message of fraternal closeness that this image promotes is effective, however, only because the distance between these two boys had been established by the mapping process of the cinematic parade. Pertile's film within her novel dramatizes the kinds of cartographic imagination that were put to the service of constituting Italian subjects.

Whereas in the previous chapter I focused on the permutations of heroism and melancholia in the context of lost father figures (particularly Garibaldi), in this chapter I will attend to the enforced de-cathexis of the "South" as a necessary abandonment of the feminine and specifically of the maternal in the constitution of national subjects. Again mobilizing the recapitulation paradigm, in which ontogeny is believed to repeat phylogeny, these books construct the Italian adult as a melancholic subject who has entered maturity and modernity by giving up and introjecting the maternal South.

The "bel paese": Petrarch and Stoppani

Father Antonio Stoppani (1824–1891) offered one of the first post-unification texts that aimed to instruct young Italians in their nation's geography and, I would argue, to construct them through it. His lengthy *Il bel paese: Conversazioni sulle bellezze naturali; La geologia e la geografia fisica d'Italia* [*The Lovely Country: Conversations on Natural Beauty; Geology and Physical Geography of Italy*] was first published in 1873, and by the time Italy entered the First World War (1915), it had reached its 94th edition. The book draws on the final lines of Petrarch's 146th sonnet for its epigram and its title: "...Il bel paese / Ch'Appennin parte, e 'l mar circonda e l'Alpe" [the lovely country that the Apennines divide and the Alps and sea surround]. Thus, the first page of the book recalls Italy's natural, physical borders. Even the mountain range that "divides" (*parte*) the country is enclosed by the protective sea and mountains that "surround" and demarcate it. These physical features both define the country and contribute to its "beauty" (the word for beauty appears three times on Stoppani's title page). At the same, however, the quotation mobilizes Italy's cultural tradition: Petrarch's words, in the Tuscan that would become the standard for the national language, signal the literary heritage going back to the "three crowns" of the early Renaissance. Thus, nature and culture, land and literature, appear seamlessly fused, the former terms (nature, land) grounding and justifying the homogeny of the latter.

The geography lessons within the text are delivered by an avuncular narrator who, beginning on the Thursday after the Feast of Saint Martin (November 11 1871) (23), describes the natural resources of Italy to a large group of nieces and nephews. The children are initially disappointed not to be hearing more fanciful tales but soon find delight in the stories that their uncle tells about "this Italy of ours" (25). When young Camilla wants to hear about her uncle's "voyages," he replies,

> De' miei viaggi?... Misericordia?...Credete forse ch'io sia stato tra gli'Indiani che muojono stringendo con gran devozione la coda di una vacca? o tra i Groenlandesi che mungono la renna e scavanci nel ghiaccio i palazzi? o tra i Chinesi, che infilzano il riso con due stecchi grano per grano, mentre noi se ne ingolla un centinajo ad ogni cucchiajata? Ovvero tra i selvaggi dell'Australia che fanno allesso e arrosto de' cristiani? (24; ellipses in orig.)

> [My voyages? Mercy me! Do you perhaps think that I have been among the Indians, who die grasping a cow's tail with great devotion? Or among the Greenlanders, who milk their reindeer and dig their buildings out of the ice? Or maybe you think I was among the Chinese, who pick up their rice one grain at a time between two sticks, instead of swallowing heaps with each spoonful like we do? Or yet do you think I've been among the Australian savages, who boil and roast Christians?]

The wealth, variety, and beauty of Italy are framed through this opening gesture of verbal border drawing and exclusion, establishing the value of Italy in contrast with the exoticism of the non-Italian. The strangeness of these "others" moves from the impractical to the violently threatening and cumulatively endorses the value and safety of "home."

The narrator begins his descriptive itinerary of Italy's geography in Belluno (the northeast), with detailed descriptions of the stunning alpine landscape. In the prefatory pages, Stoppani reinforces the link between land and language that was implied on the title page through the quotation from Petrarch. Here, the author addresses the school teachers likely to use this book and explains why he has included tonic accent marks throughout: the book is also meant to reinforce correct, standard Italian pronunciation. Indeed twice in these pages, Stoppani evokes the specter of the Tower of Babel to urge instruction in the standard tongue.[13] Just as he fuses land and language, so too does he link nation and individual. Stoppani poses a rhetorical question to the teachers: "Si può egli applicare alle nazioni quell'adagio 'nosce te ipsum' (conosci te stesso), che la sapienza dell'antichità ha posto come base della sapienza dell'individuo?L'autore di questo libro crede talmente di sì" [Can one apply to nations that adage "nosce te ipsum" (know thyself), which ancient wisdom has claimed to be the foundation of the individual's wisdom? The author of the present book believes so] (15). The need to "know oneself" is just as true for the nation as for the individual, and thus this book serves not merely as a map but also as a mirror for the young Italians who read it.[14]

A Northward Route to China: Baccini

Ida Baccini's *I piccoli viaggiatori: Viaggio in China* (1878) [*The Little Travelers: Trip to China*] develops further the links between geography and identity. The novel introduces readers to the young protagonist Adolfo who, although just 12 years old, seems fully 15 due to his studiousness, cleanliness, and respectfulness (1). The boy—who is admirable precisely for his precocious maturity—has a particular fondness for geography books. His role as model becomes indeed literal for the young readers of Baccini's geography book:

> Tempo fa lo zio, che è capitano di mare, gliene regalò uno con questo titolo: 'Viaggio intorno al globo.' Figuratevi se il nostro giovinetto fu contento! Prese una carta geografica e col suo ditino si divertì a segnare tutti i luoghi per dove era passato l'autore del libro. Così imparò molte belle cose e non mica a pappagallo, sapete? Ma assennatamente e con fondamento. (3)
>
> [A while back his uncle, who was a sea captain, gave him one {i.e., a geography book} with this title: *Voyage around the Globe*. You can just imagine how pleased our young man was! He took a map and with his little finger he had fun marking all the places where the author of the book had passed. In this way he learned many fine things, and not just like a parrot, you know? But rather wisely and in depth.]

Forcefully drawing readers into the narration through the direct address employed by the verbs in the second person plural (figuratevi, sapete), the passage offers Adolfo as a mirror for these young readers: just as Adolfo sat contentedly with his thrilling geography book (most likely the dense 1876 text by the Italian scientist Enrico Giglioli), so too the readers should learn many fine things in depth, not superficially, as they hold Baccini's book in their hands.[15] The implicit parallel between Baccini's (fictional) *The Little Travelers* and the nonfictional *Voyage around the Globe* lends the former an authoritative, scientific status: a "fondamento" [foundation], to use Baccini's word, as it were. Most strikingly, the corporeal image of Adolfo literally tracing Giglioli's voyage with his finger on a map as he reads the book itself becomes a map for readers, inviting them fully to incorporate the protagonist's itinerary.

Adolfo's itinerary—like Giglioli's, an eastward sea voyage—will indeed bring the young boy all the way to China and back, but more importantly, the geographic journey will enable a personal maturation. The protagonist, already precociously mature, will be joined by a peer who urgently needs to grow up. Lazy, dirty, and recalcitrant, Adolfo's classmate Carlino is the son of a lower-class widow, Maria, who is desperate to have her "rascal" mend his ways. Uncle Pasquale suggests that Carlino be entrusted to him for the proposed eastern journey and makes clear the goal of the voyage: "me lo darete fanciullo ed io ve lo ricondurrò uomo, e, quel che più importa, uomo di senno" [you will give him to me as a boy, and I will bring him back to you as a man, and, more importantly, as a man of good sense] (19). Echoing the earlier "assennatamente," the mature "senno" that Carlino needs can come, apparently, only from an adult man (Maria is a widow) and only through a voyage that, while seemingly eastern is, I will show, effectively a northern journey. Furthermore, Carlino's personal journey of maturation embodies also a path for Italy to take as it moves "forward."

After setting out from Florence, the travelers take to the water from the Tuscan port of Livorno. The national implications of this journey begin to become apparent here at the point of departure. In Livorno, the children see a *lapide* (plaque) commemorating a fallen hero of the Battle of Lissa, the major sea battle of the Third War of Independence that resulted in the inclusion of Venice in the Kingdom of Italy (1866). The sight of the plaque prompts an explanatory history lesson from Uncle Pasquale for the boys' (and the readers') benefit (24–26). Thus, the children's personal journey is mapped onto a national paradigm: their voyage begins with an evocation of the birth of the nation.[16] The fusion of personal and national journey is soldered when the group boards Pasquale's steamship, which we learn is named the *Italo* (29).

The ship initially travels southward, stopping at the island of Malta. Readers are told that since 1800 this island "appartiene agli inglesi" [has belonged to the English] (68). As the group travels south and then east, many of the places they see and discuss are explicitly identified as English possessions. As the imperial might of England serves as a map for the *Italo*, the erudition and moral authority of Lord Raymond, a British gentleman and father on board the ship, serves as the model for Carlo and Adolfo. When, for example, Carlo sees Etna in the distance, he thinks a city is burning. His ignorance is mocked by Raymond's daughter, Miss Mary: "'Lei non sembra molto forte in geografia, signor Carlo,' disse con tono beffardetto l'inglesina" ['Geography does not seem to be your strong suit, Mr. Carlo' said the little English lady in a mocking tone] (60). Lord Raymond then gives a detailed lesson on volcanos. In fact, the sequence of father figures has moved from Adolfo's own Florentine father Giuseppe, to his sea-faring and worldly uncle Pasquale, and now to the English Lord Raymond. It is Raymond who becomes the primary source of scientific, historical, geographic, and moral knowledge for most of the voyage.

Carlo's progress is charted in tandem with the geographic advance of the ship, marked notably by the dates and place designations that serve as headers to the letters the children write home and that constitute much of the narrative. On June 2, from Naples, Adolfo reports to his mother how Uncle Pasquale is training Carlino with a strict routine of study and hygiene. By the time they reach Malta, Carlo has made improvements, which are described explicitly in spatial terms: "non si è corretto del tutto da quella terribile infingardaggine che formava l'infelicità della buona Maria, ma siamo un pezzo avanti" [He has not corrected himself entirely of that shamefully lazy behavior that made the good Maria so unhappy, but we are at least moving a bit forward] (68–69). By June 21, as the travelers arrive at Bombay, Carlino himself can now articulate his own development and has internalized his desire to mature. The simultaneity of the paths (the boat's geographic progress and Carlino's emotional development) is underscored by the dating of the letter and the merged way in which both milestones are reported.[17] As Carlino learns the English language and encounters another English possession, he simultaneously develops his desire to progress into maturity.[18]

As the Italian boys have Lord Raymond to guide them, and the *Italo* has Britain's colonial possessions to serve as beacons on its path, the narrative merges the two journeys and charts them both on a fundamentally northern itinerary. At the same time, the boys are introduced to fellow passengers who embody "the South." Specifically, Adolfo and Carlino meet Alì, a boy who is "black as pitch" and is the servant of Raymond's daughter, Miss Mary (43). Lord Raymond's loquaciousness and informed eloquence form a sharp contrast with Alì's silences and occasional stammering.[19] It is from Lord Raymond that we learn about Alì's deceased brother Dick. The brothers Alì and Dick function in the tale as southern shadows of Adolfo and Carlino. Alì, much like Adolfo, has a good heart and noble impulses. He jumps into the ocean to save a cabin boy (86–87) and refuses to tell on the child who is the real culprit of the theft of which Alì himself had been accused (75). Dick, much like Carlino, is instead the rascally and recalcitrant child, whose adult male father figure (like Uncle Pasquale) must take stern measures with him to make him productive. However, in the case of Alì and Dick, the father figure is not a biological father or uncle, but rather an owner: Lord Raymond explains that the brothers had been two little slaves ("due piccoli schiavi" 48) of a certain "Mr. D.," a wine dealer.

In their narrative function as shadow figures of the developing protagonists, Alì and Dick are silenced and sacrificed as part of the process by which the Italian boys are northernized and as the *Italo* follows the itinerary of English colonial possessions. Dick, we learn, had been killed, eaten by sharks as he attempted to retrieve Mr. D.'s map from the dangerous waters. This act of self-sacrifice purifies the young boy, enabling him to exchange his slave's clothes for "an angel's white wings" (50).[20]

In hearing the story of this whitened black boy, the Italian youths can incorporate his nobility now that the savage body has been abjected—literally cast off. Alì, whose name in fact is a homophone for the Italian word for "wings" (*ali*), becomes a "dove" after spending time on the ship with the other children (106). The silencing, killing off, and "whitening" of these southern boys are plotted in tandem with Adolfo's and particularly Carlino's progressive maturation. Their abjection and sublimation become a way of exorcising the fear that the protagonists may themselves become as black as a chimneysweep (88).[21] Under the guidance of the British Lord Raymond, the voyage is successful, and the *Italo* brings the two boys home to their mothers as men of good sense.

Connecting by Rail: Collodi's Giannettino

Carlo Collodi's series of textbooks about the nine-year-old boy Giannettino includes his *Il viaggio per l'Italia di Giannettino* [*Giannettino's Trip through Italy*, published in three parts: *L'Italia Superiore* (1880), *L'Italia Centrale* (1883), and *L'Italia Meridionale* (1886)], which takes the young protagonist on an educational tour of the nation. In her study of postunification children's literature, Patrizia Mencarani notes that Collodi's Giannettino marks a step toward a pedagogical approach that emphasizes the child's own experience of the world as a useful source of knowledge.[22] Even before penning his masterpiece *Pinocchio*, Collodi offered protagonists who learn through direct encounters rather than relying exclusively on the word of adults, as was the more typical narrative strategy in the earlier didactic books that, for example, so relentlessly regurgitated proverbs and maxims. Mencarani states, "[l]'esperienza personale conta anche come conoscenza diretta e non solo astrattamente studiata sui libri; non è un caso che il dottor Boccadoro per insegnare la geografia al suo discepolo organizza un viaggio per l'Italia" [personal experience also counts as knowledge that is direct and not abstractly studied in books; it is not by chance that Dr. Boccadoro organizes a trip through Italy in order to teach his student geography] (31–32).[23] Mencarani here reiterates the evaluation of Collodi's works held not only by other scholars, such as Franco Fabbroni, Pino Boero, and Carmine De Luca, but also by Collodi's own contemporaries.[24] As a text itself, of course, Collodi's book is not a "direct experience" for the child reader but, precisely, the words of an adult writer. In fact, the teacher's verbal authorization of the trip gains further legitimacy through the name Collodi has invented for him: his words issue from a "golden mouth." This deed/word binary is enunciated and enacted when the teacher's proverb—his "saying"—is quoted: "Ti ricorderai che il signor Boccadoro era solito dire: 's'impara più in un viaggio che in cento libri'" [You'll recall what Mr. Boccadoro would always say, 'one learns more in a single trip than in a hundred books'] (1931, 15). The proverb here, in its verbal advocacy of deed over words (a paradox emphasized even further by the fact that the proverb is being quoted), serves as a microcosm of the book as a whole. While all books to some degree substitute for "direct experience" of the world, Collodi's narrative stages its textual status, and the tension between that status and its advocacy of experience, in ways that specifically advance the project of mapping.[25]

Il viaggio continues the educational adventures of the blond, nine-year-old character that Collodi had created in 1877 with *Giannettino* and continued in *La geografia di Giannettino* (1879) and *La grammatica di Giannettino* (1879, all published by Paggi). Collodi would continue to publish books about Giannettino until the year of his death (1890).[26] Boccadoro's sometimes naughty pupil revives and revises his more idealized namesake, the eponymous hero from the famous *Giannetto* by Luigi Alessandro Parravicini (1837). Parravicini's text was highly successful in its time, with sixty editions by 1880 (Antonelli 11). Its success, however, did not derive from any complexity or verve in its protagonist, who, "a virtuous and exemplary young boy, was little more than a vehicle for moral improvement" (Myers, *Making* 21). Rather, its utility derived from its linking of "istruzione" and "educazione," or academic instruction and moral development. Noting that for decades *Giannetto* functioned as "the prototype of the perfect text book" (13), Boero and De Luca observe how Parravicini's book successfully combines two paths, one of factual learning and one of personal growth.[27] Parravicini's *Giannetto*, in short, remained for many years a staple of the curriculum, offering a model itinerary for its readers and itself serving as a model for other texts. While Collodi's Giannettino in many ways breaks the mold of, and eclipses, his stiff, one-dimensional, and moralizing forebear, the core lessons advocated remain the same.[28] Furthermore, Collodi's book echoes the format of Stoppani's *Il bel paese*, by employing the conversation as its device to deliver geographic information. Even more specifically, Collodi modeled this *Giannettino* tale on G. Bruno's *Le tour de la France par deux enfants*, a very successful French text published three years before the first part of *Il viaggio*, and just two years after Collodi published his translation of Charles Perrault's French fairy tales.[29] Collodi, then, himself looks northward to France for a textual model of deploying geography. Thus, in spite of its overt disparagement of the value of reading vis-à-vis experience, the book emerges from and points back to a set of textual precedents (Parravicini, Stoppani, Bruno). Collodi's use of intertextuality, echoing, and mutual confirmation enables the mapping as mirroring process. As Coats writes, "this process [of 'shaping reality' and 'defining parameters of possibility'] depends on repetition—both the repetition of the same book, and the repetition of structures, images, and values across books" (6–7).

Even more significantly, the text itself is framed not as a "direct experience" but rather as a retrospective narrative account, as Giannettino shares his memories of his travels with his friends. These boys, who inquisitively listen to the storyteller, become the ideal readers. In other words, the child reader finds his (and specifically *his*) textual model not so much in the traveling Giannettino as in the listening Arturo ("Minuzzolo") and Adolfo. While the book's open advocacy of knowledge gained through the child's own interactions with the world certainly marks a difference from earlier didactic texts, *Il viaggio* stands not only as a rupture but also as a continuation and as part of a broader conversation among texts. The dichotomy it seeks to establish is everywhere undermined—the book's very structure reveals the interdependence between experience and reading (and specifically, given the book's topic, between "geo" and "graph") rather than the distinction between them.

Collodi foregrounds the issue of textuality at the outset, explaining that Giannettino has in fact written down his experiences. The book opens with the rather odd tale of the manuscript's origin and fate. Giannettino recounts to his friends that, in order to fulfill Minuzzolo's request for a monkey, he had purchased one from a beggar while in Spezia, the last stop on his northern tour before returning home (1931, 9–15). After a few days, the monkey, nicknamed "Pizzicorino" [Tickle] began imitating its new master, putting on Giannettino's clothes and pretending to write at his desk. After scribbling all over Giannettino's manuscript, which contained the accounts of his travels, the animal escapes with the help of the beggar's dog. Still donning the boy's clothes, the rascally primate rides the dog through town and laughs mockingly at those chasing after him (1931, 14). In the end, only some of the manuscript could be rescued, and Giannettino dedicates it to Minuzzolo—instead of a pet monkey, Minuzzolo gets a book. This whimsical opening scene attracts readers to a story that otherwise might appear as a dull collection of facts and figures about Italy's northern cities. Thus, the engaging romp aims to diffuse the sentiment expressed directly by one of the young characters: "'Cento fogli! Soltanto la noja di doverli rileggere!' disse Adolfo, sbadigliando" (1931, 9) ["A hundred pages! Just the boredom of having to re-read them!" said Adolfo, yawning].[30] The opening scenario thus ingratiates the child reader, while at the same time "colonizing" him as well. The monkey, like his name, "tickles" the reader. He not only provokes laughter through his antics but also creates discomfort through his disruptive and destructive potential. Deploying evolutionary imagery, the narrative explicitly casts him as the child's double and dramatizes the primitive and bestial nature to be tamed via education.

Collodi would develop the monkey-child figure in *Pipì o lo scimmiottino color di rosa* [*Beppe, or the Little Rose-Colored Monkey*], published two years after *Pinocchio* in the *Giornale per i bambini* and recalling the masterpiece linguistically and thematically: the eponymous little monkey, for example, is described as a "birba" and "monello" [imp and rascal]. In *Pipì*, several scenes of mirroring between monkey and human, and particularly between monkey and child, announce that this vivacious and gluttonous creature, who prefers to roam naked rather than be confined by elegant clothing, functions as a projection of the child's allegedly wild nature.[31] After losing his tail to a crocodile bite and repeatedly attempting to return to his primate family, thus experiencing the painful losses that will "humanize" him, Pipì undergoes his transformation. Now, "revestito tutto da capo a' piedi, s'intende bene, come un bel signore" [dressed up now from head to toe, understand well, just like a fine gentleman] (110), he boards a steam ship to accompany the human child Alfredo on "un lungo viaggio di istruzione" [a long educational trip] (110). As in *Pipì*, so too in *Il viaggio* the monkey "apes" the boy. Furthermore, Giannettino's monkey is linked through the narrative with a beggar—an adult who has not entered the system of social productivity. The destructive animal thus acts as a threatening shadow of what the boy could become, or rather what he would remain, were it not for the books that produce him as a meaningful and legible subject.

The issue of legibility becomes the overt topic in one of Giannettino's encounters. Giannettino recounts the conversations he had on the train with the Roman boy Pompilio, who asks, "Scusami, un'altra curiosità: o il dialetto del popolino di Firenze qual'è?" [Relieve me of another curiosity: what is the dialect of the people of Florence?] (1931, 37). Our narrator responds, "Il popolo fiorentino non ha dialetto; parla la lingua italiana. I Fiorentini la stroppiano un poco nel pronunziarla... ma queste sono scorrezioni di pronunzia" [The Florentine people do not have a dialect; they speak Italian. They mangle it a bit with when they speak... but these are merely pronunciation errors] (1931, 37). In fact, after being treated to Giannettino's detailed history of Florence, from the Guelfs and Ghibellines to the "splendid plebiscite" of March 15, 1860 (1894, 20), the Roman boy expresses a burst of desire to visit Florence's *libraries* (1894, 27). Clearly, then, while Giannettino as protagonist travels throughout Italy ostensibly to gather information about the nation, he is also a kind of linguistic missionary: he, like the book itself, travels the peninsula to spread the normalizing Florentine idiom and the value of education outwards from Florence.[32]

Giannettino, of course, is a particularly modern missionary, for he travels the peninsula in a train. We recall that Collodi wrote his first novel (not for children), entitled *Un romanzo in vapore; da Firenze a Livorno: guida storico-umoristica* (1856) [*A Novel in Steam from Florence to Livorno*] at the request of the publisher of the *Orario della strada ferrata* [*Railroad Timetable*].[33] The novel served as a lively guidebook to accompany the train line Firenze-Empoli-Pisa-Livorno (Boero 25, Guagnini 25–26).[34] The book was sold at train station bookshops, and its appendix listed the names of booksellers (as well as hotels, doctors, and pharmacies, among other information) in Florence, Pisa, and Livorno.[35] Thus, the mutually supporting industries of locomotion and publication benefited from and promoted the "mass travel" of modernity. Collodi revives the mechanism of the train voyage as a narrative thread; thus, the "direct experience" of the protagonist is enabled by modernity and, ultimately, in service to it. In fact, a description and history of train travel is the culminating lesson of Part 1, which reminds readers, for example, that "[l]a prima strada ferrata costruita in Italia è quella da Napoli a Portici, e fu aperta precisamente il 4 Ottobre 1839" [the first rail line built in Italy was the one from Naples to Portici, which was opened, to be precise, on October 4, 1839] (1931, 186).

At the conclusion of the volume devoted to northern Italy, immediately following the discussion of railways, Giannettino summarizes the goal of his undertaking: "perchè faccio questo viaggio? ...un po' per conoscere da vicino le più grandi e le più belle città dell'Italia settentrionale e delle nuove province, che finora ho conosciuto solo sui libri" [why am I making this trip? ...in part in order to know up close the grandest and most beautiful cities of northern Italy and of the new provinces, which up until now I have known through books] (1931, 186–87). Thus, we learn that only the cities are worth visiting and knowing, and specifically the cities that one may reach by train. Italy here is mapped, precisely, by the artery of railroads that traverse the peninsula and connect its urban centers, and the pages of *Il viaggio* are filled with descriptions of those cities, leaving the spaces in between as blanks on the map.[36] Furthermore, the assertion becomes an implicit self-authorization: the claim denies the textuality of the book actually being read, implying that Collodi's text is not a geography book (via its opposition to other books), yet also offering itself as confirmation of the validity of those other books, whose information is deepened but not contradicted by Giannettino's trip, or, more precisely, by *Il viaggio di Giannettino*.[37] Ultimately, Giannettino proudly asserts that he left Florence a boy and returns almost as a man—specifically linking the national journey (which promotes homogenization through the mechanisms of modernity) to the process of personal maturation.[38]

Africa Italian Style

Children's books mapped Italy and its citizens not only through producing verbal and visual images of the peninsula itself, but also through generating representations of Italy's "other." While, as Patrizia Palumbo has shown, the Ethiopian War of the fascist period would increase the number of children's books set in Africa and change the manner in which Africa was represented, a variety of children's books at the-turn-of-the-century period did turn their gaze to this continent. These texts were produced and circulated, some with much popular success, during a particularly vexed period of Italian imperial ambitions.[39] As I have summarized in my study of Eugenio Cherubini's 1903 *Pinocchio in Affrica*, by the early twentieth century, Italy held two small colonies in northeastern Africa: Eritrea and Somaliland. In 1887, Italy attempted to expand its colonial holdings from the Bay of Assab toward Egypt's Massaua, but the initiative was halted by the Ethiopians, who attacked and virtually destroyed a column of 500 Italian troops at Dogali. In 1889, Italy sought to establish a protectorate over Ethiopia through the bilingual Treaty of Uccialli with Emperor Menelik II. The inconsistency between the Italian and the Amharic versions of this treaty ultimately led to conflict, as the Ethiopians resisted an Italian troop build-up in the area. Sòrgoni summarizes that "[t]he 1896 battle of Adwa between Italians and Abyssinians was the biggest defeat a European army suffered in the whole colonial history of Africa. About 4000 Italians and 2000 colonial soldiers died or were captured" (77). The defeat precipitated the fall of Francesco Crispi's government that year (Truglio, "African Plots" 119).[40] Perhaps not surprisingly, children's books of this period that took Africa as their subject or as their setting often rehearsed the derogatory stereotypes Tundonu Amosu has articulated. In his study of the immensely popular adventure novels of Emilio Salgari, Amosu shows how that popular writer depicted "the blacks ... as a stupid, superstitious lot ... addicted to drinking ... harmless and ridiculous adversaries" (53). Other writers followed suit.[41] Like the advocacy of heroism I examined in Chapter 1, the denigration of actually and potentially colonized subjects has a clear utility for the state. What I interrogate here is how these overtly racist depictions were adumbrated by mapping strategies that aimed to promote—simultaneously and in mutually confirming ways—the maturation of Italian children and the modernization of the Italian nation through plotting the abjection of the "other."

Emilio Salgari's Geo-graphing

Emilio Salgari's popular texts require examination not, as some critics have recently argued, for their neglected literary merit, but because their serialized production, formulaic familiarity, and mass consumption make them a symptom and an instrument of modernization in Italy. Salgari (like most children's authors in Italy other than Collodi) has not typically been considered a writer of any great aesthetic merit. Umberto Eco, for example, claims that "Salgari never thought he was producing art" (*Open Work* 209) and cites his novels as an illustration of "closed works" that do not invite reader participation, the antithesis of his famous formulation of modern art as "open works" (see Truglio, "Wise Gnomes" 126). Other scholars in recent years have sought to foster an appreciation of Salgari's writing. Felice Pozzo has underscored Salgari's "creativity, autonomy, and freshness" claiming him as "il nostro più grande scrittore d'avventure di tutti i tempi" [our

greatest adventure writer of all times] (xxxii). Sarti, noting that
Salgari was ignored by the world of official literary criticism (1990, 9),
insists on his amazing inventiveness and scrupulous research (1990,
10). Ann Lawson Lucas vigorously advocates a recognition of Salgari's
ability to deploy effectively and powerfully the major archetypes of
western culture, positioning him along the trajectory initiated by the
Iliad and the *Odyssey* ("Archetypal" no pg.), while also claiming that
his depictions of nature can be compared to the poetry of Pascoli
("Salgari, the Atlas" 88). Thus, she claims that in spite of "borrowing
widely," Salgari offers "a new and original vision" ("Archetypal" no
pg.). Lucas refutes both literary and ideological dismissals of Salgari.
Defending not only his deft handling of archetypes like the "female
warrior" and "the cast-away," she also asserts that Salgari's "spirit of
adventure" is "Garibaldian in style (but this means generous, egalitar-
ian, altruistic), not Fascist (domineering, hierarchical, exploitative)"
("Archetypal" no pg.). Lucas's work reveals the two interrelated flash
points of critical anxiety regarding Salgari: the writer's lack of "orig-
inality" (due to his recycling of works by Verne, Dumas, and others)
and his exoticism, or perhaps better "orientalist discourse." In short,
Salgari's texts and the critical postures of attack and defense which
they provoke, I suggest, disclose the anxieties inherent to modernity
in Western culture: reproducibility and the fabrication of the "self"
via the "other," both of which suggest a loss of essence.[42] Salgari's
prose offers dense description and detailed accounts of the novels' "exotic" landscapes, and his texts often functioned as fictionalized botany,
zoology, and geography lessons. Pointing to the fact that Salgari himself
never traveled to the locales he so painstakingly describes, but rather
relied on textual sources, Lawson Lucas indeed claims that "he did not
write...to appease his longing for geographic experience, rather geography served him well in his need to write" ("Salgari, the Atlas" 80).
While Salgari's personal passions and his psychological affinity with
Darwin may account for the genesis of his prose style, as Lucas argues,
I am interested here in interrogating the rhetorical effects generated by
his earth-writing.

The following passage from the second chapter of *I drammi della schiavitù* (1896) [*The Dramas of Slavery*] typifies his approach:

> La foce di quel vasto fiume, che forma un delta considerevole che si
> estende fra il 0° 41' di latitudine sud ed il 9° 3' di longitudine est e
> 1° 17' di latitudine e 5° 56' di longitudine è intersecata da un numero
> infinito di bracci, i cui più notevoli sono il Nazareth, il Messia e il
> Fernando Vas che per lungo tempo si credettero fiumi indipendenti.
> Grandi paludi la ingombrano, tagliate da canali e canaletti in mezzo
> ai quali nuotano mostruosi coccodrilli sempre avidi di preda, ma
> più oltre si estende un bosco immenso di mangifere, che si prolunga

per parecchie dozzine di miglia entro il territorio dipendente del re Bango. (13–14)[43]

[The mouth of that vast river, which forms a remarkable delta extending from the southern latitude of 0° 41' and the eastern longitude of 1° 17' to the latitude of 1° 17'and the longitude of 5° 56', is intersected by an infinite number of branches, the most notable of which are the Nazareth, the Messia, and the Fernando Vas. For a long time, these were thought to be independent rivers. Huge swamps obstruct it, cut through by big and small canals in the midst of which swim monstrous crocodiles, always on the lookout for prey. But beyond stretches an immense forest of mango trees that extends for several dozens of miles into King Bango's territory.]

Here, textual and geographic plots merge. As the slave traders sail inland to fetch their "cargo," Salgari's precise cartography marks and locates territory, rhetorically "demarcating and diagramming that which was previously undifferentiated" (Brooks 12).[44] The encompassing purview of the authoritative narrator clarifies and brings order to confusion, containing the "vast, infinite, immense" landscape within the numbered grid of longitude and latitude lines. Like the protagonist-heroes, the narrative vision identifies and diffuses the dangers that lie hidden. As such, the novel restages European colonialist strategies of measuring, naming, and thus bringing to light the hidden wonders, dangers, and resources of the Dark Continent.[45]

The river-scape cited here comes into focus early in Chapter 2. The pages leading up to this moment depict the lookout boat and its crew nervously peering through the nighttime darkness, as the characters search for the signals from their potential traders and for any sign of the British or French ships that might try to intercept them, hang them, and free their cargo. These opening pages brim over with verbs of seeing (*guardare, vedere, scorgere, osservare, esaminare, sorvegliare, scoprire* [look, see, discern, observe, examine, survey, discover]) and with references to instruments of sight (mirrors and telescopes). Indeed, at least five times in just a few pages the narrator describes the crew and its leader as casting their gaze across the coastline.[46] The book's first illustration, furthermore, shows sailors Hurtado and Vasco staring intently off to their right. Illustrator G. G. Bruno depicts Vasco pointing to the distance and Hurtardo with hand to forehead as if to help him focus his view. Discernment, in short, becomes the obsessive theme of the opening chapters, and we as readers are commanded to penetrate the darkness of the African coast through the "sharp" eyes of the "negrieri" [slave traders]. The very first line of the novel is an imperative addressed to the crew in the *voi* [plural you], but as an opening line, and through the use of "ragazzi" [boys] seems addressed also to the readers: "Adagio ragazzi e aprite bene gli occhi!" [Take it easy boys and open your eyes wide!] (3). In short, the novel opens with nothing short of a dramatization of the life-and-death stakes attendant upon positioning oneself as the subject and not the object of gaze.

Through Salgari's novel, middle-class Italian readers of adventure novels can safely open their eyes and adopt the perspective of western discernment and rationality, casting their gaze over the potentially threatening yet fruitful lands, whose dangers are revealed, controlled, and contained within the carefully plotted rhetorical grid.[47] While these strategies certainly typify the devices of orientalism, I underscore here two points specific to this case. First, *I drammi* reveals how this *plotting* can be at work even if the *story* is about the moral conversion of a character away from the evils of the slave trade.[48] Second, the passages show how the details of this one novel are implicated within a general discourse of mapping that not only justifies colonization of its object but also enables the melancholy maturation of its subjects, as becomes evident in other texts of the period that echo Salgari.[49]

Becoming a Man at Elephant Lake

Eugenio Cherubini's novel *Pinocchio in Affrica* (1903) reverberates with one such echo. In fact, like Salgari's *I drammi*, it was illustrated by G.G. Bruno. In this spin-off of Collodi's masterpiece, Cherubini uses the home-away-home code to structure the puppet's journey from Italy to Africa and back. Drawing on Peter Brooks' Freudian analysis of plot, I have argued that the effects of mapping a "no-place" (a utopian "away") onto a real place (Africa) offered readers a more satisfying, meaningful ending than history itself had provided (Truglio, "African Plots" 119, 122). Specifically, I contend that "Pinocchio's trajectory from Africa back to Italy becomes a textual *fort-da* that insists on the subject's ability to choose and control the experience of loss" and that redefines Africa as an "undesirable mirage-utopia" (134). Similarly, *Al lago degli elefanti: Avventure di un italiano in Africa* (1897) by Jack La Bolina (pseudonym for Augusto Vittorio Vecchi) draws on verbal and visual mapping strategies as a way to work out anxieties about the other within the self.[50] Published at a time in which emigration out of southern Italy, and, simultaneously, Italian attempts to extend colonial holding in Africa were both reaching crisis points, and when scientific discourse was apparently affirming the determinative links between physiognomy and moral character, *Al lago degli elefanti* seeks to exorcise the specter of unredeemable primitives within Italy's own borders while simultaneously asserting the superiority of Italians over Africans by aligning Italy with the northern (i.e., "superiore") European powers.[51]

The troubling links between Africans and southern Italians emerge at several points early in this adventure story. First, we learn that the

Genoese ship captain, who takes the young protagonist to Africa, has never participated in the slave trade himself, but that he has seen many desperate southern Italians sailing to the Americas as indentured servants (14). Soon after, Giorgio Varini, the blond protagonist from Turin, bluntly remarks that the "Negro" with whom he travels could easily be mistaken for a Calabrian were it not for his wooly head and big lips (22). Mobilized at the beginning of the story, these historical and physiological associations between southern Italians and Africans might account for the story's virulent project of progressively decoupling Italians from the "primitive" inhabitants of Africa.

Al lago degli elefanti follows the journey structure so typical of children's and young adult novels. Young Giorgio must leave school and earn money by working with a business venture in Cameroon. Giorgio sets out from Genoa accompanied by Giuseppe Acqua, a Negro prince who has been educated in Europe, and Gaspare Schroeder, a German boy. They sail from Italy to Cameroon and then undertake inland journeys that include doing battle with elephants, confronting poisonous fish, and circumventing the plots of treacherous tribal allies. It appears, then, that the maturation process being mapped as a physical journey is here headed southward, where I have asserted that Italian texts typically urge a northward journey in order to plot maturation and modernization together. The novel, however, positions itself within the body of texts that dramatize a giving up of the "the South" as a necessary abandonment in the creation of modern, melancholy Italian subjects. Giorgio, much like Baccini's Adolfo and Carlino, travels south only to be tutored under a series of northern father figures: his teacher in Turin, a former "garibaldino" named Pietro Ceroni, sets the journey in motion, and Giorgio is then put into the care of the Genoese Captain Giuseppe Ponza. In Cameroon, he meets Antonio Millich, the Austrian friend of Giorgio's Turinese teacher who owns the farm where Giorgio will work, and finally Mr. Peterson, the Norwegian supervisor of a farm farther inland. Giorgio's educational journey consists of absorbing the lessons adumbrated and modeled by these northern men, against the backdrop of the increasingly threatening African landscape and its inhabitants.

The text opens with a visual map of Western Africa and Western Europe as the frontispiece (see Figure 2.3). A rectangular frame parallels the physical edges of the page, the longitude and latitude lines are clearly indicated and labeled numerically at the borders, and Italy appears in the top right corner. A dashed line marks an ocean pathway connecting Genoa and Cameroon, going southwest across the Mediterranean, through the straits of Gibraltar, hugging the western coast of Africa, and entering through the "Golfo di Guinea." The very center of the map, in capital letters, is labeled as "Africa Occid. Francese" [French West Africa]. Following this physical and political map, the first black and white illustration in the book offers a photograph of the port of Genoa. These illustrations, in

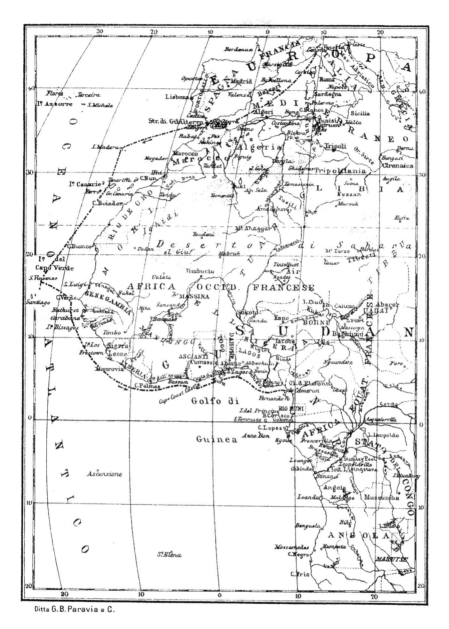

Figure 2.3 Frontispiece from *Al lago degli elefanti* by Augusto Vecchi [Jack La Bolina].

addition to conveying information, should be read along the terms delineated by John Stephens in his analysis of landscapes in children's books. Stephens asserts that "[l]andscape in picture books is never simply present, or never just 'ground' or background, but always moves viewers on from representation ('what is there') to interpretation of what is there" (98) and that "the social and ideological force of such landscapes lies precisely in their apparent depiction of an ordinary reality" (99).[52]

The map and image that open Vecchi's text, then, perform several functions. First, their level of detail and their purported representation of actual places suggest that the book they adorn should be read as realism rather than fantasy. Furthermore, the scope of the first map announces that Italy is here being positioned in a broader geographical (if not fully "global") context, extending south of the equator. In other words, Italy is being constituted via its relationships with other nations. Finally, the dashed line indicates that the protagonist's journey has in fact already been mapped out—while adventures and challenges certainly await, the path itself has been preordained to be followed (not to be blazed) for the boy-protagonist and the reader.

The ensuing narrative reinforces these effects. The story brims over with detailed geographical and historical information, including the history of the slave trade, the development of steam ships, and the abolition of slavery in Brazil. Vecchi's wealth of botanical, geographical, and anthropological information goes even further than Salgari's predilection for detailed description.[53] Like Salgari, then, Vecchi plots his setting with extreme precision—we should note that he speaks not primarily of "Africans" but of the Cru (Kru), Dualla, Bakundu, and other peoples—and drenches his narrative with authoritative detail. Further, the deployment of a particularly literary lexicon, including poetic terms like *ivi*, *meco*, *beltà*, *coniugi*, *uopo*, and *dimora*, seems to guarantee the narrator's erudition.[54]

The issue of authority emerges early in the novel, in a description of Giorgio's parents' first meeting with the captain of the ship that will take their son to Cameroon:

> Sulla fede dei romanzi scritti, come suol dirsi, di maniera, essi sinceramente credevano che avrebbbero trovato nel capitano dell'Enotria un vecchio burbero, dai capelli irti e della barba arruffata, cogli anellini d'oro agli orecchi, ruvidamente vestito, e che non sapesse dir quattro parole senza punteggiarle con un sagrato. (11)

> [On the basis of novels written, as they say, in a certain style, they sincerely believed that they would find in the captain of the Enotria a coarsely dressed grouchy old man, with bristly hair, disheveled beard, and golden rings hanging from his ears. Indeed they expected he would not be able to say even four words in a row without swearing.]

Instead, the captain proves to be an elegant, educated, and articulate man. Vecchi here playfully reproduces the stereotypes of sailors disseminated by popular adventure novels, only to pull the rug out from under the characters' and readers' expectations. This debunking of other popular novels posits the existence of a reading community whose shared texts have generated cultural expectations—here, a clichéd image of rough-and-tumble sailors. Giorgio's family models Vecchi's readers as members of that community. The subversion of those textually grounded expectations implies that *this* book is grounded not in fantasy but in reality: Vecchi offers his readers not just another predictable adventure novel, but also an authentic portrayal based on empirical evidence. This claimed authenticity, reinforced by the abundance of historical and botanical facts and visually underscored by the detailed map and photograph, lends the whole book an aura of truth and reassures the reader that this book does not traffic in stereotypes. The appearance of authority extends to the assessments of racial characteristics asserted in the text.

The *bildungsroman* recounts not only Giorgio's development from boy to man through his successful display of physical prowess and mental acumen in Cameroon, but also, through his accumulated experience, his eventual acceptance of the racism he had initially resisted. This coupled development (maturation into a man linked to acceptance of racial stereotypes) is the narrative equivalent of the dashed line preordained for him to follow. Specifically, Giorgio slowly comes to embrace the "truth" in his comrades' and mentors' conviction that Africans (embodied most notably in the European-educated prince returning home to Africa) are essentially inferior and barbaric. Even here, Vecchi's strategic use of a scientific-like precision comes into play, as the narrator claims that each individual African tribe has its own unique defects: whether it be cowardice, sneakiness, superstition (such as believing that the poisonous fish are magical fetishes), or inability to do math.[55] This particular shortcoming, linking Africans to young children, puts them at a distance from the cartographer who skillfully mapped the route from Genoa to Cameroon. Intellectual inferiority is paired with moral inferiority, as Acqua, for instance, does not feel any remorse after killing a man, as opposed to the disquiet experienced by Giorgio (Chapter 3).

Over the course of the novel, Giorgio must come to accept that while his comrade's bestial nature may be temporarily obscured by a veneer of European manners, his primitive essence will always inevitably re-emerge. Giorgio's adult, northern mentors express this sentiment by means of metaphorical language that is particularly telling. First Captain Ponza remarks, "Le confesso che non ripongo gran fiducia nell'innesto dell'educazione europea sulla pianta-uomo esotica. Se ne ottiene dei semi-barbari che sono peggio dei barbari sinceri" [I confess to you that I do not place much faith in the grafting of European education onto an exotic human-plant. You end up with a bunch of semi-savages that are even worse than pure ones] (15). Later Peterson asserts, "Grattateli un pochettino questi negri che si mandano alle scuole europee, e sotto la vernice ritroverete il legno d'ebano di cui si è fatto commercio per tanto tempo" [scratch them a bit, these Negroes that they send to European schools, and right under the paint you'll find the same ebony wood that was bought and sold for so many years] (89). Using images of plants and of wood to represent people clearly dehumanizes the subjects of these metaphors. Further, the specifically botanical language here locates these assertions about the inefficacy of educating Africans within the scientific discourse deployed by the text in its discussions of literal botany, making these claims appear equally "scientific." Finally, the use of plants and trees as images for people implies that these people, too, are naturally rooted in their land, determined in their essence by the soil from which they spring, no matter how one may try to spruce them up or transplant them. The reference to Acqua's other tribe members as his "conterranei" (35) ["fellows," but with use of the root word "terra" or land] reinforces this concept.

At the same time, however, these metaphors, which usefully serve the novel's racist agenda, also rather problematically suggest that education itself may be an artificial and superficial process, like painting and grafting. Given the clearly pedagogical aims of the text, whose wealth of lessons should be fully absorbed and integrated by readers, and given the state's strenuous efforts to promote education in the period, these images open troubling questions. Indeed the previous associations between southern Italians and Africans brings the issue "home," especially in light of the fact that results from educational reform in the South seemed to be lagging. The novel attempts to resolve this issue through the progressive distancing between Giorgio and Giuseppe, the latter receding ever further back into his primitive origins, and the concomitant strengthening of the link between Giorgio and the German Gaspare. Education will "take," the plot suggests, if planted in the right (i.e., northern) soil. The text takes pains to emphasize the deep respect that German and Austrian characters develop for their Italian neighbors and to insist on the felicitous outcome of Giorgio's educational journey, which results in the triumphant discovery of gold. The plot in short closes (rather than resolves) the vexing issue it opened by suggesting that an Italian boy can be educated even if an African boy cannot.

Giorgio, whose Italian birth apparently makes him capable of attaining real education, must relinquish his friendship with the "primitive" Giuseppe Acqua, and abandon his naïve and childish belief in human equality in order to be embraced by Gaspare and named the heir to Peterson's fortune. Giorgio's gradual "progression" toward this view, mapped against Acqua's increasing "regression" into primitivism, correlates with the blond Turinese boy's development of physical prowess. The narrative and illustrations manifest this development particularly in Giorgio's encounters with elephants, as highlighted by the novel's title. In Chapter 2, one of these indigenous African creatures chases Giorgio, grasps him in its trunk, and quite dramatically swings him about and hurls him into the water. The boy is subsequently tormented by bad dreams, indicating that this episode carries the force of trauma in Giorgio's development. Later (Chapter 6), Giorgio participates in the hunt organized by Peterson and the community. After successfully killing four elephants, the men celebrate together. Learning to master the indigenous elephants, then, parallels the abandonment of attachments toward the primitive friend, and both become necessary steps along the itinerary of attaining manhood and a place in the community.

Furthermore, Giorgio's heteronormative white masculinity is confirmed by the transfer of his affection from the savage boy Acqua to the native woman Wataba, an appropriately servile Dualla who becomes Giorgio's companion: "Wataba lo consolò offrendosi colla devozione speciale della donna negra per l'uomo bianco" [Wataba comforted him offering herself with the special devotion of the black woman for the white man] (110).[56] As he abandons Acqua and takes possession of Wataba, Giorgio assumes his place among his father figures, and Italy takes its place among the European powers. Indeed the novel, near its conclusion, offers a comforting image of a canoe floating down the Mungo River adorned with the Austrian, Norwegian, and Italian flags (133). Ultimately, the novel feminizes Africa and at the same time imagines women as a resource, coding both women and Africa as available for harvesting by Europe, via the supposedly honorific entitling of the gold mine: "*Società anglo-germanica-italiana delle miniere Wataba del Camerun*" [The Wataba of Cameroon Anglo-German-Italian Society of Mines] (143).

The fusion of Giorgio's personal itinerary and Italy's national trajectory, both of which are enabled by the paradoxical rejection (via Giuseppe Acqu) and possession (via Wataba) of Africa, culminates and is authorized by the paternal words of the old Garibaldino. In the penultimate chapter of the novel, as Giorgio fields multiple offers for collaboration on the gold mine initiative, he receives letters simultaneously from his father and his former teacher:

> Tra quei messaggi *di affari*, ne giunsero anche due molto più graditi, uno del babbo Varini da Torino, ed uno da Cantù. L'antico garibaldino di Bezzecca non aveva dimenticato il giovanotto che, mercè sua, era ormai divenutuo un uomo nel senso più alto della parola, e gli spediva una laconico consiglio: 'Ricordati essere italiano; della tua lieta ventura profitti anzitutto l'Italia'. (137; italics in orig.)

> [Among the *business* correspondence, two other much more welcome messages arrived: one from his dad Varini, from Turin, and

one from Cantù. The old Garibaldino from Bezzecca had not for-
gottton the young man who, thanks to him, had already become a
man in the best sense of the word. He sent a laconic word of advice:
"Remember you are Italian: from your fortunate adventure, may
Italy above all proft."]

The passage puts into proximity and links the personal coming of age
for Giorgio (he hears from his "babbo" and becomes a "man") and the
national development of Italy (his teacher is not called "his mentor"
or "Mr. Ceroni" but rather is designated by his association with the
father of the nation, and reminds him of his national duty). In short,
Al lago degli elefanti strives to insist authoritatively that Italians are
white Europeans, to affirm Italy's mature place among the community
of European nations, and to map the parallel paths of personal and national growing up through the process of abandoning and introjecting a
feminine "South."

"A Sweet and Melancholy Melody": Capuana's *Scurpiddu*

In Chapter 1, I discussed how the "Calabrian boy" of De Amicis's *Cuore*
silently appeared in all his dark swarthiness in Enrico's northern classroom. Similarly, the Calabrian-like Giuseppe Acqua inevitably regresses
into his primitive "nature" in Jack La Bolina's *Al lago degli elefanti*. Both
characters work as a kind of foil for their Piedmontese protagonists and
specifically function as devices for Enrico's and Giorgio's maturation.
Sicilian writer Luigi Capuana (1839–1914) gives readers another southern boy in the title character of his *bildungsroman, Scurpiddu*, which
appeared in 1898.[57] Written by and about a Sicilian, the book was published in Turin in standard Italian for a mostly northern reading public.
Thus, Capuana's eponymous hero, while the protagonist of the tale and
subject of maturation, also functions as an instrument of maturation for
the young, primarily northern reader.

   Capuana was one of the major theorists and practitioners of *versimo*
(regional realism), which grounded its approach in a positivist method
of meticulous empirical observation. As I noted in the Introduction,
Capuana was well versed in the work of Cesare Lombroso. Capuana's
own fairy tales, as critics have established, are deeply indebted to the
extensive research of folklorists Giuseppe Pitrè and Lionardo Vigo,
and Capuana pays homage to the former by naming a character after
him anagrammatically as the magician Tre-pi in *C'era una volta* and
Il Raccontafiabe (Boero and De Luca 108). We can discern Capuana's in-
vestment in such research and the cultural and political issues at stake in
his review of Salvatore Salomone-Marion's 1897 study *I contadini siciliani* [*Sicilian farmers*]. Discussing the book shortly after its publication,
Capuana notes that this "talented folklorist" was carrying forward the

work of scholars like Pitrè, Vigo, and Serafino Guastella (Capuana, *Gli 'ismi'* 176). In this review, Capuana reveals his dedication to precision in anthropological studies: he critiques the author, for example, for having assumed that the peasants around Palermo, who are of Phoenician and Arab-Norman ancestry, would share customs and traditions with the peasants from other regions in Sicily, like the "Greek-Siculo" race from the Catania area. Just as crucial, though, are his concerns about the potential loss of customs, values, and characteristics unique to the variety of Sicilian *contadini* as a result of Italian unification. In fact, he opens his review by asserting that the book should have been called "*I contadini siciliani di tempo fa*" [*Sicilian farmers of time past*] (176) since the effects of unification, especially through conscription, had already significantly changed the habits of the people described in Salamone-Marion's book. *Scurpiddu*, in a sense, can be read as Capuana's attempt to intervene in this process and to navigate the apparently conflicting demands of national unification and preservation of local identity.

Scurpiddu becomes an extraordinary example of a text that plots the passage from child to adult and specifically from boy to man, onto a national map that demands the melancholic loss and simultaneous introjection of the South as a path to modernity. *Scurpiddu* is notable for the way in which it so seamlessly solders the rural, the local, the feminine, and the primitive together and codes them all as aspects both of childhood and of antiquity. Where the Garibaldian hero tales that I analyzed in Chapter 1 staged a movement from epic to novel, here the pastoral is evoked but left behind. Like the "dolce e malinconica melodia" [sweet and melancholy melody] (19) that Scurpiddu plays on his panpipes while tending his flock, the pastoral world leaves a faint echo to be enjoyed nostalgically in the pages of the novel.[58] Vittorio Spinazzola has characterized the text as a "harmonization" (the musical register perhaps inspired by the image of the pipes) of "realisticità psicosociale e favolismo idillico" [psychosocial realism and idyllic fable] (151). Coming from the pen of the great theorist of *verismo*, the tale assumes the authoritative voice of the scientist dispassionately recording reality.

The opening scene overtly deploys the strategy of mapping as the narrator locates the protagonist's geographic position. The first line reads: "Massaio Turi aveva incontrato il ragazzo una sera nel punto dove finisce, sul ciglione della Arcura, la scorciatoia che dal mulino di Catalfàro conduce a Bardella" [Farmer Turi had met the boy one evening on the embankment of the Arcura, at the point where the by-way which leads from Catalfàro's mill to Bardella comes to an end] (3). The protagonist, then, occupies a specific place we are invited to envision as a point or a dot on the map of Sicily. The clearly marked coordinates from which the protagonist starts his itinerary contrast with the quality Pavlik has observed in literary maps in children's books. In these kinds of maps, Pavlik argues, "[t]here are no 'You are Here' signs, and there are rarely ever 'tracings' to indicate the direction of the characters' movements" (33).[59] Unlike, then, the open-ended quality typical of the kinds of maps Pavlik analyzes, Capuana's text does provide readers with a "you are here" pointer, using proper place names to produce the effect of geographic specificity, even if most readers, who would have been from the more literate North, would not have been familiar with the rural Sicilian setting.[60] Spinazzola rightly points out the double valence of Capuana's strategy of using precise toponyms without, however, providing the reader who is not a native of the Catania region with any sense of where exactly to find these "contrade sconosciute" [unknown districts] (151): it simultaneously produces the effect of realist precision and of fable-like universality, conjuring a general "elsewhere" for the non-Sicilian reader. I would argue that this vagueness provides an opening for the reader to identify with Scurpiddu, while the precise toponyms underscore the "southernness" of the tale. The indication of location, working in a way contrary to the literary maps Pavlik discusses, *does* seek to orient the reader and trace his path, thus becoming the starting point of the novel's didactic strategy. Using the language of the journey, Andretta asserts that in *Scurpiddu* (and in his other novel, *Cardello*) "[l]'iter va dall'abbandono alla conquista di una coscienza sociale e civile" [the itinerary progresses from state of abandonment to the conquest of a social and civic consciousness] (53). As Scurpiddu begins his story at the "end of the road," he finds himself precisely in need of the paternal figures who will guide him out of his personal impasse into to the "social and civil" order.

Farmer Turi immediately poses four questions that open overtly the issue of identity and reveal the criteria according to which identities were to be grounded: "Dove vai? Che fai qui?... Come ti chiami? Di chi sei figlio?" [Where are you going? What are you doing here? What is your name? Whose son are you?] (4). In other words, one's goals, function in a society, the possession of a name, and a lineage become the cardinal points that define the subject. In response, the nine-year old boy reveals that his mother abandoned the family during a famine, that his father died by falling out of an olive tree, and that he, a barefoot beggar, is doing nothing and going nowhere. He gives his name as "Mommo," a diminutive of Girolamo. The boy's inability to respond satisfactorily to the farmer's questions implies that he is ungrounded. The proper place names used to designate his location contrast with and thus highlight the improper and inappropriate responses offered by the boy. The encounter dramatizes that the boy at this point is very much a "subject in process," the double sense of being "on trial" and "in formation" is evidenced by the interrogation to which Farmer Turi subjects him and by the command to continue journeying ("vieni con me") rather than to remain at this ambiguous point.[61]

Farmer Turi takes pity on young Mommo, and brings him to his farm to tend the turkeys in exchange for room and board. In fact, while scholars describe *Scurpiddu* as an example of how Capuana deployed "verismo" in his children's literature, Andretta has noted that in southern Italy it was rather unusual for families (other than the aristocracy) to employ boys as servants living in their home.[62] Thus, it is not in service to his realist ideology of literature but rather as a didactic strategy, I would argue, that Capuaua depicts the young Scurpiddu's unusual adoption by the farmer and his wife. The boy's position in the new home appears specifically as a kind of consolation in the wake of the death of the farmer's son, who was carried off within the space of five days by a fever two years previous to Scurpiddu's arrival (5). Both the farmer and his wife are moved by the resemblance of the wandering boy to their "lost son" (17).[63] The invocation of the deceased boy at the beginning of the story casts a melancholic shadow over the narrative, underscored by the reference to the farmer's wounded heart (5). At the same time, the suggestion that Mommo can take the place of the other, unnamed boy implies a potential interchangeability of subjects. Indeed this same interchangeability allows the reader to take Scurpiddu's place. The assumption by the orphaned Scurpiddu of the dead boy's vacated position affirms that the family unit is the microcosmic matrix of subjectivity. The family will ultimately both cede to and naturalize the state's role in positioning him as a proper subject.

Soon after, the character "Soldato" (Soldier) re-christens him "Scurpiddu," a dialect name that references his slender build and that the protagonist initially resists but ultimately accepts (13). The opening four questions begin to receive more concrete answers: the change of name coincides with the change of father figure and with Scurpiddu's trajectory from ungrounded wanderer to functioning member of a society. As he accepts the name bestowed on him by another, he in turn assumes the right to name the turkeys over whom he functions as little patriarch. Initially, Scurpiddu chooses names of people he knows on the farm: the turkeys are named after the boy's local community members (10). As he grows and is given books of Italian history to read, he chooses names in homage to "Garibaldi" and "Victor Emanuel" (85).[64] The transition here signals a growing consciousness that moves from local to national, and the names that point to historical father figures help solder the connection between the personal and the national.

Facilitating the widening scope of the protagonist's (and readers') awareness, Soldato takes his turn as the boy's surrogate father figure. Having returned from his military duty and thus having seen many of Italy's great cities [Milan, Bologna, Turin (28)], Soldato personifies Italy's post-unification conscription law, and the use of "Soldato" as his name signals that this role is indeed his very identity. He acts as a lens for Scurpiddu to the world outside the rural farm. It is Soldato who helps Scurpiddu learn to read (21) and who takes him on a trip to the city Catania (74–75). Spinazzola has argued that, in the novel, Catania functions not merely as a city but as "The City," the urban universe as opposed to country life (151). In The City, then, Scurpiddu reacts with uncritical marvel at the progressive innovations—the railroad, telegraph, and seismograph—that are modernizing Italy. In the same way, he eagerly embraces the opportunity to learn to read: "Voglio comprarmi un sillabario, un bel libro per imparare a leggere" [I want to buy a spelling book, a nice one to learn to read] (76). Introduced through the same character (Soldato) and embraced with the same sense of marvel, reading and modernization are thus linked.

Through the process of learning to read under Soldato's tutelage, Scurpiddu transforms from bestial child to functioning citizen.[65] As a boy, he was particularly adept at imitating animal sounds and would often amuse his farm companions by mimicking dogs, cats, and cows (19) and is referred to lovingly as an "ape" (17).[66] While tending the turkeys, he plays the reed pipe and keeps constant company with a jackdaw bird he named Paola, who remains with him day and night. Over time, as Scurpiddu begins to acquire literacy, he learns in particular, for example, that "tacchino vuol dire nuzzu"—that *tacchino* (standard Italian for turkey) means *nuzzu* (dialect word for turkey) (79). In other words, he leaves behind simultaneously his animal mimicry and his local dialect, thus the text implies an analogy between the two. As he comes to master and be mastered by the standard written Italian, he begins to abandon his childish playfulness and to plot seriously the course of his future. His affinity with nature and the animal world gives way to his desire to experience the city and its marvels, and this transition is equated with growing up and taking on mature adult responsibilities. In other words, these trajectories are "mapped" simultaneously, and thus each of the various attachments that must be abandoned becomes a metaphor for the others.

Don Pietro, the local priest, seems poised to embody the role of another surrogate father. However, when the priest tricks the boy into handing over some coins, Scurpiddu discovers and exposes the deception, pointing out the hypocrisy of one who preaches against the sin of theft. Don Pietro's authority—and that of the church he represents—deteriorates further when he is unable to maintain logical continuity in an argument with Soldato. Don Pietro insists on the evils of military life but cannot defend his pacifist argument when reminded that until quite recently the Pope himself was a "king" who commanded armies (81–82). Scurpiddu's rejection of Don Pietro mirrors the contemporary secularism and anticlericalism of the Italian state. The Coppino Law of 1877, for example, required that communes offer religious instruction but gave students the right to opt out if they so chose. Later, a regulation of 1908 made it obligatory for communes to provide this education only if families requested it (Stewart-Steinberg 313).[67]

In addition to the Church, another path offered to and rejected by Scurpiddu is that of banditry. Two thieves arrive on the farm demanding food from Farmer Turi. Scurpiddu traffics with them at first, accepting their money in return for his silence, on Farmer Turi's advice (30–31), but later he foils their midnight attempt to steal one of the farmer's mares by screaming to alert the whole community and courageously rescuing the horse (44–45). The scene offers clear echoes of Collodi's Pinocchio who, while forced to act as a as the guard dog for a farmer, refuses to be bought off by the thieving polecats. Rather than colluding with them, Pinocchio barks loudly to alert the farmer as they attempt to steal his chickens (Chapter 21). Putting Scurpiddu in the role of the famous puppet—indeed Scurpiddu pretends to bark like a guard dog just prior to the thieves' arrival (42)—underscores that the young Sicilian, too, is on the path to becoming a proper boy and that the values he embraces on this path accord with those promoted by the Tuscan model. The thieves represent life outside the law and outside the confines of regulated, hierarchal structures like those Soldato explicitly praises: namely, the farm and the barracks. Each of these regulated communities, Soldato explains, functions properly and maintains the well-being of all the members. The transgressive, ungrounded, mobile life of the bandit is offered to but rejected by Scurpiddu in favor of the models endorsed by Soldato.

Both of these tested but rejected paths—the Church and "criminality"—were identified in this period specifically as characteristic elements of *southern* culture. We can recall, for example, that Lombroso founded his discipline of criminal anthropology by examining an anomaly in the skull of a Calabrian brigand, and his publications continued to lend support to the stereotype of southerners as more inherently criminal. The continued influence of the Church in the South, even after the unification, can be seen as operating within the school system. The statistics of teachers in public and private schools who were clergy indicates a percentage significantly higher in the South in post-unification years than in the North. In 1862–1863, more than half of the public school teachers in each of Abruzzi, Sicily, Calabria, and Basilicata were members of religious orders, while the national average was only 35.5% (Mencarani 115–17). While that figure certainly indexes the enduring power of the church in public life, it is the negative interpretation of that power that *Scurpiddu* dramatizes. The wild, untamed violence of *brigandaggio* and the stultifying effects of a superstitious and still medieval attachment to Catholicism were two of the dominant images of the South circulating in the period. Thus, the rejection of Don Pietro and of the bandits signifies not only the move into a regulated and legitimate subjectivity for the boy, but also the renunciation of the most "backward" and dangerous aspects associated with the "Mezzogiorno."

The course of Scurpiddu's path forward, then, includes taking on certain father figures (Turi, Soldato) and rejecting others (Don Pietro, the thieves). Simultaneously, he sustains and masters a series of losses of female figures, most notably that of his mother. His mother had

abandoned the family before Scurpiddu was nine, as we recall from his
first responses to Farmer Turi. Later, she reappears on the Turi farm
(26), only to die from tuberculosis shortly after her return. Scurpiddu
learns of her death by accidently witnessing her funeral (58), and he
seems to manage this second loss by trying to stay in the present: his
memories of her are "[v]isioni d'un istante, che gli facevano battere
rapidamente le palpebre e tremare un po' il cuore. Poi il presente lo
riafferrava, lo distraeva" [momentary visions that would make his eye-
lids flutter rapidly and his heart tremble a bit. Then, the present would
grab him again, would distract him] (80). The traumatic loss of the
mother is replayed in yet other losses. The text associates through con-
tiguity and parallelism the loss of the mother with the loss of Paola,
his beloved pet bird. When his companion leaves him to fly away with
a flock of jackdaws, he responds to her "abandonment" by calling her
an "ingrata" and "infamaccia" [ingrate, horrible villain] (84–85), renouncing her vehemently rather than keeping her in his memory. The
flight of Paola symbolizes the surmounting of his childhood association
with nature in order to become civilized; a repression of the feminine
on his trajectory toward manhood and another repetition of the loss
of the mother, all of which become necessary to his inauguration into
melancholy maturity.[68]

The rejection of the feminine, furthermore, is dramatized in the
hair cutting that functions as a kind of secular baptism for Scurpiddu
(11–12). Soon after his arrival, Farmer Turi calls to him, "Vieni qua,
tu che sembri un gufo con quei capellacci!" [Come over her, you who
look like an owl with that crazy hair] (11). Turi then takes the boy on
his knee ["Se lo mise tra le ginocchia" (11)], puts on an apron, and goes
at that crazy hair with his scissors. Described as both an "owl" and a
"sheep" (12) during the process, Scurpiddu comes out of the shaving
"un'altro" [a new man] (12). Long, disheveled hair in this period con-
noted both femininity and unruliness. Contemporary book illustrations
of boys tend to show them with shorter hair. We can think, too, specifically of Gertrude's lock of hair jutting out from her habit as a sign of
her defiance in Manzoni's classic *I promessi sposi* [*The Betrothed*] and
of Yambo's eponymous Ciuffettino whose rascally lock of hair becomes
the marker of his impish identity ("ciuffettino," the protagonist's nick-
name, means little tuft of hair). Indeed, Cesare Lombroso suggested
the link between abundant hair and femininity and its role as signaling
atavistic degeneracy. The esteemed criminologist cites "l'abbondanza
enorme e la nerezza dei cappelli" [extremely abundant black hair] as an
attribute of "il tipo criminale" [the criminal type] in a prostitute and
murderess that he examines (*Donna* 342). In Capuana's novel, then,
the haircutting ritual marks simultaneously Scurpiddu's integration
into to the farmer's family and his abjection of the feminine. A memory
described later in the novel reveals that Scurpiddu associated his hair

specifically with his mother, who used to comb it for him putting his head on her knee (22).[69] The echoed language indicates that Turi has literally taken the place of the mother.[70] Thus, the boy's mother in essence functions for Scurpiddu much as Giuseppe Acqua did for Giorgio: the "regression" of those figures indexes and enables the progression of the protagonists.

Ultimately, the state takes on the role of final father surrogate, as Scurpiddu leaves the farm and Turi assumes a new name—the "correct" form of Mommo—and a clear rank and role as bersagliere: the last sentence labels with precision and confidence who the protagonist has become: "Scurpiddu diventava Scaglio Girolamo nel 3° reggimento bersaglieri, 1ᵃ compagnia" [Scurpiddu became Private Girolamo in the third bersagliere regiment, first company] (95). But Scurpiddu's itinerary does not map a seamless assimilation into the patriarchal symbolic order—here specifically the anticlerical monarchy, which imposed conscription and promoted literacy in the standard idiom. Scurpiddu's final name also honors another character, Girolamo the cattle herder who was said to be able to communicate with witches and predict the future. Up until the very end, Scurpiddu believes in this power and consults Girolamo for advice, thus he does not renounce the ancient spirituality of his local culture, even as he enters the service of the modernizing state. While the subject Scurpiddu eagerly imports the standard language, the novel *Scurpiddu*, with its dialect title and explanations of local customs, sent Sicilian culture into Italian homes. In the book, readers learn, for example, that Catania's piazza contains a statue of an elephant that symbolizes the city and that those born on June 29, the feast of St. Paul, are believed to be immune to snake venom. While Scurpiddu learns that *tacchino* means *nuzzu*, Florentine children reading Capuana learn that *nuzzu* means *tacchino*. The protagonist's itinerary from lost child to identifiable adult coincides with trajectories from local to national, from antiquity to modernity, from rural to urban, and from pastoral—as Battistelli associates *Scurpiddu* with the "poesia di Teocrito non spenta ancora nelle campagne siciliane" [the poetry of Theocritus which is not yet extinguished in the Sicilian countryside] (93)—to novel.[71] While the latter terms in this series dominate as the outlines of subjectivity and the coordinates of desire, the former terms are incorporated and disseminated nostalgically by the text.[72]

In her 1923 account of children's literature, Battistelli gives Capuana's novel high praise. She enunciates clearly its chronotopic and nostalgic effects, which invite readers to conflate childhood and the premodern with rural and southern spaces:

> episodi di vita rustica, ingénue, ma forte e buona, che ci fanno sorridere di compiacenza, di simpatia verso il *nuzzaru* e i suoi amici e ci fanno rivivere la meraviglia e la gioia della nostra vita più

semplice, più lontana. È un libro che diverte, interessa i bambini e ringiovanisce i grandi, un libro di cui non è permessa l'ignoranza nè a piccini nè a grandi. (94; italics in orig. signifying the "foreign" Sicilian word)

[scenes of rustic life, naive, but strong and good, that make us smile with satisfaction, with sympathy toward the *turkey herder* and his friends. The scenes let us relive the wonder and joy of our lives when life was simpler, far-away. It is a book that entertains and interests children and rejuvenates adults, a book that niether kids nor grown-ups should be allowed to skip.]

Thus, Capuana's novel is extremely useful for all of "us"—we who perhaps have never even experienced a similar rural environment but now can appropriate it as a source of rejuvenation as we smile at the southern boy and his friends. The novel becomes a medium through which both childhood and the rural South may be nostalgically and safely accessed while simultaneously enabling the very renunciation of those "places." As Scurpiddu could take the place of the dead son of Farmer Turi, so now we as readers stand in his place, for "a bit," as he looks back on the past/South with a deep and melancholic sadness: "Scurpiddu non si era mai immaginato che quel verde, quel silenzio e quei campacci potessero dare tanta tristezza" [Scupiddu had never imagined that that green, that silence, and those old fields could make him so sad] (94).[73] It is this ability to look back on the abandoned time of childhood troped as a left-behind place that generates the particular pleasure of reading children's literature, according to Nodelman ("Pleasure and Genre"). This effect of melancholia becomes, I suggest, the way in which Capuana navigates the conflict between the cultural homogenizing of post-unification Italy and the protection of unique local identities.

As does Freud in his analysis of melancholia, Capuana uses the metaphor of ingestion: the peasants and the other classes of Sicily who "sono già entrate, lievito di attività, nell'organismo della nazione" [have already entered the national organism like an activating yeast (i.e., a catalyst)] will maintain "quest'elemento primitivo" [this primitive element], whose "tenacity" and "persistence" will not be fully "absorbed" or "transformed" (*Gli 'ismi'* 180–81).[74] Rather than the successful de-cathexis carried out by the work of mourning, the always incomplete mechanism of melancholia as experienced by Scurpiddu and as enacted by *Scurpiddu* was deployed to allow the individual child and the "national organism" to mature. In short, the novel enacts the structure of melancholia by its incorporation of lost objects, while it simultaneously reinforces the recapitulation paradigm by mapping this melancholic maturation process on fused personal and national trajectories.

Inverting the Map: Garibaldi Returned

The children's novel *La storia di Pipino nato vecchio e morto bambino* [*The Story of Pipino, who was Born Old and Died Young*] by the Crepuscular poet Giulio Gianelli (1879–1914) exemplifies the process of mapping.[75] Because its ideological agenda is to resist rather than promote modernization, it renders this mapping process particularly legible.[76] Gianelli's protagonist first appears as a dwarf-like clay statue, magically infused with life from the loving heat of a nearby pipe. "Pipino" is thus miraculously born at age 65 and becomes younger each day until he ultimately ascends into heaven as an infant, accompanied by his beloved and humanized Pipe-mother.[77] Living a reverse life, then, he begins in a state of melancholia, as he remarks "Mi prende la melanconia e non so perchè" [I am seized by melancholy, and I don't know why] (13). Born as an adult into a modern Italy—the first pages describe the middle-class trappings of the writer's studio and then narrate a labor strike being conducted by ants in the garden—Pipino's itinerary takes him down South and back into his youth in order to heal that melancholia by restoring a lost wholeness.

This children's story was first published in installments by the Turinese Catholic weekly *L'adolescenza* in 1910 and was issued as a volume the following year by the Società Editrice Internazionale, a Turinese Catholic press. *La storia di Pipino* deploys the same mechanisms of recapitulation and melancholia that we have seen operative in the secular books discussed so far, but in an effort to resist and critique Italy's modernization. Gianelli, through his protagonist's many adventures, dramatizes a nostalgic regression in order to counter the perceived threats of urbanization and secularism. The tale asserts that these forces were thrusting Italy and its children into a premature decadence, portrayed chronotopically by the dystopian "Paidopoli," the city of aged children, who drink and smoke until they are saved by Pipino. Gianelli maps Pipino's chronologically "backward" voyage from advanced age to childhood onto the Italian geography. The story culminates with Pipino's quest, as he leads a group of one thousand children from the North to the South in order to liberate the dying fairies of poetry. Gianelli's hero is allegorically both a new Christ and a reverse Garibaldi, seeking to redeem Italy by retrieving the primitive South and thus liberating the nation from modernity.

The imaginative narrative offers its readers many overt references to Roman Catholicism.[78] Specific Catholic prayers and the Creed are advocated openly as the best educational tools for children. Later in the tale, when the rescued fairies ask about the religion of the children who have saved them, they show particular preference for the Catholics of the group. Pipino's young followers, furthermore, are born out of a pomegranate. In Christian iconography, this fruit, "especially when cut open to show the seeds inside," becomes a symbol of new life and resurrection—precisely the hope embodied in the thousand young pomegranate-seed children (Murray and Murray 197).[79] Most broadly, Pipino's role as a Christ figure permeates the tale, from his prophesied and miraculous birth, to his preaching and his years as a shepherd, to his work of salvation, and finally his ascension into heaven.

The heavy-handed promotion of Catholicism may have been motivated in part by the publishing venues. As Catholic enterprises, the journal *L'adolescenza* and the press SEI, which had been founded by the Salesians in 1862 and which was consolidated the same year in which it published *Pipino*, were under the watchful eye of the Church.[80] Gianelli, furthermore, was writing on the heels of the 1907 papal encyclical *Pascendi*, in which Pius X detailed the "errors of the modernists" and called for renewed vigor in the routing out of antitraditional writings. Near the conclusion of the encyclical that vigorously defends the unquestionable authority of the Church, Pius writes, "[i]t is also the duty of the Bishops to prevent writings of Modernists, or whatever savors of Modernism or promotes it, from being read when they have been published, and to hinder their publication when they have not" (60). Gianelli may have included such specific moments that aggressively advocate orthodox Catholic practices—among the most infelicitous and artificial in the book—to conform to the expectations of the text's publishers, particularly in light of biographer Farinelli's discussion of Gianelli's own "modernist inclinations" (26) and his close affiliation with Father Giovanni Genocchi and other leading Catholic modernists (26). Farinelli also reports that Gianelli sought a different publisher for the book after it had been issued by SEI. However, even without the overt references to Catholicism, whatever Gianelli's motivations for including them, the overall structure and effect of the text bespeaks a deep and multifaceted nostalgia. Indeed, this strategy mirrors and inverts the secular discourses at work in other children's books that urge Italy's modernization during the same period.[81] Gianelli forges the very same set of analogies that we have seen in other children's books that deploy the recapitulation model but flips the value judgment attendant on the terms of the binary. Gianelli's *La storia di Pipino* laments the loss of supposedly primal, natural modes of being and dramatizes true patriotism as a return to a childlike faith. As Pipino's mother tells him, "la tua vita non è a rovescio, ma, come vuole la virtù, è più diritta che mai. Sono gli altri uomini che vivono a rovescio" [your life is not going backwards, but rather, as virtue would have it, is heading straight forward. It is other men who are going the wrong way] (11).

As noted in the Introduction, German zoologist Ernst Haeckel (1834–1919) provided a particularly forceful exposition of the recapitulation model in his 1874 *The Evolution of Man*. Italian translations of Haeckel's works on evolution were published in Turin in 1892, 1895, and 1908. In the *Evolution of Man*, he adamantly defends his notion of the

First Law of Biogeny, and, in particular, blasts the Catholic Church for what he considered its medieval resistance to it.[82] Furthermore, Haeckel notes that because ontogeny is the brief and compressed reproduction of phylogeny, the first becomes the visible text of the latter. He, in fact, uses the simile of the philologist, who must be able to separate the "original text from interpolations and corrupt readings" (11).[83] Haeckel, that is, argues that from the "available empiric material supplied by Ontogeny," the scientist can read "the long extinct historical processes of tribal evolution" (11). While, then, the Darwinian basis of recapitulationist thinking was perceived as antithetical to Catholicism to the point that the foremost disseminator of recapitulation looked upon the Church as the most formidable enemy of this enlightened thinking, Gianelli, in order to mount his defense of Catholicism, actually employs this very mode of thinking. Just as, for Haeckel, the smaller scale of ontogeny renders visible and legible the much broader and thus harder to discern processes of phylogeny, so too Pipino's individual life trajectory—from maturity to youth to infancy—becomes a textbook and a map to urge all Italy to reverse course socially and politically. Pipino, in other words, renders more visible, more legible, especially for a young audience, the broader, longer- term movements and shifts in late-nineteenth- and early-twentieth-century Italy. In conjunction with Pipino's individual, physical recuperation of youth, the text maps other, social trends that must be reversed.

In order to rescue the endangered fairies, Pipino, along with his mother and the group of children called *i mille* (the Thousand), under-take a southward march. Gianelli includes specific geographic markers to chart their progress (or better, "regress") as they make their way down the peninsula on their voyage of redemption. Beginning in north-ern Italy, the unlikely band follows the coastline of the Ligurian and the Tyrrhenian Sea. Moving southward along the peninsula's western coast, the protagonists discern a ship returning from across the ocean— "Un giorno in riva al mare egli [i.e. Lauretto, the tallest] scoprì una corazzata che tornava dall'America" [One day on the sea shore Lauretto spied a ship that was returning from America] (172–73)—and greet it with shouts of patriotic fervor. As the group continues, Gianelli provides more geographic coordinates: after a week, they reach the vicinity of Naples, traveling under its blue sky and by its even bluer sea (173–79). In this charting of the southward journey, the text rewrites not only the standard stereotypes of southern squalor, underscoring the beauty of land and sea, but also the painful contemporary history of these locales, as if in an attempt to reimagine and heal the wounds of recent real-ity. Just as the narrative reverses the humiliation of mass emigration to America through the enthusiastic waving of the tricolor flag to greet the returning (rather than departing) ship, so too does it reimagine the se-ries of natural disasters suffered in the South—particularly the Messina earthquake of December 28, 1908—as Vesuvius erupts before their eyes, not with lava but rather with flowers, so the children may bring bouquets to the fairies: "non più fumo, ma fiori, fiori scaturirono dalla bocca del Vesuvio" [no longer smoke, but flowers, flowers sprung from the mouth of Vesuvius] (179).[84] Turning inland, the "army" continues south and finally arrives at the "enchanting" coast town of Taranto, in the southern region of Apulia, from where they launch on eggshell boats into the Ionian Sea (184). The narrative, then, dramatically reverses Giuseppe Garibaldi's famous 1860 campaign with his Thousand (northward from Sicily with his Redshirts). At the same time, it reverses the trajectory of many children's books of the period, as I have been discussing in this chapter. Pipino, in other words, is not only going backwards through time, but also "backwards" through space as it has been imagined in Italy since the unification: delving on his voyage deeper and deeper into the most morally, politically, and industrially "backward" realms of the nation on his mission of salvation, seeking to undo the trajectory of history and rewriting its effects.

Like the feminized vision of the South enacted in *Scurpiddu* through the narrative association of rural Sicily with the mother, the female bird, and the boy's long hair (all to be abandoned), so here the South is feminized as the voyage downward, marked by flowers and "enchanting" landscapes, brings the group ever closer to the female fairies. These fragile feminine figures must be reclaimed and saved by the increasingly virile Pipino who sees his strength growing as he un-develops from old age to manhood, and by his two privileged boy companions, Mario and Ugo. The construction of the South as a feminized-infantilized space offering the restorative power of fairy tales can already be found in Capuana's work. In his preface to *La reginotta* [*The Princess*], Capuana recalls how, as a child, he was enchanted by the tales his Aunt Angela would weave, which captivated him and his siblings: "intanto la Zia Angiola, filando in piedi, raccontava, senza mai stancarsi, le sue storie meravigliose, stavamo, cheti come l'olio, a bocca aperta, incantati per ore e ore" [meanwhile Aunt Angiola, standing and spinning, would never tire of telling us her marvelous tales, and we would listen, quiet as oil, our mouths hanging open, enchanted for hours and hours] (*Tutte le fiabe* 1: 149). Overtly linking the weaving of tales with the weaving of textiles, Capuana here recalls the feminine sources of his Sicilian stories, tales that have the inexhaustible power to bewitch and to silence their listeners. Capuana, furthermore, also suggested the power of such tales to work, specifically, as a curative for the malaise that assails the modern, male adult. In the preface to *C'era una volta…fiabe* [*Once upon a Time…Fairy Tales*], he narrates how the composition of his tales became a cure for an ailment that he describes with all the hallmarks of melancholy: "In quel tempo ero triste ed anche un po' ammalato, con un'inerzia intellettuale che mi faceva rabbia" [At that time I was sad and also a bit sick, with an intellectual inertia that infuriated me] (*Tutte le fiabe* 1: 27). Sad, sick, inert, and self-reproaching, the male writer is rejuvenated through his excursion into fairy tale land.[85] The ambivalence codified by Capuana in the prefatory passages to his tales typifies the orientalizing of the South as both a desired, feminized space of plentitude and creativity and as a feared Medusa with the power to silence and petrify. This bifurcation, too, marks exactly the ambivalent attitude that, according to Freud, the melancholy subject holds toward the lost and incorporated object of cathexis. This image of the South disseminated by Capuana's popular texts becomes the ambivalent space-time Pipino and his Thousand enter and attempt to reclaim for the salvation of Italy. At this point, however, Gianelli imagines that the fairies no long dwell even in Italy's South, but beyond the southern borders of Italy, *through* the South and further still into "Asia Minor," implying that indeed all Italy has by now fallen into modernity.

Gianelli's tale was published just six years after Italy's Orlando Law (1904) had raised compulsory education to age 12, and shortly after the regulation that gave communes the choice to offer religious instruction, mandating this instruction only if requested by parents (Stewart-Steinberg 313). From beginning to end, Gianelli's text consistently and overtly rejects academic instruction while promoting a sort of spiritual rejuvenation. Pipino is born in the home of a man who, "avendo molto studiato, non sa più nulla" [having studied a lot, no longer knows anything] (8), as we learn from Mother Pipe. The prematurely aged children who have been freed from the dragon-guarded and dystopian city of Paidopoli promise Pipino: "Non studieremo troppo, sta sicuro, e saremo buoni" [Don't worry: we won't study too much and we'll be good] (112). Pipino is hailed as an ideal teacher, not in spite of his illiteracy but because of it, teaching instead with the alphabet of the soul (125). Finally, as the thousand children born out of the pomegranate travel together, their education is thus described, as I noted above: "I mille bambini si divertivano, imparavano, stringevano fra loro amicizie fratene. Quelli francesi si esercitavano nella nostra lingua, così pure quelli delle altre nazioni. Il 'Padre nostro,' 'l'Ave Maria' e il 'Credo' rappresentavano il libro di testo per i bambini di tutte le razze" [The Thousand children had fun, learned, and formed brotherly friendships. The French children practiced our language, as did the ones from other nations. The Our Father, the Hail Mary and the Creed were the text books for the children of all races] (171–72). The voyage south and the return to youth are thus linked to yet another kind of backward motion. Here, the text seeks in effect to counteract the various efforts of the Italian state to overcome its high rates of illiteracy in order to catch up with more advanced European neighbors. This is not, I would say, the kind of jocular antiacademic attitude that children's writers sometimes use in order to ingratiate their young readers. The tone throughout is far too earnest, melancholy, and totally devoid of that kind of authorial winking. Nor, I think, can we read this stance too literally, first of all, because Gianelli did, after all, write a book that in itself requires and works to promote literacy in the standard Italian, and because he contributed to the efforts in the Agro Romano to educate the children of the poor as a remedy against exploitation.[86] Rather, this overtly antiacademic stance seeks to recuperate a Romantic notion of the child and to posit that primal purity and wholeness as a resistance to the modernizing forces that were turning children into nothing but so many machines, as the fairies lament.

The condemnation of dehumanizing academic instruction is grounded in the idealization of supposedly primal forms of language. The fairies who are so threatened by modernity personify this idealized view. The various domains of the fairies include love, forgiveness, prayer, smiles, and sleep, as well as "the word." The fairy of the word is "quella che mette sulle labbra ancora poppante la sillaba *ma*, che poi si radoppia in mamma, e la sillaba *pa*, che poi si radoppia in papà" [the one who places on the lips of the still nursing children the syllable *ma*, which then doubles into mama, and the syllable *pa*, which then doubles into papa] (222). The description of this fairy recalls quite closely a passage from the essay *Il fanciullino* by symbolist poet Giovanni Pascoli. Addressing the "eternal child," who represents the spirit of poetry, Pascoli writes, "fai come tutti i bambini i quali ... quando sono ancora poppanti ... con misura e cadenza balbettano tra sè e sè le loro file di *pa pa* e *ma ma*" [you are like all children who, while still nurslings, rythmically babble to themselves their strings of *pa pa* and *ma ma*](36).[87] Following Pascoli, Gianelli evokes infantile language as a kind utopia of wholeness before specific languages inaugurate differences. Gianelli in fact goes even further. When rendering a child character's speech, Gianelli writes "l" instead of "r." He uses the same spelling technique to transcribe the speech of the flowers.[88] Making the voices of flowers and the voices of children phonetically and graphically echo each other in this way reaffirms the Romantic analogy of child-as-nature. The glorification of a primal form of language reaches a kind of climax near the end of the book, when Pipino has un-grown almost to infancy. At this point, he lives in the woods with his mother, who has transformed from a pipe to a woman (signaling the restoration of more a truly human world, as well as the feminizing effects of the southern voyage). The pair receives a letter from Ugo and Mariù, the most favored and beloved of the Thousand children. Because neither Pipino nor his blessed mother can read, a fairy helps them understand the note. Because they cannot write, they kiss the letter and send it back to the children, who understand its meaning. Responding to the kissed letter, Ugo and Mariù arrive in time to witness Pipino's ascension into heaven. In the image of the kiss that is fully legible, imprint replaces symbol. The imprint becomes for

Gianelli a semiotic form that promises immediacy, embodies presence, and conjures a reunion.

Similarly, the privileging of oral over written speech further promotes the idealized view of a natural, primal language. Pipino teaches the children by means of face-to-face storytelling, and the faires lament, "che sarà il mondo senza le belle fantasie ispirate da noi, raccontate dai nonni e ascoltate dai bambini?" [What will become of the world without the beautiful fantasies that we inspire, the stories that grandmothers tell and children listen to?] (44). Pino Boero, in his essay on Gianelli, argues that "scrivere costituisce per Gianelli un'appendice di raccontare" [writing for Gianelli is an appendix to narrating] (24), and speaks of the author's attraction to the "la concreta magia della voce" [concrete magic of the voice] (25). Indeed, whatever the real origins of the Pipino story, both Castellino and Farinelli, though differing in some details, claim that Gianelli first narrated this story orally to his adopted children Ugo and Mariù, to whom the written text is dedicated. In other words, both these critics find it important to assert the primacy of the oral, face-to-face origin of the story, perhaps in part because the story itself asserts that importance so vigorously.[89] The deep nostalgia for oral over written language, for imprint over symbol, for universal infantile babble over learned articulation in a specific tongue, all bespeak a desire for a natural language of wholeness and immediacy that would collapse distances and erase absences.

All these manifestations of spatial and temporal regression (lifespan, geography, education, language) coalesce to generate a deep nostalgia for presence. In this regard, not only the poet Pascoli but also evolutionary scientists such as Piero Giacosa inform Gianelli's thinking.[90] In the opening paragraph of his study of anaerobic respiration at the cellular level, entitled "Un postulato meno avvertito della dottrina dell'evoluzione" (1913) [A less-perceived hypothesis on the theory of evolution], Giacosa insists that the back bone of modern biology is the concept of a common descent for all living things: "Senza di questa scoperta [of the cell as fundamental morphological unit] mancherebbe la prima base alla dottrina della unità sostanziale delle forme viventi e delle loro derivazioni da un tipo comune primordiale, dottrina che … costituisce la spina dorsale di tutti i concetti moderni biologici" [without this discovery we would lack a basis for the tenet of the substantial unity of living forms and of their derivation from a common primordial type: the tenet that constitutes the very back bone of all modern concepts on biology] (385). Building on his work from 1909, he argues for the cell as the fundamental functional as well as structural unit. He goes on to assert that "per la dottrina dell'evoluzione è necessario che si mantenga la unità fondamentale strutturale e funzionale che è naturale in un ceppo unico di discendenza" [for the theory of evolution it is necessary to maintain the fundamental structural and functional unity that is natural in a single origin of descent] (390). In discussing the sometimes invisible commonality between higher- and lower-order life forms, he notes how in the process of evolution functional systems are "sviluppata e complicata e suddivisa" [developed, complicated, and subdivided] (391). For Gianelli, then, these principles of evolution speak on a social scale. The vision of a common, shared point of origin becomes a longed-for utopia. Over time, we have "developed and become complicated and subdivided," traveling ever farther away from that primal unity. Such subdivisions and differentiations obscure our fundamental oneness as we "progress" through history.

The total absence of Pipino's father in the story suggests that this yearning for presence emanates from a perceived paternal lack and, given the saturation of the text with Catholic imagery and messages, becomes a sign of the absence of *the* Father. The text marks the absence of the Creator-Father as a loss: early in the story, Pipino's mother teaches him: "Egli ha creato dal nulla tutte le cose, il sole, le stelle, le piante e i fiori, e poi ha dato agli uomini gli occhi per contemplarle. Per contemplare nelle creature il Creatore. Ma gli uomini non sanno più guardare" [He created from nothing everything that exists: the sun, the stars, the plants, and the flowers, and then he gave to men eyes with which to behold these things. To discern the Creator within his creation. But men no longer know how to see] (14). The modern world has made men forget how to read the book of nature. All the journeys backward become attempts to remember this forgotten language of presence and wholeness. In this light, the prayers used to instruct the children not only nod to the Catholicism of the publishing venues, but also seek to reconstitute the family: the Our Father, Hail Mary as mother and the child-self of the "I believe." The rescued fairy of the word echoes this utopia, as the first syllables on a child's lips announce and validate the nuclear family: papa and mama. Most overtly, the novel's ending stages an apotheosis of total reunification with mother and father. The story casts the presence of the patriarchal family as memory and as telos. The individual human family becomes the visible sign of the divine, and the loss of one implies the loss of the other.

Gianelli may well have been drawing from his own life experience, but his personal loss is in fact typical of the national demographic phenomenon alluded to in the image of the ship returning to Naples from America: the loss of so many fathers to emigration. Emigration to the Americas of men, including often young fathers, left these generations of children to associate "father" quite literally with "loss." In his *Pagine autobiograficahe* [*Autobiographical Pages*], Gianelli muses on the repurcussions of his father's 1881 emigration to Argentina to find work: "Quando mi ripenso bambino nella più remota infanzia se cerco di rivivere quella che era allora in me l'impressione circa la parola'babbo' non ricompongo che la più vaga idea. ...Ancora ricordo che alla parola 'padre' si univa la parola 'America'" [When I think back to when I was a boy in my earliest childhood, if I try to revive what was then my impression of the word 'daddy' I can only manage to recreate a very vague idea. I do still remember that the word 'father' was linked to the word 'America'] (qtd. in Farinelli 150). Gianelli was 2 years old at the time, and his father never returned.

The return to religion, to the South, to preliteracy, to nature, to childhood, to paternalistic political and social structures (Pipino puts down a strike by three thousand ants by convincing them of their ingratitude) becomes a remedy for the loss of pure presence. The recourse to recapitulation enables this kind of reading: the story of an individual (Pipino) serves as the visible text of an invisible narrative, namely, the story of Italy's fall from grace and the loss of its paternal core—the loss indeed of its very heart (as the tale is dedicated to Ugo and Mario, "two hearts in my heart"). This fairy tale then seeks to heal a foundational wound of modernity. This desperate, cosmic desire to turn back time is given its most daring narrative form in the image of the fairies who physically lift the children high into the air so that the earth may spin beneath their feet, bringing Italy back to them.

Peppered with patriotic exclamations and images of the tricolor flag, the text seeks to imagine an alternate vision of a possible "Italy." As a new Christ, Pipino redeems Italy by undoing the damage of modernization. Because all of Italy's ills are located in this primal loss, the hero must return all the way to the origin and reunite with mother and father in a prelapsarian utopia. All of the "progress" that Gianelli's tale resists—growing up, going North, scientific progress, secularizing—had become so tightly mapped together and so tightly associated with the project of "making Italians" that even in critiquing them by reversing the hierarchy of their values, Gianelli only reinforces and further naturalizes these isomorphic associations.

The tales I have examined here narrate the journeys of Adolfo, Carlino, Giannettino, Giorgio, Scurpiddu, Sussi and Biribissi, Pipino, Mario and Ugo, Pinocchio, and other boys as they progress into manhood and take Italy with them into (or out of) modernity. Noticeably absent here, clearly, are the journeys of girls. Even when the author of the book was a woman, as in the case of Baccini, her traveling protagonists were boys. Girls, I will argue in my next chapter, do not journey themselves. When they are present at all, rather, they facilitate, guide, enable, or encourage the journeys of their male counterparts. Pin's Maria, Falco's Topolina, Giorgio's Wataba, the Little Chick's Marietta, Pipino's mother all inspire journeys or become the reward for a successful journey. As I will argue in the following chapter, the girl does not need an itinerary because she is, paradoxically, always already an adult and permanently a child.

Notes

1 "The word 'Italy' is a geographical expression, a description which is useful shorthand, but has none of the political significance the efforts of the revolutionary ideologues try to put on it, and which is full of dangers for the very existence of the states which make up the peninsula." [In a letter to Austrian ambassador to France of April 1847]. See also "Klemens von Metternich"and Seward's chapter "The Storm," 228–47.

2 Dickie asserts that the "notion of Italy as a natural geographical entity, a distinct part of the Mediterranean, dates back some 22 or 23 centuries. For almost as long, much has been made of the boundaries provided for Italy by nature: to the North, the *chiostra alpina;* to the West the Mediterranean; to the East the Adriatic. However ... Italian geography is an unreliable criterion of historical analysis. ...Ultimately, we cannot write a history of Italy without taking into account the historical force of the various 'imaginary Italies'" (19).

3 Anderson is here quoting Thai historian Thongchai Winichakul's 1988 "Siam Mapped," a work that, according to Anderson, "traced the complex processes by which a bordered 'Siam' came into being between 1850 and 1910" (171). In his section on "The Map" in *Imagined Communities* (170–78), Anderson summarizes Thongchai's findings. Before 1851, only two kinds of maps were available in Siam, both handmade: a vertical cosmography for "mapping" salvation and a multi-perspectival military map, neither of which included borders. After mid-century, print-capitalism enabled reproducible maps displaying boundaries, which converged with a "new conception of spatial reality" (175). Doumanis explains that the first "fully detailed official map" of Italy was not completed until 1907. However, the *Istituto geografico militare italiano* produced less detailed maps for schools prior to this (94).

4 On Ferraguti, who illustrated both *Cuore* and Virginia Treves's *Piccoli eroi,* see Faeti, *Guardare* 110–18.

5 This will not be the last time that Garrone's individual experiences are mapped onto a national paradigm. Later in the school year (in April), this boy will endure the loss of his mother. The teacher consoles him by quoting the words of Giuseppe Mazzini. It is not surprising that Garrone, the student most frequently held up in the book as a role model for the other boys, would also be subjected to this particularly traumatic loss, and that his personal mourning would be mediated through the words of one of the heroes of Italian unification.

6 Pavlik draws on the work of Baudrillard, de Certeau, Lefebvre, and Deleuze and Guattari in his analysis of literary maps in children's books. Ultimately, Pavlik argues that through strategies like multiple perspectives, elimination of frames, and uneven fit between visual map and verbal text, these images encourage the active participation of readers in the construction of meaning and elicit the imaginative creation of multiple possible worlds. The mapping that goes on in the Italian books I analyze here works differently, as these works instead seek to inscribe the borders both of their reading subjects and the nation.

7 See Chapter 1 for a more detailed discussion of Nuccio's historical novel. Set in 1859/1860, the novel clearly seeks to make the argument for "irredentismo" as a continuation of the unification movement.

8 Paratextual maps have been mobilized in children's books to various effects. Ciara Ni Bhroin, in her study of the work of O.R. Melling, argues that the

"map of Ireland in the paratext" of a particular edition of *The Hunter's Moon* "serves as a metaphor for an ideal (unified) Ireland" (92).

9 Ubertis Gray writes, "La loro anima è ancora raccolta in sè stessa. … La vedranno a modo loro; intima, circoscritta, qualche cosa che sia un po' più della casa, una specie di cerchia. … Questa cerchia, di cui immaginano i confini, sarà materiale e morale … sarà fatta dalla vaga idea che c'è una linea di montagne, di fiumi, di mari, qualche cosa di sensibile, di visibile che li chiude in sè, li raccoglie, li numera, li protegge" [Their souls are still wrapped up in themselves. They will see it [i.e., the homeland] in their own way: intimate, contained, something just a bit bigger than their own house, a kind of circle. This circle, whose borders they imagine, will be material and spiritual. It will be created by the vague notion that there is a line of mountains, rivers, or seas—something tangible and visible, that surrounds them, gathers them in, counts them, and protects them] (8).

10 Patrizia Mencarani concludes her study of Italian children's books between 1860 and 1890 by citing this "mirror" scene from *Memorie di un pulcino*. She reads the scene as an illustration of the way in which Baccini and almost all other texts of the period favor an idealized and sentimental realism (figured as mirrors) over fantasy (figured as windows). Such books mirror to the child reader a domestic reality to be dutifully accepted rather than opening a window for the reader onto a realm of possibilities and desires (440–47).

11 The chick remarks, "Sicuro, la Marietta che leggeva tanti libri con le figure, avrebbe potuto spiegarmi un po' più chiaramente la cosa" [Certainly Marietta, who read so many illustrated books, could have explained all this to me more clearly] (40).

12 In his seminal structuralist analysis, Vladimir Propp asserted the crucial importance of the hero's departure from home as a function for the fairy tale: "The structure of the tale demands that the hero leave home at any cost" (37). Maria Nikolajeva, in her discussion of a semiotic approach to the history of children's literature, writes, "The basic pattern in children's literature is the circular journey, that is, the plot development home—departure from home—adventure—return home. This pattern, which has its origin in the European Romantic philosophy, can be traced in practically any children's text…The purpose of the journey is the maturation of the child (protagonist as well as the reader). But the return home is a matter of security" (46). Nikolajeva argues that the circular code has given way to a linear pattern (home—away), which is more open ended and more modern. Perry Nodelman has argued that the return home is not so much a matter of "security" as a strategy of colonization: "It's no accident that the vast majority of stories for children share the message that, despite one's dislike of the constraints one feels there, home is still the best, the safest place to be" ("The Other" 30).

13 To become a great nation, Italy must not repeat "la storia della famosa Torre" [the story of the famous Tower] (6); he later exclaims, "Che babilonia pel semplice dato e fatto d'una cattiva pronunzia!" [What a Babylon for the simple fact of poor pronunciation] (8).

14 Olindo Giacobbe, in his 1923 guide to children's literature, praises this early text, noting that "sotto forma di 34 conversazioni serali ai nipoti, illustra le bellezze e le ricchezze d'Italia, ha contribuito a formare quella coscienza della propria terra e delle proprie origini che sarà certamente di sicura guida nel cammino della vita ai giovani d'Italia" [in the form of 34 evening conversations with his nieces and nephews, he illustrates Italy's beauties and riches. It has contributed to forming that consciousness of one's own land and one's

own origins that will certainly be a trusted guide on the path of life for Italy's young people] (54). This endorsement mobilizes the trope of life as a journey and suggests that this journey requires the presence of a guide (both Stoppani's and Giacobbe's books) to prevent the potential deviations and wrong turns. Giacobbe, too, establishes a link between the child's life and his or her land. The repetition of the word "proprio" makes this land/ life link appear as an appropriate, proper relationship. Giacobbe suggests that the written word needs merely to "illustrate" the natural way in which the abundant land defines the life of its citizens. In 1923, then, Stoppani's text is made useful in urging this view of national identity, in which the con- structive quality of the text is denied as it is presented as a mere instrument revealing natural truths.

15 Given how pleased he was, young Adolfo most likely received from his un- cle Enrico Hillyer Giglioli's *Viaggio intorno al globo della r. pirocorvetta italiana "Magenta" negli anni 1865–1868 sotto il comando del capitano di fregata V.F. Arminjon* [*Voyage around the Globe of the Italian Royal Steamship "Magenta" in the Years 1865–1868 under the Command of the Navy Ship Captain V.F. Arminjon*], published in Milan in 1876, just a few years before Baccini's novel appeared. The text narrates the sea voyage of the author, who was an Italian zoologist and anthropologist. The *Magenta* was the first Italian military ship to circumnavigate the globe. Leaving Naples, it sailed east, with China on its itinerary, and returned to the port of origin three years later. The dense *Voyage* includes Giglioli's botanical, zoological, meteorological, and anthropological observations in the form of a ship diary (see Cappelletti). Paolo Mantegazza, a noted anthropologist of the period and supporter of Darwinian evolutionary theory, penned an "ethnological introduction" to the book, which sported a wealth of paratextual material, including, notably, folded maps. Giglioli's scientific tome clearly provided the blueprint for Baccini's fictional children's book. The ship *Magenta,* furthermore, takes its name from the Lombard city where a major battle of Italy's Second War of Independence was fought in 1859. Thus, Baccini's paradigm text celebrates Italian unification and Italian scientific progress.

16 Here, as in the many instances I explored in Chapter 1, the narrative de- scribes the birth of Italy as enabled by the death of a hero (in this case Alfredo Cappellini, 1828–1866). As the protagonists stand in front of the stone plaque, the acknowledgment of martial heroism is again portrayed as mourning rather than as celebration.

17 "dopo ventun giorni di navigazione, siam qui, proprio qui, a Bombay che come saprai, è un bel porto dell'Asia meridionale, appartinente agl'inglesi" [after twenty-one days of navigation, we are here, really here, in Bombay which, as you will know, is a lovely port in southern Asia, belonging to the English] (104).

18 Here again, as in other texts like *Un piccolo eroe*, maturity is synonymous with becoming a man and figured in part as the capacity to support women (in this case, Carlino's widowed mother): "ho una gran voglia di tirarmi avanti onestamente e di guadagnar tanto da mantener te, me, e magari qualche poverello se ci capiterà ...Che ne dici?" [I feel a strong desire to make my way forward honestly and to earn enough to support you, me, and any poor soul who might come to us for help ... what do you say?] (105). In the next chapter, I will revisit this novel in order to analyze more specifically the gendering at work in this "mapping of maturity."

19 Regarding Alì, we read: "Un'occhiata del padrone impose ad Alì di allon- tanarsi"[At a glance from his master, Alì left the scene] (47); "volle parlare,

scolparsi, ma non gli uscirono dalla gola che suoni inarticolati e rauchi che parevan singhiozzi" [he wanted to speak, to show he was innocent, but nothing came out of his throat but rough and inarticulate sounds that seemed like hiccups] (67); "balbettava fra i singhiozzi" [he stammered between sobs] (73); "elesse di soffrire e...tacque" [he chose to suffer and remained silent](75).

20 "il povero Dick ha cambiato la divisa della schiavitù con le bianche ali dell'angelo" [poor Dick changed his slave's uniform for the white wings of an angel] (50).

21 As the *Italo* goes through the Suez Canal, the narrator takes the occasion to talk a bit about "this blessed Africa" [quest'Affrica benedetta] where the sun "in pochi giorni far diventar neri come tanti spazzacamini" [in a few days can make you as black as so many chimneysweeps] (88).

22 We should note the very division of the text itself into three sections according to northern, central, and southern Italy reproduces and reinscribes the historical political division of the peninsula, and also the way in which the peninsula continued to be conceived by, for example, the politicians whose letters Moe has analyzed. The constant repetition of this north-central-south map makes it difficult to imagine Italy in other ways (East/West, coastal/mountain, etc.). Part Three of *Il viaggio* recounts Garibaldi's expedition with "The Thousand" as Giannettino travels to Palermo.

23 Mencarani argues that Collodi would go on to revolutionize Italian children's literature with *Pinocchio*, because here he replaces the idealized "literary child" protagonist typical of writers such as Ida Baccini with the "real child," including his faults and weaknesses. For a succinct account in English of Collodi's journalistic and literary production in its political context, see Boylan.

24 Boero and De Luca describe the *Giannettino* books as "il primo caso di scardinamento del sistema ideologico che sacrifica l'infanzia all'altare della morale borghese" (23) [the first case of a text that unhinges itself from the ideological system which sacrifices childhood on the altar of bourgeois morality]. In 1883, an education committee tasked with evaluating texts to be adopted by the schools advised against Collodi's *Giannettino* because it was too entertaining, and its "gay" and "sweet" character risked detracting from its otherwise admirable pedagogical mission (Boero and De Luca 22). We might perceive here the official preference for melancholic tones in children's literature.

25 There is no doubt a gender tension being played out here as well. The book unfolds in an exclusively masculine world, and Boccadoro's proverb seems a reiteration of the old Italian saying that "deeds are masculine and words are feminine." The hierarchy of deed over word established here, then, also works as a repression of the feminine.

26 The year 1890 saw the publication of *La laterna magica di Giannettino*, which I explored in Chapter 1 and will discuss again in the Conclusion. John Welle recently analyzed this text in light of its intermediality, i.e., "the participation of more than one medium of expression in the signification of a human artifact" (178, quoting Werner Wolf). Collodi's text puts illustration, narrative, and the magic lantern into play. Welle, who points out that the magic lantern had become a nearly ubiquitous instrument of education and entertainment by 1890, insightfully reveals how the novel's illustrations and verbal text misrepresent this technology. The book describes the lantern as if the images were in the lens rather than projected onto a screen. Collodi and Mazzanti (the illustrator) depict the children

looking into the crystal in order to see the images of Giotto, Garibaldi, and the other illustrious men of Italian history that Giannettino shows them (see Figure 1.1). Welle argues that the novel thus "re-mediates" the lantern, erasing its history and striving to create an effect of immediacy in order to focus attention on the objects of representation (i.e., the great men) (186). I would, in fact, argue just the opposite: by describing in words and showing in illustrations the children looking *at* the lantern (rather than their backs to it and observing a screen), the novel makes this modern technology itself one of the "objects of representation." Like the trains in *Il viaggio*, the lantern here is not only the medium but also the message. Indeed, when the children express their marvel and wonder upon seeing a slide image, they are not only in awe of the men represented, but they are also amazed by the "reality effect" of the technology.

27 "intreccia due percorsi, uno nozionistico ed enciclopedico, l'altro narrativo e 'morale'" [weaves together two itineraries, one factual and encyclopedic, the other narrative and 'moral'] (13).

28 Mencarani draws extensively on both *Giannetto* and *Giannettino* to illustrate the most common didactic themes and approaches of children's books from 1860 through 1890. Both books overtly discourage, for example, gluttony, laziness, and vanity and promote thrift, hard work, and obedience. Antonelli notes "[i]l successo di *Giannetto* viene fermato solo dalla concorrenza del *Giannettino* di Collodi" [*Giannetto*'s success was halted only by the competition from Collodi's *Giannettino*] (11).

29 See Giulia Donato and Mariella Colin. Donato reports that *Le tour de la France par deux enfants*, published in1877 by Belin in Paris, met with great success. Appearing not long after Prussia's annexation of Alsace and Lorraine, it was read as a patriotic gesture. G. Bruno was the penname of Mme Augustine Fouillè (18). Collodi was not unique in this regard. Colin asserts that "Italian children's literature was …indebted to French influence from its very origins" (83). She documents how publishers, beginning with Emilio Treves in Milan and with others following suit, sought translations of French texts which became extremely popular. The works of Jules Verne in particular found great success in Italy. Translations retained their appeal even as they were followed by imitations, such as Collodi's *Il viaggio* and Emilio Salgari's adventure novels that echoed the work of Verne (Colin 80–85). Lorenzini (Collodi Nipote) playfully thematizes the popularity of Verne in his 1902 *Sussi e Biribissi*, having his young protagonists attempt to undertake their own journey to the center of the earth through Florence's sewer system.

30 The destruction of boring scholastic books by comical animals anticipates the well-known scene in *Pinocchio* in which the fish gobble up the items thrown into the sea by the battling boys. But even the fish turn away from the tedious text books that land in the water, including Baccini's *Pulcino*, and—with typical irony—Collodi's own *Giannettino* and *Minuzzolo* (Chapter XXVII).

31 "Vedendolo così di prim'acchito, si poteva quasi scambiarlo per un ragazzino di otto o nove anni" [Seeing him that way at first glance, one could easily mistake him for a little boy of eight or nine years] (24); "Ma la più grande passione di Pipì volete sapere qual'era? Era quella di scimmiottare tutto quello che vedeva fare agli uomini" [But do you want to know what Beppe's greatest passion was? Aping everything he saw men doing] (24).

32 Collodi was a member of the commission that was created by Emilio Broglio, the Minster of Public Education, in order to address the "language question" in the new Italy. Headed by Alessandro Manzoni, the commission published

its report in 1868 and advocated the use of a cultured, spoken Tuscan as the national language to be taught to and by public school instructors (Boero and De Luca 19, 20; Richardson 64–70). A survey taken in 1910 showed that, even decades after Manzoni's report, teachers were still using dialect in the classroom (Richardson 69). The report elicited much debate on the most appropriate form for a national language to take and the most effective means by which to promulgate it. For an analysis of the developments and permutations of how language was perceived to relate to "national identity" from the Renaissance through the nineteenth century, see Gambarota.

33 John Welle has pointed out that Collodi wrote the *Giannettino* series and his translations of French fairy tales on the request of the Paggi Brothers, "who understood the profits to made in the emerging market of children's literature" (180). Welle argues that seriality (as in the Giannettino books) and the new relationship in the "cycle of production" in which the publisher interprets reader demands and solicits appropriate texts from authors (rather than the author creating a book and then finding a publisher to distribute it to readers) both mark a significant shift in the Italian culture industry. These shifts are indicative of children's literature as a product and disseminator of modernization.

34 The rail line had been completed in June 1848 under Grand Duke Leopold II, for whom the line was named. Lorenzini's novel became part of an emerging railroad genre, preceded by Carlo Chirici's *Guida del viaggiatore sulle strade ferrate da Firenze a Livorno e da Firenze a Prato* (Mergerione 16, 17). Elvio Guagnini notes that this "patchwork" text cannot be classified as a mere guidebook because of its sophisticated weaving of multiple genres, its use of parody, and particularly the way in which it takes some of the symptoms of modernity as targets of its ironic approach ("Introduzione"). Giovanni Verga's "Malaria" (1883), set in Sicily, offers a potent rendition of the train as symbol of modernity and a compelling account of those left behind in the "forward" march of modernization.

35 French children's books, too, were marketed at railway bookstores in the second half of the nineteenth century (Colin 82).

36 Doumanis discusses the connections between railroad construction and unification going back to the 1840s. He notes that "[s]upporters of unity, such as Cattaneo and ... Cavour,had foreshadowed that crucial role that railways could play in effecting an Italian confederation. Railway construction was a key subject at the Congress of Italian Scientists in Genoa in 1846 ... The railway question did, however, confirm the extent to which national unity was regarded more as a means to other ends, as most schemes did not include economically under-developed central or southern Italy" (62).

37 The effect is similar to that created by the photograph of Civenna and its accompanying geographical data at the beginning of Lino Ferriani's tale, as I will describe in note 52.

38 "sono ritornato a casa, se non già un uomo fatto (sarebbe troppo pretendere) ma per lo meno un omino avviato bene" [I have returned home, if not already a fully grown man (that would be too much to claim) at least a little man well on my way] (1931, 15).

39 Palumbo notes that "Fascist educators and officials, however, were instrumental in the move away from this literary cliché of a mysterious and dangerous Africa; they encouraged Italian writers and artists to represent Africa as a ploughed and cultivated land marked by the dignified white houses of the Italian colonists" (226).

40 See also Clark 99–101 and Saladino 44–51, 74–84.

41 In his analysis of *Pinocchio in Affrica*, Thomas Morrissey accurately describes
Cherubini's depiction of black Africans as "savages incapable of governing
themselves...brutish and gullible cannibals with the judgment of monkeys"
(Wunderlich and Morrissey 146–47). Cherubini would not be the last Italian
writer to send Pinocchio into Africa. Anna Franchi published a children's
novel in 1930 with Salani entitled *Pinocchio fra i selvaggi* [*Pinocchio among
the Savages*] in which Pinocchio, now a real boy, travels to Africa for adventure. In 1939, Marzocco issued an anonymously authored story called
Pinocchio istruttore del Negus [*Pinocchio, the Ethiopian King's Teacher*], set
in what was by then the fascist colony of Abyssinia. Caterina Sinibaldi has analyzed these texts through the lens of translation theory, showing how they, as
intralingual and intertemporal adaptations, "contributed to the fascist project
of remodeling and re-interpreting the past to attain national regeneration"
(351). Franchi, who was a leftist writer, adopted a paternalistic attitude in
her novel toward the Africans who are aligned, verbally and visually, with
animals. The Marzocco text, in which the protagonist is mistaken for an
Abyssinian because he is covered in chocolate, deploys a "hostile nationalistic
attitude" that mirrors and reinforces the newer racial theories which "placed
additional emphasis on the irreducible alterity of Africans" (348).

42 See John Welle's comments on Collodi's series, note 33. In regard to Salgari
specifically, see especially della Coletta on this point. As part of her analysis
of the discourse of world's fairs, she argues convincingly that Salgari's "pre-
fabricated" literature "reflected the exposition mentality" (126–27). These
issues come to fore in a particularly forceful and dramatic way in a study
by Paola I. Galli Mastrodonato. Her essay urges scholars to take Salgari
seriously and specifically advocates a historical approach to Salgari's texts.
She begins by summarizing the existing body of Salgarischolarship, underscoring how even critics who do study his work tend to reinscribe the mass
culture vs. high culture divide established by Eco. She then offers an analysis
of Salagri's representation of the Sepoy rebellion (The "Great Mutiny" of
1857) in his novel *Le due tigri* (1904). She contrasts Salgari's depiction of the
event with primary sources in Britain at the time of the mutiny, underscoring how Salgari, unlike the British, provides a more nuanced, accurate, and
far less demonizing representation of the Hindu and Muslim Indians. What
interests me here is how Galli Mastrodonato's discourse actually *reproduces*
that of Salgari, to whom she refers as "il nostro Maestro" ["our Master"].
She sets the stage for a battle between the elitist gatekeepers of high culture
(as she says, "l'establishment accademico-letterario" [the academic-literary
establishment]) in terms that liken them to the domineering and exploitative
British as depicted in Salgari's novels, while Salgari himself, like his own
Sandokan or Black Corsair, becomes the master of the underdogs and hero
the of the masses (here, the marginalized scholars of mass culture). Her essay
is replete with the rhetorical devices of adventure and melodrama: "Ahimè,"
she interjects at least twice; she asserts that "la rivolta contro l'opressione
è sempre sinonimo di coraggio e bellezza" [the revolt against oppression is
always synonymous with courage and beauty] with a perhaps unintentional
double reference to the British oppression of the Indians and the cultural
elite's oppression of Salgari and his followers. She issues a challenge as if de-
fying readers to a duel: "Sfido chiunque a trovare un qualche passo..." [I dare
anyone to find a single passage...], and the essay concludes with an ecstatic
vision of the master's spirit smiling over Italy, now bustling with turbaned immigrants. The essay, I submit, testifies to the power of Salgari's discourse to
map its readers onto the power dynamics of self and other that it constructs.

43 This adventure novel is not part of the Sandokan series but is typical of the adventure genre. Illustrated by the popular Giuseppe Garibaldi Bruno, who would also illustrate Cherubini's *pinocchiata*, the novel uses the slave trade as a thematic springboard for a tale of conversion, betrayal, and revenge. This cited scene describes the passage of the slave-trader ship's lookout boat from the west coast's Bay of Lopez into the interior. There the sailors will exchange casks of alcohol for 500 slaves from the local King Banga, described as an "ubbriacone" [big drunk] (10).

44 "previously undifferentiated," of course, for those now doing the mapping.

45 Such as Swedish surgeon Mungo Park who was hired by the British to map the Niger River and who published an account of his explorations in 1797 as *Travels in the Interior Districts of Africa*. As Cristina della Coletta insightfully argues in her analysis of Salgari's "toponymic precision" in the context of exposition narratives, "[h]aving reached the fixity of the map and the atlas, Salgari's exotic emporia reproduces the totalizing and all-encompassing logic of the mind, and the unchanging closure of the text" (129, 132). She establishes how Salgari's "evaluative inventories" arrange humanity hierarchically (131).

46 Uses of the word "glance" include: "mastro Hurtado ...gettò...un acuto sguardo" [master Hurtardo cast a sharp glance] (7); "I marinai gettarono un lungo sguardo sul versante opposto" [the sailors cast a long glance on the opposite side](7); "Il maestro, dopo aver lanciato uno sguardo sospettoso sull'orizzonte occidentale" [The boss, after having cast a suspicious glance toward the western horizon](8); "Mastro Hurtado, con un acuto e rapido sguardo percorse la costa" [Master Hurtardo, swept the coast with a sharp and rapid glance](8); and "il maestro, che gettava degli sguardi inquieti verso l'ovest" [the boss, who was casting some troubled glances toward the west](9).

47 See Chapter 1 for a discussion of melancholia in Salgari and his use of Garibaldi as model for Sandokan. Vittorio Sarti (1990) provides an excellent bibliography of Salgari's immense production and a succinct biography, noting in particular how the author did not benefit financially from his incredible popularity due to the exploitative "noose contracts" with his publishers (10). Salgari killed himself in Turin on April 25, 1911. Recent scholarship, making use of documents in the Giunti archive, has sought to establish that Salgari's contracts with Bemporad were in fact generous in comparison with others of the period (Cappelli and Zangheri 64, 65).

48 Palumbo notes that only a few of Salgari's many novels are set in Africa, and that "he made no reference to any of the Italian colonial campaigns undertaken during this period" (226). Palumbo and Lucas both explain how Salgari's novels were revived and re-packaged by the fascist regime for aggressively propagandistic purposes ("Salgari, the Atlas," 79; Palumbo, 226).

49 The beautiful 1992 edition by Viglongo reproduces the first edition of the novel (Rome: Voghera, 1896) with the illustrations by G.G. Bruno. *I drammi* was reprinted in 1897, 1923, and 1928 (see Sarti 1994, 48).The Viglongo edition also contains the illustrations that adorned subsequent printings of the novel and inserts additional visual material, including, notably, several maps. A nineteenth-century map of Africa appears as the frontispiece. Although these visual maps were not part of the original novel, the publisher's decision to add period maps, including one for the privileged position of the opening page, attests to the powerful "mapping" rhetoric of the verbal text.

50 *Al lago degli elefanti* was published by G.B. Paravia in Turin. See note 29 in Chapter 1 for a brief account of the author.

51 Specifically, 1893 saw the increasingly violent uprisings of the Sicilian Leagues (*Fasci siciliani*), which were eventually quashed by the state in 1894, a repression that triggered increased emigration to the Americas (see Clark 101–103 and Alcorn). Bencivenni summarizes that in the U.S. alone (i.e., not accounting for emigration to Argentina and Brazil), in 1880 the "census counted only 44, 230 foreign-born Italians, but in 1900 the number had increased to 800,000. By 1920 about four million Italian immigrants lived in the country" (14). Cesare Lombroso published the third edition of his *L'uomo delinquente* in 1884, in which he used the phrase "born criminal" for the first time, and with co-author Guglielmo Ferrero published *La donna delinquente, la prostituta, e la donna normale* in 1893. The battle of Adwa took place one year before Vecchi's novel's publication. Finally, 1898 saw the publication of Alfredo Niceforo's *L'Italia barbara contemporanea (studi e appunti)*. In his note "to the reader," dated 1897, which serves as a preface, Niceforo (1876–1960) remarks that Lombroso, Ferrero, and Scipio Sighele have signaled their approval of his "abbozzo di una fisiologia dell'Italia meridionale" [sketch of southern Italy's physiology] (5) and asserts bluntly "la Sardegna, la Sicilia e il Mezzogiorno rappresentano tre popoli ancor primitivi, non completamenti evoluti, meno civili e raffinati delle popolazioni del settentrione e del centro d'Italia" [Sardinia, Sicily, and the South represent three peoples that are still primitive, not completely evolved, less civilized and refined than the populations in central and northern Italy] (3), a fact that any dispassionate soul ("anima spassionata") would acknowledge as self-evident ("tanto obiettivo e tanto evidente di per se") (3).

52 This visual recourse to the land itself is at play also in Lino Ferriani's *Un piccolo eroe* (1905). Pin thinks back on his small hometown of Civenna on Lake Como, and describes the town in natural terms as "il caro nido" [the dear nest] (13). The image brings "un sorriso melanconico" [a melancholy smile] (13) to his face. The novel in fact opens with several photographic images of Civenna and of Lake Como and provides geographic details on the town, such as its height above sea level. Such gestures reassuringly ground the fictional *bildungsroman* in factual data and recognizable, measurable reality. The landscape images that adorn the opening pages of the book serve to generate a reality effect and thus naturalize the contours of the "melancholy heroism" that I analyzed in the previous chapter. Stephens analyzes a broad array of Australian picture books mostly from the 1980s and 1990s to show how, especially through repeated visual depictions of the nineteenth-century cottage, such texts often implicitly condition an attitude that embraces "human domination of nature" (110).

53 The pedagogical merits of the book found favor with Olindo Giacobbe in his critical survey of Italian children's literature (1923). Giacobbe writes approvingly of the text, explaining that "racconta le fortunose avventure di un italiano in Africa e tratta della flora e della fauna indigena, oltre che degli usi e degli varie costumanze degli abitanti" [narrates the adventures of an Italian in Africa and discusses the indigenous flora and fauna, as well as the traditions and various customs of the inhabitants] (75). The book saw several editions during the fascist period, including printings in 1922, 1939, and 1943.

54 More common Italian words would be *lì* (there); *con me* (with me); *bellezza* (beauty); *bisogno* (need); and *casa* (abode, dwelling).

55 Early in the novel, Giorgio writes home to his father: "Il capitano mi assicura che tutti i negri sono così; che le matematiche sono troppo ardue per il loro cervello. Egli sostiene che appartengono ad una razza inferiore. Che sia

vero?" [The captain assures me that all Negroes are that way, that math is too hard for their brains. He claims that they belong to an inferior race. Could that be true?] (24). We should recall that Pinocchio's inability to complete his 12 sums at the opening of Cherubini's novel indicated his immaturity. In both cases, the mastery of numbers marks a fully developed, rational adult, an ability lacking in children and Africans, according to these texts.

56 In this way *Al lago degli elefanti* follows the pattern analyzed by Tribunella in many American children's and YA novels. In widely read works such as *A Separate Peace* and *The Outsiders*, the male protagonist must lose his attachment to a male friend and then introject, often ambivalently, the qualities of that lost friend, in order to attain melancholic maturity. Giorgio clearly must incorporate some of Acqua's martial fierceness but deny his "primitive" qualities. In discussing the construction of maturity in S.E. Hinton's two novels, Tribunella writes "[t]hese adolescents manage to achieve this state [i.e., of knowing adulthood] by being disciplined through the loss of their friends" (*Melancholia* 51). Given Acqua's particularly childish qualities, his loss not only signifies the rejection of primitive Africa, but also, as Tribunella argues, since it is "the child...who operates as the lost object for the reader," Giorgio's rejection of Acqua also implies that "ultimately it is childhood itself that must be lost" (125).

57 Capuana produced a significant body of work for children. The 73 original fairy tales he penned with inspiration from the oral traditions of Sicily were published in *C'era una volta...fiabe* [*Once Upon a Time...Fairy Tales*] (1882);*Il regno delle fate* [*The Kingdom of Fairies*] (1883); *La reginotta* [*The Princess*] (1883); *Il Raccontafiabe* [*The Fairy Tale-Teller*] (1893), *Schiaccianoci* [*The Nutcrackers*] (1897); *Chi vuole fiabe, chi vuole?* [*Who wants Fairy Tales, Who Wants Them?*] (1908); and *Le ultime fiabe* [*The Last Fairy Tales*] (1919). His prose narrative for children includes *Scurpiddu* (1898); *Cardello* (1907) and *Gli "Americani" di Ràbbato* (1912). See Boero and De Luca 107, 362; Miele 302–303; and Canepa, "Capuana" 160.

58 The edition that appears in the 1972 collection, edited by Inturrisi, reproduces the 1898 text, but parts of the novel are abbreviated. Page number citations throughout refer to the 2014 printing noted in the Bibliography.

59 Pavlik here is using the concept of "tracing" as described by Deleuze and Guattari in contrast with the "mapping" of the rhizome.

60 In fact, as the Inturrisi edition explains in a note (p. 13), the very first word of the novel, "Massaio," is a specifically southern term for "farmer."

61 In her essay on the adolescent novel, Kristeva clarifies that "[w]hen I say 'adolescent,' I mean less a developmental stage than an open psychic structure. Just as biologists speak of the 'open structure' of living organisms that renew their identity by interacting with another identity, it could be said that the adolescent structure opens itself to that which has been repressed" (*New Maladies* 136). If Scurpiddu begins with the openness of adolescence, it is the project of the narrative to turn that permeable structure into a developmental stage and bring its openness to a close. By the end of this *bildungsroman*, the process, described very clearly as progress, is fulfilled when the protagonist has forged an appropriate and legible identity.

62 On *versimo* and Capuana's children's literature, see Giacobbe, *Note di letteratura infantile* 61–64; Boero and De Luca 362; and especially Muñiz Muñiz. Andretta writes "Pochi erano i maschi servitori che mangiavano e dormivano nella casa del padrone" [very few male servants would eat and sleep in the master's house] (53). It was common for girls to be employed as domestics in this way. Male farmhands were typically paid and lived in their

own homes. Capuana's use of verist techniques like authorial impersonality contributes to the illusion of the novel's status as a truthful documentary rather than a pedagogic fiction.

63   "In quella commozione entrava un po' il ricordo di un figliolo perduto due anni addietro, a nove anni, bruno e magro come quel ragazzo. Una febbre maligna gliel'aveva portato via in cinque giorni, e gli aveva lasciato una gran piaga nel cuore" [Into that poignant emotion entered a bit the memory of a dear son lost two years previously. He was nine, dark and slender like that boy. A terrible fever had carried him off in five days, and he had left a deep wound in the farmer's heart] (5). "Più di tutti gli voleva bene la massaia, un po' perchè le rammentava il figlio perduto" [More than anyone, the farmer's wife loved him, in part because he reminded her of her lost son] (17). The use of the phrase "un po'" ["a bit" or "in part"] in both these descriptions seems to soften or mitigate the association of Scurpiddu with the dead boy, as if the narrator wanted to deny that the farmer and his wife would or could entirely replace their son. However, the namelessness of the dead boy in the narrative makes that empty space available to be filled in by the boy who takes on a series of new names.

64   Muñiz Muñiz perceptively notes the way in which the various name changes function as an index to the educational parabola of the text. She argues that the "completa integrazione del fanciullo nella vita civile del paese...è l'unico modo che un ragazzo senza nome...possa avere per meritarne uno" [the complete integration of the child into the civic life of the country is the only way a boy without a name could manage to earn one] (290).

65   Muñiz Muñiz very persuasively contrasts Capuana's Scurpiddu with Verga's young Jeli, specifically on the issue of their relationships with scholastic instruction. Jeli dismisses literacy while Scurpiddu eagerly acquires it. The differing attitudes toward reading and writing held by these two otherwise similar protagonists become a lens onto the fundamentally different ideologies of Capuana and Verga, the latter convinced that "true communication" between the natural world of the peasant and the artificial world of the "signori" is never possible (290–91).

66   "instancabile e allegro buffone come uno scimmiotto" [a tireless and happy clown like an ape] (17).

67   See Clark 105–109 for a discussion of the ways in which the mutual hostilities between "liberal Italy" and the Church were manifested, such as the 1889 erection of a statue in Rome in honor of Giordano Bruno (1548–1600, whom the church had executed as a heretic) and the reorganization of charities under Crispi.

68   Muñiz Muñiz notes that the progression of Scurpiddu can be charted against the regression of the memories of his mother and the world she represents (291–92). Although Muñiz Muñiz does not draw on psychoanalytic theory, she uses the image of the "umbilical cord" to describe the protagonist's links to his mother and the "old world" and thus effectively illustrates the way in which the text ties together maternal associations with a host of personal and cultural cathexes to be severed in order for the subject to enter, melancholically, into modernity and maturation. Spinazzola perceptively points out that Paola does not die but willingly abandons her companion. Her flight away from the boy and into the open sky also becomes, then, a model for Scurpiddu to break from "ogni vincolo protettivo" [all protective ties] and enter a "mondo più vasto" [larger world] (149).

69   In his analysis of *The Outsiders*, Tribunella places some interpretive weight on the cutting of hair as well, pointing to that ritual-like act as a marker

of imposed identity: "by choosing to cut their own hair first, the boys are refusing to allow anyone else to do it" (*Melancholia* 59–60).

70 "Si rammentava con dolcezza dei giorni in cui ella lo pettinava al sole su lo scalino della porta di casa, tenendogli la testa fra le ginocchia" [he would recall with sweetness the days when she would comb his hair in the sunlight on the little step outside the door to the house, holding his head on her knee] (22).

71 Capuana himself in his dedication to Michele La Spina speaks of his desire that Scurpiddu should embody the Pan-like spirit of ancient Sicilian shepherds with their pipes (3).

72 In this way, the "realist" *Scurpiddu* functions similarly to Capuana's contemporary fairy tale production. Inspired and informed by the local oral traditions that folklorist Giuseppe Pitrè was philologically documenting in those years, Capuana's linguistically Tuscanized tales marketed for children rather than scholars disseminated those traditions northward. *Scurpiddu*, a kind of modernized fairy tale charting a boy's initiation into manhood, performs a similar cultural function.

73 See Tribunella on the dynamic of characters and readers as a mechanism of melancholia in his analysis of *Number the Stars* (*Melancholia* 118–120).

74 Postulating that in melancholia (unlike in mourning) the ego identifies with the abandoned object, Freud writes that the process represents "a regression from one type of object-choice to original narcissism. ... the ego wants to incorporate this object into itself, and, in accordance with the oral or cannibalistic phase of libidinal development in which it is, it wants to do so by devouring it" (249–250).

75 The "crepuscolari" or twilight poets, writing in the early twentieth century, were influenced by D'Annunzio and Pascoli and noted for their mixture of melancholy and irony.

76 In 1910, *L'adolescenza* published the tale in installments and with illustrations by "Golia," pseudonym of artist Eugenio Colmo (1885–1967), who also illustrated Gozzano's work (Farinelli 176; on Golia see Zipes, *Oxford Companion* 255 and especially Faeti, *Guardare* 2011, 202–210). SEI published the volume in 1911 with its dedication to "Ughetto e Mariù," and the book was a "success" (Farinelli 178). Later editions of the text were illustrated by Massimo Quaglino. Olindo Giacobbe lauds this book in the 1937edition of *La letteratura infantile*, including it in his recommended reading list for the fifth grade. Giacobbe underscores Gianelli's unhappy biography—orphaned young, he battled illness through his life—and notes that the book's many good moral lessons and sense of love for the "Patria" make it "among our best and most felicitous books for children" (144). In 1935 Onorato Castellino contributed a "presentation" of the text, included in the 1942 edition (the edition from which I quote). Castellino praises Gianelli's work in 1908 with Giovanni Cena and Sibilla Aleramo educating the destitute inhabitants of the Agro Romano, one of the "luoghi tristi che oggi il Governo fascista ... ha redento totalmente" [sad places that today the Fascist Government has completely redeemed] (x). Castellino anachronistically appropriates Gianelli and his novel for Fascism, seeing a kind of pre-fascism in the text's critique of Liberal Italy.

77 In Umberto Eco's *The Mysterious Flame of Queen Loana*, the protagonist Yambo (named for the children's writer Enrico Novelli who used the pen name Yambo) suffers from amnesia. At one point, he begins to recall the plot of *La storia di Pipino*, since his condition allows him to recall what he has read but not what he has actually experienced. Pipino's backward voyage becomes an analog to Yambo's re-tracing of his own life in an attempt

to restore his memories (98–99). He mis-remembers Pipino as having been born in a cabbage.

78 In her insightful reading of *Pipino*, Myers classifies this novel as a "microcosmic fantasy"—one of several texts written between 1908 and 1915 that played with scale as a strategy to critique contemporary society. Likely inspired by Vamba's 1895 novel *Ciondolino*, in which the young protagonist becomes a tiny ant, Gianelli's text adumbrates his Catholic viewpoint via his diminutive protagonist. Similarly, Giuseppe Fanciulli launches his nationalist critique in *L'omino turchino* (1912) [*The Little Indigo Man*] and Lombroso Carrara enacts her socialist critique in *Un reporter nel mondo degli uccelli* (1911) [*A Reporter in the Bird World*] using this microcosmic structure, which effectively employs scale and perspective to set in opposition real and possible worlds, utopias and dystopias (Myers, *Making* 65–83).

79 Both Sandro Botticelli and Jacopo della Quercia depicted the Madonna and Child with a pomegranate. The idea of rebirth recurs to Greek and Roman mythology, which links the pomegranate to springtime, the season enabled by the joy of Ceres when she reunites with her daughter Persephone. Thanks to my colleague Bob Blue for drawing my attention to this symbolism. Quaglino's illustration shows precisely the pomegranate split open with the seeds spilling out and transforming into children.

80 On SEI, Manson notes "Their growing success in publishing for schools at the end of the century constituted a notable exception to the general decline of the Catholic presence compared to the reinforcement of secular publishing for schools, whose strong points were the Milanese editorial centre or Bemporad" (191).

81 On the differences and affiliations between aesthetic modernism and Catholic modernism, see Somigli and Moroni's Introduction in *Italian Modernism*. They remind us that "in Italy, as in France, the term 'modernism' was introduced at the beginning of the twentieth century to indicate the movement within the Catholic Church which sought to 'democratize' its structures and, most importantly, suggested an 'evolutionary' view of dogma" (4–5).

82 His rhetoric is indeed militant: "In this spiritual warfare...reason and culture, evolution and progress on the one side, marshalled under the bright banner of science; on the other side, marshalled under the black flag of hierarchy, stand spiritual servitude and falsehood, want of reason and barbarism, superstition and retrogression" (xxii).

83 Haeckel here is talking specifically about the interference of the kenogenic process, or adaptations (10).

84 The Messina earthquake is fundamental to the genesis of the text. Gianelli went to Messina after the disaster in the capacity of newspaper correspondent and White Cross soldier. He stayed from December 30 through January 8 (1909) and brought back with him to Rome the two children to whom *Pipino* is dedicated and who figure as Pipino's special friends in the narrative, namely, the "abandoned" Morosi brothers, Mario (age 11 at the time of the quake) and Ugo (age 9). Gianelli became their caretaker and even resisted attempts by their mother to reclaim them (Farinelli 168–70). The abduction of these children, justified as a rescue, betrays disturbingly paternalistic attitudes also evident in the text where the children are fictionalized characters. Invernizio would take up the theme of the South's rescue and adoption by the North in the opening tale of her 1915 short story collection. Here, little Italo, whose parents and sister are "buried in the rubble" ["seppelliti sotto le rovine" (8)] of their home in Sicily, is rescued by the wealthy Florentine merchant, Mr. Labardi. Labardi, we are told, had

recently lost his wife and son, and so the adoption of the Sicilian boy by the Florentine father is made to seem a natural reconstitution of the family (much as Mommo replaces the unnamed dead boy in *Scurpiddu*).

85 "The distinguishing mental features of melancholia are a profoundly painful dejection, cessation of interest in the outside world, loss of capacity to love, inhibition of all activity, and a lowering of the self-regarding feelings to a degree that finds utterance in self-reproaches" ("Mourning and Melancholia" 244).

86 In 1908, Gianelli worked with Giovanni Cena and Sibilla Aleramo in the Agro Romano region. Farinelli (166–67) recounts Gianelli's observations of how self-interested priests and landowners sought to deny them education and the joy Gianelli experienced in helping those children learn to write.

87 Pascoli drew much of his discussion of childhood speech from James Sully's 1895 *Studies of Childhood*. Pascoli possessed the 1898 French translation of the psychologist's work. Gianelli published an analysis of Pascoli's poetry in 1905 ("Leonardo Bistolfi e Giovanni Pascoli" in *L'Artista Moderno*, see Farinelli 37–38), and he met Pascoli in 1906 (Farinelli 162). Myers notes the influence of Pascoli on Gianelli and the other microcosmic fantasy writers (77–79). Boero too remarks on the "deteriore" [second-rate] pascolianisms, including the calls to find contentment in small things (21).

88 Gianelli's approach here is rather uncommon. I have found only one other children's book of the period that uses a kind of "baby talk." Pertile's *Il trionfo dei piccoli*, which I analyze in Chapter 3, at one point transcribes the three-year-old Mario as saying "butta cignola" (62) for "brutta signora," or "ugly lady," in a moment of anger toward his mother's friend. It is not surprising that books that aimed to disseminate literacy would avoid validating what was considered incorrect speech.

89 Castellino x–xii. Giuseppe Farinelli, in the 1973 edition of Gianelli's complete poetry, cites Raimondo Canavasso's words from a conference on Gianelli (176). See also Boero 22–24.

90 Farinelli suggests that Gianelli, while in Turin during 1907, very likely attended meetings organized by Giacosa to discuss the biological basis of religious conscience (26). His brother, the writer Giuseppe Giacosa, participated in 1880 Turin conference I discussed in the Introduction.

3   A Beatrice for Modernity
Girls in Italian Children's Literature

Ma io sono un uomo, e non ho la bambola

[But I am a man, and I don't have a doll]

—Pertile, *Trionfo dei piccoli*, 49

The seven original fairy tales in the 1905 collection entitled *L'ultima fata* [*The Last Fairy*] by "Cordelia" (Virginia Treves) link femininity to abundance and domesticity. In the first tale, which shares its name with the collection, the young orphan Pervinca wanders through a cottage that has been magically prepared for her. She is amazed by the wealth of provisions that fill up the house, each in its appropriate storage space: "E non mancava nulla di ciò che è necessario ad una vita comoda, nè le stoviglie lucide nella credenza, nè la biancheria profumata nei cassettoni, nè ricche vesti negli armadi; nella dispensa c'era una provvista di viveri e nella cantina una schiera di bottiglie di vino generoso, tanto da poter vivere parecchi anni" [The house was full of everything necessary for a comfortable life: shiny dishes in the cupboards, perfumed linens in the drawers, fine clothes in the closets, in the pantry was plenty of food, and in the cellar a row of bottles of fine wine, enough to last several years] (16–17).[1] The cottage becomes a *locus amoenus* Pervinca will inhabit, whose abundance will enable her to welcome her wandering brother at the end of the tale, saving him from his desperate situation. At the same time, I will argue, this house and its spaces function as figures for the girl herself.

In the first part of this study, I analyzed the use of Giuseppe Garibaldi as a heroic fetish from a by-gone age that Italian children were urged to remember but also abandon. In the second section, I examined books that use cartographic imagery (such as those that include visual maps as illustrations), that tell stories about journeys, or that aim to teach geography. These various mapping devices depict the South as a source of abundance to be integrated into the new nation, but also as a primitive danger that Italy must overcome. Both of these strategies (heroism and mapping) couple the recapitulation paradigm with a melancholic structure. In advocating the isomorphic parallelism of the individual's development from unruly child to productive adult on the one hand, with Italy's maturation from rural to modern society on the other, these books insist that such processes entail an abandonment and introjection of manly epic heroism (as figured by Garibaldi) and of the feminine, primitive South (both beyond and within Italy's new borders).

Italian does not have a gender-neutral word for "child." Can we nevertheless see this process of subject formation through recapitulation and melancholy as operating for all subjects in process, both boys and girls? This chapter will argue that Italian children's books did not deploy a gender-neutral strategy in this regard. Rather, the narratives of the period insist that all these developmental trajectories—ontogenic, phylogenic, or cartographic—be forged by a male subject: or more precisely, that the Italian male subject is in fact produced by these itineraries and by their imaginary fusion. The texts I analyze in this chapter suggest that women, instead, do not develop, progress, travel, mature, or modernize. Rather, women are immobilized within history, atavistically attached to (imagined) origins, paradoxically permanent children and always already adults, and typically maternal adults. "She" enables the maturation of the male subjects and of Italy.[2]

The conclusion of Giuseppe Nuccio's historical novel, which I analyzed in my discussion of Garibaldi, forcefully illustrates this gendered maneuver. In this adventure-filled novel about Garibaldi's liberation of Sicily, the young local boys who have joined with the Red Shirts to overthrow the Bourbon monarchy must, after this successful revolt, adopt a new identity from their northern saviors. These "picciotti," in other words, learn that local attachments must give way to national affiliations. Nuccio codes this moment as a deeply melancholic transfer of devotion. The boys must withdraw their attachments from *La Talia*, an anthropomorphized mother figure whose name had often been invoked alongside that of the local female patron Saint Rosalia, in order to embrace *Italy*, an abstract concept figured on the map that is carried by the boy from Trieste:

> Pispisedda baciò l'Italia e poi la diede a baciare a Roccco, a Ferraù e a Turi mormorando, con gli occhi gonfi di lagrime: 'Ci fossero Fedele, Sautampizzu, Cacciatore...' e ripensò a quelle sere dell'ottobre dell'anno avanti e dell'aprile e del maggio, quando avevano gridato, tutti insieme: "Viva la Talia!". Ora avrebbero gridato il nome giusto, tanto più dolce: L'Italia; ma le labbra dei morti non più. ... (243; ellipses in orig.)

> [Pispisedda kissed [the map of] Italy and then offered it to be kissed by Rocco, Ferraù, and Turi as he murmured, with his eyes full of tears, 'If only Fedele, Sautampizzu, Hunter were here...' and he

thought back to those evenings in October of last year, and in April
and May, when they had cried out, all together, 'Long live La Talia!'
Now they would have cried out the correct name, a name so much
sweeter: Italy. But the lips of his dead friends could no longer cry
out. ...]

Here, as in other books, the narrative overtly employs the feminine function as inspiration: the ancient and maternal "Talia" elicits the passion
and patriotism that prompts the boys' revolutionary actions, but then
cedes her place to "Italy." Similarly, we recall how the young protagonist
Pin in Lino Ferriani's *Un piccolo eroe* becomes a productive adult husband in order to provide for his childhood sweetheart Maria, who waits
at home while he travels to England. But while the girl inspires the boy's
(and Italy's) maturation, as if in the role of a modern-day bourgeois
Beatrice, she also embodies that which is abjected in the constitution of
a melancholy adult citizen.

In his discussion of G. Stanley Hall's 1904 study of adolescence, children's literature scholar Kenneth Kidd suggests that "[t]he girl represents
for Hall not so much the boy's opposite but rather a particular (hopefully
temporary) stage in his evolution; for Hall, as for so many other practical
theorists of recapitulation, femininity, like savagery and criminality, is
not an identity or experience in its own right, but rather an evolutionary
stage or phase through which boys must pass in order to become men ...
she is the abject of masculinity" (157). Hall's 1904 study of adolescence
shares this perspective with slightly earlier and highly influential Italian
criminological studies by Cesare Lombroso and his followers, to whom
I will refer in more detail. In this chapter, I will analyze 11 children's
texts from 1878 to 1921 in light of the role of the girl child, not as
maturing subject but as enabler and as *repository* of attachments abandoned by boys and by Italy as they march into maturity and modernity.
The detailed and almost obsessive catalogue of specific domestic spaces,
each one reassuringly full of its appropriate provision, that we saw in
Virginia Treves's description of the enchanted cottage—kitchen cup-
board, dresser drawer, closet, pantry, cellar—offers, I suggest, figures
for the girl herself as a repository of the premodern and infantile past.

Divesting the Feminine: Vamba's Gian Burrasca

The child/nation isomorphic link, deployed in a specifically gendered
fashion, emerges in the very popular book *Il giornalino di Gian Burrasca*
(1907–1908 in installments, 1912 as volume) [*Johnny Whirlwind's
Notebook*] by "Vamba" (Luigi Bertelli). The opening page emphatically
and visually announces the recapitulation paradigm (see Figure I.1).[3]
The illustration that greets the reader is a sketch of the calendar page for
September 20th. This day marks the Italian National Army's conquest

of Rome in 1870 and the definitive moment of national unification as the secular government claimed the Eternal City for itself, wresting it from the Papacy ("1870. Entrata delle truppe italiane in Roma"). The illustration of the calendar page also notes that September 20th is the feast of Saint Eustazio, soldier and martyr, thus attesting to the continued presence of Catholic culture and practices in the new secular nation. But of course, most importantly, September 20th is the protagonist's birthday. Gianni Stoppani, nicknamed by his parents "little Johnny Whirlwind," shares his birthday with Italy. The superimposition of the little boy's birth in 1897 ("Nascita di Giannino," whose name is visually underscored and in bold print) with that of the whole nation in 1870 comically highlights the protagonist's charming and endearing narcissism: he makes sure that everyone sees the calendar, so that they remember to bring him gifts. The juxtaposition also announces (and I think comically subverts) the vigorously asserted coincidence of the above trajectory: the naturalized story that Italy is growing up alongside, in tandem with, and through its children.[4]

Il giornalino di Gian Burrasca explains its own genesis: on his ninth birthday, little Gianni received an empty notebook to be used as his journal. The device of the diary clearly functions as a comical and cheeky send-up of Edmondo De Amicis's very earnest *Cuore* (1886) [*Heart*]. This book, structured as the diary of a boy in Turin through an academic year, was already a wildly popular text and a staple of the Italian curriculum by the time Vamba was writing—indeed, it was already in its 97th printing by 1890. *Cuore* preached hard work and obedience, and envisioned the schoolroom as a space that would overcome divisions of economic class and geographic region.[5] The diary structure in De Amicis's text documents the daily learning process of the boy protagonist under the paternal guidance of father and (male) teacher and literally under the gaze of the king, whose image hangs in the front of the classroom.[6] In Vamba's comic and subversive rendition, Gianni's diary instead records all the moments in which the impish boy's innocent fauxpasses reveal adult hypocrisy.

In addition to signaling the paternal text the novel subverts, the diary itself becomes the instrument of a fairy-tale-like rite of initiation: as a birthday gift, the diary functions as a blank slate onto which Gianni will write his own story. The suggestion that the boy can become a man by authoring his own story, however, is quickly deflated, much as Vamba's irony deflates De Amicis's earnest moralizing, for young Gianni can think of nothing to say. Desperate to fill the blank pages with something, he decides that his only recourse is to copy his sister's diary into his own. He finds a diary entry that itself clearly appropriates, and uncritically reiterates, all the *topoi* of nineteenth-century melodrama. Replete with exclamations of "povero cuore mio" [my poor heart], a coerced engagement to an unattractive but financially secure man, and secret amorous relationships, Ada Stoppani's lovelorn and hyperbolically tragic prose becomes comedy as it passes verbatim through little Gianni's pen. In short, the boy transcribes his adolescent sister's already clichéd rhetoric. Rather than constructing his own subjectivity, then, Gianni is inaugurated into adulthood as the copy of a copy. The comically disastrous consequences of this inept transition into the symbolic order enact a critique of the ideology of self-creation implied by the empty notebook. Such an ideology, I suggest, was at play in the work ethic so vigorously promoted in children's literature of the period with an eye to moving Italy's economy "forward."[7] The sister's financially advantageous match is threatened when Gianni innocently reads these copied pages from his diary in front of Ada's rich and rotund fiancé, signor Capitani, whose extreme financial wealth seems to be registered and critiqued in his body as excessive corpulence.

The scene certainly achieves engaging comic effects, and through that comedy enacts one of the book's many critiques of "social conformism and the hypocrisy of the adult petite bourgeoisie."[8] At the same time, I suggest, this false start also tells us that a girl's diary cannot be the model of this boy's development. Typical of the repetitions that structure this narrative, a similar false start follows soon after. Gianni tries on his sister Luisa's clothes and makeup not long after having tried on Ada's rhetoric, and with similar consequences. "Che bella signorina ero diventato" [what a beautiful young lady I had become] (11), he marvels in self-satisfaction as he gazes into the mirror to admire his rosy cheeks and pretty skirt. But instead of envy—"che invidia, avranno di me le mie sorelle!" [how jealous my sisters will be of me!] (11)—he elicits only more scolding and slaps from his family. Having conjured the recapitulation paradigm through the prominent positioning of the calendar on the first page, *Il giornalino*, in addition to its cutting and repeated social and political critiques, dramatizes that the boy's subjectivity must be inaugurated with and by the rejection of the feminine.[9]

"A Mothering Kind of Pedagogy"

Broadly speaking, in Italy in the late nineteenth and early twentieth centuries, the field of children's literature was one of the few discursive spaces in which women could operate as major players without significant censure. While, perhaps not surprisingly, the two works that have received the most critical acclaim (*Cuore* and *Pinocchio*) were written by men, women penned a vast body of work, many as popular or almost as popular in their time as those two classics. Ida Baccini (1850–1911), for example, authored the novel *Memorie di un pulcino* in 1875, which rivalled *Pinocchio* in popularly (and in fact is mentioned in *Pinocchio*). Other women writers who found receptive audiences for their children's books included Eva Cattermole Mancini ("Contessa Lara") (1846–1896),

Virginia Treves ("Cordelia") (1849–1916), Emma Perodi (1850–1918), Carolina Invernizio (1851–1916), Sofia Bisi Albini (1856–1919), Gemma Rembadi-Mongiardini (1857–1916), Anna Franchi (1867–1954), Annie Vivanti (1868–1942), Paola Lombroso (1871–1954), Laura Orvieto (1876–1953), Arpalice Cuman Pertile (1876–1958), Corinna Teresa Ubertis Gray ("Térésah") (1877–1964), and Carola Prosperi (1883–1981). Indeed, women intervened not only as authors of books for both school curricula and for pleasure reading, but also as editors for children's periodicals: Emma Perodi from 1883 directed the *Giornale per i bambini* [*Children's Paper*]; in 1884, Ida Baccini assumed leadership of the magazine for young girls called *Cordelia*, which she directed for almost 30 years, until her death in 1911 (*Cordelia* was founded in 1881 by Angelo de Gubernatis, who named it for his daughter, and it ran until 1942); Sofia Bisi Albini directed the *Rivista per le signorine* [*Young Ladies' Magazine*] from its founding in 1894 until its merger in 1913 with *La nostra rivista* [*Our Magazine*]; Paola Lombroso helped found *Corriere dei Piccoli* [*The Little People's Courier*]; and Virginia Treves was at the helm of the *Giornale dei fanciulli* [*Newspaper for Kids*] for a decade, and served also as director of *Margherita*, an illustrated magazine for girls.[10] The supposedly "natural" association of women and children, and the notion that women, with their sentimentality and sensitivity, are not only suited to be nurturers of children but are indeed *like* children, underwrite this legitimization.[11] Lucia Re has pointed out how "[i]n the education of children, women were supposed to be the principle agents for the inculcation of 'good feelings' such as a sense of obedience, respect for authority, parsimony, and charity" (163).

A New Dido: Ida Baccini's *I piccoli viaggiatori*

Ida Baccini's *I piccoli viaggiatori* [*Little Travelers*] (1878), which I examined in the previous chapter in terms of its use of mapping strategies, embodies the notion of women as permanently infantile and charts the stakes of this link (that is, women/children) for Italy's educational and modernizing goals. Baccini here reincarnates one of Italy's core foundational myths—none other than Virgil's *Aeneid*. She illustrates how the ancient struggle between Dido and Aeneas, where "woman" is perceived as a tempting trap that immobilizes men and prevents their forward progress, could be redeployed for the specifically modern project of (re)founding Italy. As fitting for a children's book, the protagonist's mother, Luisa, replaces Aeneas' lover, Dido. When Luisa's husband Giuseppe enthusiastically approves the plan for their 12-year-old son Adolfo to undertake a sea voyage to China with his Uncle Pasquale, Luisa is terrified. She sees only dangers and is beside herself with worry to the point that Adolfo, despite his eagerness for this adventure, is ready to cancel the plans. Luisa, however, as a proper mother, relents and entrusts the boy to his uncle, though with much trepidation. Luisa, then, embodies Dido insofar as she, as a woman, threatens to hold back the male protagonist from the roaming (and also perhaps "Rome-ing"—we recall that Uncle Pasquale's boat is named *Italo*) to which he is called. Luisa, ceding to the desires of the three men in the family, must reconcile herself to the fact that her son must leave home to become a man. Unlike her Adolfo and his friend Carlino, Luisa and Carlino's mother, Maria, do not go away, but remain home, and thus do not undergo the development that the voyage enables. In addition to the women's immobile and potentially immobilizing roles, the text provides other markers that indicate the perpetual infancy of the female figures.

Early in the novel, just before the voyagers set out, Carlino's mother, who is of a lower class than Luisa and Giuseppe, is put into the role typically filled by one of the children. Specifically, Maria asks a naïve question that serves as a prompt for one of the adult men to provide a scientific disquisition in order to illuminate the characters and the readers. In this instance, Maria expresses her fear that the ship may encounter a group of Sirens, creatures she believes to be half-fish, half-women, and her inquiry provides the narrative opening for the ship captain (Pasquale) to give a marine biology lesson: "[l]a sirena ... non è altro che la foca, o vitello marino" [the sirens are just seals, or sea-calves] (34), followed by a long discussion of the characteristics of this fascinating animal. Through this scene, readers are not only taught many facts about the seal, but also made to see how childish Maria is. Pasquale points out that "a'tempi di prima, i marinai non erano istruiti" [in olden days, seamen were not well educated] (36). They relied on "fandonie" and "favole" [foolish tales and fables] to describe the natural phenomena that science now has properly explained.[12] In short, Maria, chronologically an adult woman, structurally occupies a role typically held by the children in the novel (asking a question that initiates the didactic passages of the book) and thematically is childlike in her adherence to fairy tales and fables rather than science. We should note too how the sailors "of long ago" are like the children of today, in a move typical of recapitulation. Finally, the specific content of this early example of a "teachable moment" solidifies the gender issues at play. Before leaving the port, and soon after the strenuous and tear-filled objections of Luisa had been overcome, the specter of the Sirens is conjured by the other mother in the book—that is, another image of the female as entrapment to the male sea voyager. The sirens, like Dido/Luisa, are effectively exorcised by the modern scientific knowledge of the adult, modern, male captain, who then shuttles off the young boys, leaving behind Luisa and Maria. Indeed, the evocation invites us to read the text also as a modern-day Odyssey, where the mothers patiently wait at home for the return of their little heroes.

The final chapter narrates the long-awaited return of Uncle Pasquale with his charges, who are now ready to assume their roles as productive men. Tellingly, the reunion of Adolfo and Luisa is described not in words but by two full lines of ellipses. The narrator then comments, "Perchè tutti quei puntolini? Perchè certe cose non si possono raccontare, bambini miei, altro che co' baci e le lacrime; domandatelo alle vostre mamme!" [Why all these periods? Because certain things cannot be expressed, my little ones, except with kisses and tears; go ask your moms about it!] (190). Maternal love, then, is described as inarticulate, as a nonlinguistic, corporeal, fluid "semiotic" that reminds us of Julia Kristeva's formulations. Where Kristeva theorizes such a polyvalent semiotic fluidity as potentially subversive of phallocentric, symbolic discourse, here, instead, this maternal nonlanguage is rendered primarily as silence and linked again to infancy in its impotence rather than its potential. Whereas the adult men of the novel produce the articulate and edifying discourses about everything from marine biology to the silk industry in China, which fill almost all of the book's 200 pages, Luisa's contributions are primarily limited to the frightened tears that seek to hold her son back and the two lines of silent and tearful *puntini* that greet his return.[13] Indeed, these *puntini* have the narrative effect of sparing the reader from having to endure pages of prose describing the carrying-on of a tearful mother. Baccini, in other words, while ostensibly paying homage to the preciousness and ineffability of maternal love, in fact erases it from the text. Indeed, as a woman writer, Baccini herself (as we are reminded by the occasional intrusion of the narrative voice) is actually the author of all the many historical and scientific passages diegetically attributed to male characters. In other words, this woman writer, according to the gender dynamics the book itself establishes, in essence ventriloquizes the male voice. Thus, her silencing of Luisa at the conclusion functions more as a refutation than as a celebration of the Kristevian "semiotic."

Furthermore, by means of these ellipses, Luisa emerges not only as a new Dido or as a modern Penelope, but also as another figuration of Alì, the black former slave child whose character I analyzed in the previous chapter and who is also rendered silent throughout the novel. First, we should note that the command to the readers to "go ask your mom" implies that all mothers will give the same response. The protagonist's crying mother exemplifies mothers in general who, like the inarticulate speech they produce, are undifferentiated, interchangeable, and also ultimately and indeed by definition disposable: "le mamme, o chinesi, o francesi, o turche son tutte eguali; e anzichè far patire i loro figlioli, io scommetto si lascerebbero mettere a pezzi" [moms, whether they be Chinese, Turkish, or French, are all alike; and rather than have their dear children suffer, I bet that they would let themselves be ripped to pieces] (132). This observation is offered by the narrator, who elsewhere has cast herself as a mother figure. She is commenting on her childhood memory of being told that if she were naughty, her parents would send her to China where bad children are thrown into the sea and fed to the fish. The narrator dismisses this threatening story, now that she knows that no mother, even a Chinese one, would hurt her child. Indeed, she claims—and her own maternal identity seems to authorize the claim— that all mothers would sacrifice themselves rather than see their children hurt. The statement draws on and reinscribes the assumption that while men are unique individuals, women, because of their reproductive role, are all essentially the same. Moreover, the claim exchanges one explicitly violent fantasy with another: the child's body is pulled out of the water and replaced with the body of the mother, who will be ripped to shreds in her child's place, precisely in the water, recalling the inarticulate tears that mark maternal language.

The fantasy of the naughty Chinese children who are fed to the fish, deployed as a strategy to elicit proper behavior in Italian children, links to other moments in the novel in which specific bodies are cast into the water to be devoured by maritime creatures. Readers had earlier learned from the proper English gentleman Lord Raymond, who tells the tale not with sighs and sobs or ellipses but "con bel garbo" [in very fine taste] (48), that Alì's brother Dick had been eaten by a shark while serving his master. Dick, we learn, had jumped into the water to re- trieve his master's map. Dick's tragic story prompts the learned Lord Raymond to provide a detailed science lesson on sharks. He concludes his display of erudition with a description of the practice of some white Europeans who use a "circle of black slaves" to protect themselves from these ocean predators. The unfortunate ones [*disgraziati*] indeed are of- ten attacked, giving their masters time to get away, and it is they who end up "lacerati e divorati" [lacerated and devoured] instead of their padroni (52).[14] First, we should note how Raymond's speech, like the white padroni he describes in it, is itself encircled by black bodies be- ing devoured—it begins with the narration of Dick's violent death and ends with the sociology lesson just described. Indeed, his discourse was literally enabled by the sacrifice of a black body: Raymond insists that it would be too upsetting for poor Alì to narrate the story of his brother's sad fate and with a look sends Alì away so he himself can tell the tale. Like the image of devoured Chinese children that instills good behavior in young Italians, like the lacerated slaves that protect their padroni, like the silenced Alì and his dead brother his who make way for Raymond's edifying scientific discourse, mothers, too, have disposable bodies that are made available to be sacrificed for the protection, edification, and maturation of their children: their inarticulate and corporeal language of tears, sobs, and kisses must be cast overboard in order for the boys to be become men.

Yet at the same time, this language must to some extent be preserved, incorporated into the discourse that enables the male subject to mature. For Baccini's text, I suggest that this work of simultaneous abjection and incorporation is clumsily accomplished specifically through the passages that frame the didactic pages, or the feminine "sugar coating" that renders the masculine medicine of science and history lessons more palatable. Perhaps, however, this sugar coating was far too thin. In a reversal so typical of all of Collodi's profound subversions, Baccini's own book, like the Chinese children, the black slaves, and all mothers, is ultimately thrown overboard to be eaten by the fish. Chapter XXVII of Collodi's *The Adventures of Pinocchio*, we recall, includes Baccini's *Memorie di un pulcino*, among the dry, pedantic schoolbooks jettisoned into the sea by the naughty boys. It is so unpalatable, however—precisely because its edifying discourse had evacuated all pleasure—that even the fish refuse to consume it. Linguistically, structurally, and thematically, then, *I piccoli viaggiatori* dramatizes the maternal function as both necessary and threatening to the male subject's maturity and Italy's modernity.

A Talisman Against Modernity: Cordelia's *L'ultima fata*

Fairy tales, as well as realism, were harnessed by writers of the period to engender proper subjects. Virginia Tedeschi Treves, who wrote under the Shakespearean pen name "Cordelia," was already well known in the domain of children's literature by the early twentieth century. She had established herself as the director of the children's periodical *Giornale dei fanciulli* (1881–1891) when she published her best-known children's book *Piccoli eroi* [*Little Heroes*] in 1892 with Milan's Treves Brothers.[15] *L'ultima fata* [*The Last Fairy*], a collection of seven fairy tales, was first published in 1905, with the third edition (consulted here) in 1909 by the major Florentine press Bemporad. The collection (from which I quoted at the beginning of the chapter) includes 37 black, white, and red illustrations by the liberty artist Duilio Cambellotti.[16] *L'ultima fata* did not, as far as I have been able to establish, reach the popularity of her earlier *Piccoli eroi*. I have not found more than three editions, whereas many other children's books of the period had more numerous printings. However, the book was one of several collections of fairy tales, folk tales, and fables marketed for children in Italy at the time.

In fact, the post-unification period saw a surge in research on local folklore, undertaken by scholars such as Giuseppe Pitrè working in Sicily. The use of fairy tales as children's literature is itself to some extent a product of recapitulationist thinking: the notion that the traditional, oral, popular tales of the "folk" should be appropriate material for children is grounded in the idea that children are like primitives and vice versa.[17] The literary fairy tales of the Neapolitan writer Giambattista Basile (1566–1632) were decidedly not for children but for the court, as both Nancy Canepa and Jack Zipes make clear. By the late nineteenth century, fairy tales had been appropriated for children and marketed for pleasure reading. Other notable Italian fairy tale collections for children of the period include Luigi Capuana's multiple volumes published between 1882 and 1919, starting with *C'era una volta...fiabe* [*Once Upon a Time...Fairy Tales*]; Emma Perodi's *Novelle della nonna: Fiabe fantastiche* [*Grandma's Stories: Fantastic Fairy Tales*], which appeared in 1892; Luigi Bertelli's (Vamba) translated and adapted versions of Alexandre Dumas' French tales *Contes pour les grands et les petits enfants*, published by Bemporad in 1906 as *Novelle lunghe* [*Long Short Stories*]; Carlo Collodi's translations of Charles Perrault's and other French fairy tales (1875); and the Turinese poet Guido Gozzano's fairy tales, which came out in children's periodicals between 1909 and 1914.

The translation (in the sense of carrying over) of fairy tales from the forest and the court to the nursery and the school room had at times the effect of a "betrayal" [*traduttore-traditore*] of this genres' most engaging, nuanced, and potentially subversives qualities. Carola Prosperi's three fairy tales are a particularly clear case in point. Her slender 1910 collection *Tre fiabe* [*Three Fairy Tales*] was published in Turin by the Unione dei maestri elementari d'Italia [Italy's elementary-school teachers' union] and thus clearly had an instructional aim. Each of the three tales concludes with a very overt utilitarian educational message that not only deflates any sense of magic and wonder in the tales but also leaves many of the ambiguities and nuances opened up by the tales unaccounted for. Prosperi's rendition of Anderson's "The Little Match Girl" ["Fata Bianchina"] concludes with the protagonist, Michele, not only safely walking back home, but smugly able to dismiss his wonderful dream of the snow fairy because "sapeva bene, poichè era andato a scuola, come si formava la neve lassù" [he knew full well, since he had attended school, how snow was really made up there] (12). Thus, not only is any sense of "mystery" ("la fanciulla sorrise misteriosamente" [the snow fairy smiled mysteriously] (11)) summarily swept away, but so, too, any potentially troubling questions about why a young child would be trying to sell matches at night in the snow are abruptly foreclosed. Similarly, her "Pennadoca" ["Goose feather"] tale narrates how a rather spoiled princess is cured of her malaise by using the magic feather from a white goose as a pen. The conclusion offers the narrator's analysis: "Io credo...che la reginotta guarì per mezzo del lavoro, che è il farmaco insuperabile e divino contro la noia e le malinconie. Non vi pare?" [I believe that the princess was cured through her hard work. There is no better medicine than this divine drug for fighting off boredom and melancholy, wouldn't you agree?] (9). With the "non vi pare," the narrator enlists her readers into ignoring other questions raised by the tale—for example, why the princess had the right to demand that a local poor old woman hand over her beloved pet—and coerces them into repressing the potential double meanings of a "farmaco." In short, fairy tales of the period at times were pressed into the service of promoting obedience and work at the expense of their more powerful aesthetic and ethical potentials.

In this milieu, the fairy tale genre seems particularly useful for Treves, given its typical setting among royalty. Royal figures can be read, of course, as players in a psychological "family romance," as Freud and Rank suggest. In this formulation, kings and queens from literature and dreams function as figures from infantile memories, representing all parents who once seemed omnipotent. Certainly, Treves invites all the young children reading the tales to identify with the protagonists. Given the literacy distribution and economic realities of Italy, these readers would have been primarily middle- and upper-class children mostly in the north of Italy. However, for Treves, this regal scenario also takes on a more literal and historical sense. Her seven tales play out among royal characters and most conclude with a coronation and with the establishment of harmony in well-ruled kingdoms. Such a setting enables Treves to dramatize a deeply conservative political view.[18] In these the tales, Treves mobilizes sympathy for and justifies the rights and privileges of monarchy. Young Fiordiligi, about to marry into the royal family, is shocked by what he learns: "non avrebbe mai creduto che i sovrani invece di godere la vita, avessero infinite preoccupazioni d'animo e non potessero neppure mangiare in pace, nel timore di essere avvelenati" [he would have never believed that the sovereigns, instead of enjoying life, had infinite spiritual cares and worries, and could not even eat in peace without fearing that they would be poisoned] (28). Princes Aurora hardly bats an eye as she surveys the carnage caused by the war that her father launched to protect her from the Cave King, since, after all, the soldiers are "lieti di dare la loro vita per la bella prinicpessa" [happy to give their lives for the beautiful princess] (138). The fighting, poverty, squalor, illness, and other miseries in the city encountered by Prince Valorous during his travels are explained quite simply: "[q]ui non c'è nessun re" [here there is no king] (221).

The tales, then, register nostalgia for a lost social order and articulate an antagonism toward the liberalism that was reconfiguring the Italian state.[19] In addition to these general apologies for monarchy, Treves conjures the specter of specific Italian historical events, presenting them in a way that reveals deep anxieties about more liberal distributions of power. The first tale, for example, evokes the assassination of King Umberto in 1900 by anarchist Gaetano Bresci and the Milan bread riots that precipitated that retribution. After months of agitation, the malcontent people explode in revolution: "Il re fece un ultimo atto di coraggio presentandosi al popolo esortandolo alla calma, ma venne ucciso barbaramente" [The king made a final act of courage coming before the people and begging them to return to calm, but he was barbarically murdered] (29). Similarly, a summary of the Risorgimento is offered by the mage Barbadoro [Golden Beard] to Prince Valorous (221–22). He explains that the area they are visiting was once divided into many small kingdoms, always at war with each other. Ultimately, "[i]l popolo, stanco di guerre, fece la rivoluzione, furono scacciate tutte le famiglie regnanti che si rifugiarono ... Qui il popolo governa, ma ... la guerra continua" [the people, tired of war, revolted and chased all the kings away. Now the people rule, but the fighting has not stopped] (222). The tales usually avoid any real place names, using instead designations like "Happy Island" or "the Valley of Kings," a gesture that itself produces the legitimizing effect of timelessness and universality. However, readers are simultaneously invited to see the connections to their homeland. Indeed, the first tale figuratively plants an Italian flag over the collection. Here, a ruby, diamond, and emerald gemstone that had been a gift from one character to another provides the visual inspiration for a red, white, and green flag. This flag, with its three colors that "go so well together" (36), flies over Pervinca's utopian kingdom. Through such oblique invocations of contemporary Italian events, Cordelia harnesses the timeless fairy tale genre to concrete political anxieties, using the genre as a vehicle to resist modernity (understood as the growth of political liberalism) and imaginatively to arrest this kind of historical development.

The red, white, and green gem is referred to as a "talisman" in Pervinca's tale. In addition to using royal characters as an instrument for justifying monarchy and class privilege, Treves employs another generic feature of fairy tales to forward her conservative agenda, namely the "magical agent" that comes from a "donor." Vladimr Propp, in his seminal structuralist analysis *Morphology of the Folktale*, defines the "donor" as the *dramatis persona* whose function is to test the hero and then offer him or her "some agent (usually magical) which permits the eventual liquidation of misfortune" (39, 43). Maintaining this common generic feature, all seven tales include an enchanted object that is gifted from a mage or fairy to the hero, sometimes via an intermediary.[20] Treves displays her creativity in offering readers an impressive array of quotidian objects with extraordinary powers: walnuts that when cracked open release birds or flying insects that lead the hero to his wish; a diamond that in the hands of the good hero emits a guiding light but burns the hands of evil doers who grasp it; a walking staff with glowing eyes that can revive petrified men and cause the cold-hearted heroine to fall in love with the staff-bearer; a golden book which, when consulted, generates words on its pages to suit the situation at hand; a basket full of white kittens who warn the hero and heroine of approaching danger with their meows; a phial containing a narcotic and a bundle holding a bear skin that enable to the hero to access the last drop of healing water; and finally, a small silver box with three packets: a sleeping potion used to escape the cannibals, an explosive used to free the ship from the crags, and a perfume that makes the heroine smell so bad that the unwanted prince rescinds his marriage proposal. Many of these magical objects take the form of a container or receptacle of some kind, visually and functionally echoing the storage spaces in Pervinca's cottage and thus connecting them to the concepts of life and abundance that those domestic spaces implied.

In the fourth tale, the talisman-container takes the form of a magical book, specifically, a little book of gold, given by a wise hermit to Princess Aurora to consult for good advice. Duilio Cambellotti's cover image of *L'ultima fata*, which depicts a young woman bent attentively over an open book, places Aurora and her talisman in a privileged role (see Figure 3.1). The image not only illustrates a particular moment in the fourth tale but also stands as the emblem of the collection as a whole and serves to greet the readers who pick up Cordelia's book. While the image illustrates Aurora pensively engrossed in the act of consulting her magic talisman, I suggest that this cover illustration also works more broadly as a mirror: it reflects "us" as the readers of this book we hold in our hands. In this way, the image constructs the ideal reader as a girl and models her as she consults Cordelia's book closely. Furthermore, this image and the many other references to books throughout (fairies, mages, and wise old women often consult books before giving advice or issuing prophecies) suggest that Cordelia's collection itself should be received as a kind of talisman. The book is offered as an enchanted object that promises to protect its bearer (here, the child readers) and to ward off threats and dangers, to liquidate misfortune, as Propp puts it. If, as I am suggesting, we see Cambellotti's image as modeling not only Aurora but also the reader, and if we therefore consider the collection as a talisman, then Virginia Treves herself assumes the role of the "donor." Specifically, Treves becomes the donor named by the collection, the Last Fairy herself. She is the *last* fairy, we learn from the narrative, because all her fairy-sisters have been chased away by the mage named Progress. In short, this talisman book that has been given to us (female) readers by the Fairy Treves will liquidate, precisely, the misfortune of progress: the forces of modernization depicted as a threat.

The first tale informs us that Progress has chased away all but one of the good fairies. The last tale ends with the renaming of an island: after the inhabitants have adopted all the technologies developed by science, their island is rechristened as "Progress," whereas previously it had been "Happy." Not only does the content of these names announce the political message (a lament that happiness gives way to and is replaced by progress), but also this transparent and allegorical-like *use* of names becomes, I suggest, one of the ways in which the fairy tales seek to resist the forces of modernity. Semantic reliability and legibility are proffered as an antidote to the confusion wrought by progress: King Good is good; the bear king will eat you; Splendore is quite splendid, the hope inspired in him by Princess Speranza does not fail; Prince Valoroso learns to live up to his name through his brave quest, inspired by his shining star, the princess Stellina, and so forth. To contextualize and highlight how these proper names work as anchoring points that tether

Figure 3.1   Duilio Cambellotti, from *L'ultima fata* by Virginia Treves [Cordelia].

word to world, I would draw a contrast with the comically illogical manner in which Geppetto chooses a name for Pinocchio: he selects a name that was borne by an extremely poor family, in order to bring the puppet good luck (97). Perhaps even more than his name, the instability of Pinocchio's nose, if we try to understand it as a barometer of whether his words correspond to reality or as an expression of his inner truth, marks the kind of semiotic crisis that Cordelia's text strives to remedy.

Suzanne Stewart-Steinberg has forcefully articulated this instability in Collodi's novel. Considering interpretations of the nose as a "phallic symbol," she argues, "[i]ndeed what the tale lacks, in the absence of moral progress, is a master signifier, or at least a signifier capable of grounding the tale in some ultimate significance. Given this fictionality, the fact that words and things live in an unstable relationship, Pinocchio's lies, as symbolized in his nose, cannot be led back—or at least not in an obvious manner—to the genital apparatus.... His nose makes its appearance not only in connection with his lies. Pinocchio's nose is far more duplicitous, an unstable signifier of his desire and of his will. His nose points to the phallus and not genitality, but only if the phallus is understood as the point of coincidence between omnipotence and total impotence." Rather than attesting to "an interiority or privacy of the subject," the unreliable and uncontrollable nose puts precisely this notion of the subject into crisis (45–46). The deeply threatening nature of this instability, I think, is registered in the fact that so many subsequent representations of Pinocchio have so vigorously attempted to lock down this image. Emer O'Sullivan, surveying the abundant field of Pinocchio translations and adaptations across cultures, with particular emphasis on German (and "Germanized") versions, takes issue with the notion that in spite of all changes, updates, and modifications, somehow "the authentic story of Pinocchio has not been lost" and that its "mythoic core" remains discernible. Rather, O'Sullivan asserts that "the only similarity" many an adapted Pinocchio "bears with the original is that he is a wooden puppet with a long nose" ("Does Pinocchio have an Italian Passport?" 152–53). I would extend this to suggest that, in fact, the "growing nose=telling lie" syntagm has become the unproblematic synecdoche of Pinocchio's very essence (whereas for Collodi it is the impossibility of such an equation to which the nose attests, if it attests to anything). Treves's obsessively proper use of proper names, which seeks to restore a reassuring knowability of the subject and legibility of language, attempts to remedy the kind of perceived crisis that Collodi exemplified in Pinocchio's nose.

In addition to the use of proper names, Treves dramatizes the natural grounding of language in various scenes of reading. The link between text and nature emerges, for example, in the mage who writes on the water with his poplar-branch pen (narrated on page 109, illustrated on page 113), and "wise maxims" written in "words of fire" that Barbadoro urges Valoroso to read (214). Nature itself sings through the birds who celebrate the birth of Princess Aurora, and the interspersed onomatopoeia renders their song "authentic" without sacrificing legibility: "Tirì tì tì bella fanciulla / Siam le voci del bosco" [Tiri ti ti beautiful little girl / we are the voices of the forest] (104). The complete clarity of every textual moment in the book obtains even in phrases that we might expect to be enigmatic or polyvalent, such as prophecies or spells. When Marinella reads the label to the third potion, it tells her "se sul tuo corpo mi spargerai, tutti gli uomini allontanerai" [if you sprinkle me on your body, you will chase away all men] (294), and indeed that is exactly what the smelly perfume does. Such moments, even when poetic (as in the rhyming potion labels) overtly seek to stabilize meaning and to dispel any potential ambiguity.

I would suggest along these lines, too, that the lack of a frame narrative works in a similar fashion to announce the transparency, naturalness, and reliability of language. Many other fairy tale collections of the period employ the device of a frame narrative, a practice that goes back to the earlier literary tale collections, including notably *The Thousand and One Nights*, as a way to dramatize the "fruitful interaction between oral storytelling and literary reproduction and invention" (Zipes *Tradition*, xii). In the Italian tradition, the frame tale of Princess Zoza in Basile's *Lo cunto de li cunti,* as Nancy Canepa has insightfully argued, serves as "a hermeneutic key to the entire collection" (81). Canepa unpacks how the frame tale, constructed in a "self-referential" way, "allegorized Basile's own hybrid telling project" (82).[21] The books marketed for children at the turn of the twentieth century carry on this tradition. Emma Perodi's collection stages the telling of her "novellas" in the humble home of a countryside grandmother who recounts the tales to her family. Similarly, Vamba sets up his translations of Dumas's fairy tales by depicting a scene of reading in which the narrator—Luigi Bertelli's own alter ego as the author of *Ciondolino*—reassures his young listeners that he won't bore them with a long disquisition of the history of fairy tales.[22] While each text uses its frame in a unique manner, in one way or another the frame often serves as a strategy to contain and guide interpretation. In Perodi's text, for example, after the Grandmother tells the third tale ("Narbona's ghost"), the adults of the family reassure the frightened grandchildren that in spite of what they just heard in the story, they do not really need to fear ghosts.[23] The *lack* of a frame in Treves's collection may imply that no such interpretive grid is needed: the tales speak clearly for themselves, without need of mediation, containment, or direction.

In fact, the tales speak clearly in a very correct, modern, and standard form of Italian. Unlike the antiquated and literary lexical forms that can be found in Perodi—for example, *ivi* for *lì* [there], *cerusico* for *chirurgo* [surgeon], *mentovare* for *menzionare* [mention], and *ita* for *così* [so]— and unlike the Sicilian flavor deployed by Capuana in his tales, no trace of temporal or regional linguistic specificity appears, such as might have been accomplished by the use of local proverbs, phrases quoted in dialect, proper names typical of particular locations, metalinguistic discussion, or other strategies of nuancing Italian with geographical or historical markers.[24] Access to and command of correct standard Italian was of course one of the privileges of the privileged classes, and Treves here implicitly validates this form of the language as the clearest and most appropriate means of a top-down communication that is not open to interpretation. Treves opens here a paradoxical situation. The language adopted by Treves in her conservative project is precisely the form of the language that the new liberal state sought to promote and disseminate as a unifying and modernizing strategy throughout the new nation. And, the growing access that women had to this language was also an effect of modernizing initiatives of the state.[25] What the tales, then, perhaps unwittingly disclose is how these "modernizing" initiatives were not in fact necessarily democratic or "liberal" but rather could have the effect of silencing the already disenfranchised.[26]

The *questione della lingua*, as Treves here makes clear, is always a question of power. Her utopian figuration of language—of a pure and timeless national idiom that provides reliability and fullness of meaning, that speaks "naturally" and "transparently" without opening itself up to potentially anarchical polyvalence—sought to counter the "head-spinning" confusion brought about by historical changes.[27] We have seen how the questioning of the natural rights of monarchies presented one such threatening change. The decoupling of the supposedly natural causal links between sex and gender was another. Even in their deeply antimodern gestures, Cordelia's stories reinscribe the kind of gendering at play in contemporary texts that advocate progress. Specifically, in spite of apparent gender complementarity, Treves codes "progress" as the domain of men and entrusts the conservation of the past to women.

Many of Cordelia's tales seem to offer a kind of parallelism between boys and girls through pairings of a brother and sister, husband and wife, and, in one story, a male-female pair of villains. In the first tale, Pervinca and Fiordiligi are brother and sister who are orphaned, and each one receives the same gift from the woodland fairy; the fifth tale introduces Farfallina e Caprettino, underscoring their symmetry, as "[u]n bambino e una bambina [che] erano nati nel medesimo giorno a due povere donne che abitavano la stessa casa ed erano amiche" [a boy and a girl born on the same day to two poor women who lived in the same house and were friends] (151). Of course, these pairings are not unusual in the fairy tale tradition. Perhaps the most well known, the Grimm Brothers' Hansel and Gretel, has its seventeenth-century Neapolitan antecedent in Basile's "Ninnillo and Nennella," where the parallelism is even more evident in the echoing names. In *The Uses of Enchantment*, the classic Freudian analysis that passionately advocates for the psychological utility of fairy tales for young readers, Bruno Bettelheim analyzes brother/sister pairs within his general psychological framework (78–83). For Bettelheim, paired siblings offer to the child reader a path by which he or she might unify "our dual nature" (78). He argues that "[s]uch fairy tales begin with an original lack of differentiation between the two siblings: they live together and feel alike, in short, they are inseparable" (79). Certainly, this scenario is at play in these two tales from Treves. Bettelheim goes on to argue that, through the course of the narrative, we see "the fairy

tale's symbolic way of rendering the essentials of human personality development: the child's personality is at first undifferentiated; then id,
ego, and superego develop out of the undifferentiated stage. In a process
of maturation, these must be integrated, despite opposite pulls" (79).
Bettelheim, who draws primarily on the Grimm tales, subscribes to a
maturation model that initiates from an undifferentiated point of origin.
For him, fictional "boys" and "girls" represent different parts of the
human subject (male or female), parts that each subject ("the child")
must learn to integrate into a healthy whole. He claims that fairy tales
give children a safe imaginary space in which to navigate that process.
What we see in Cordelia, and in other Italian texts of the period, is that
this developmental process is not symbolized through the paths taken
by the brother-sister or other male-female pairs with the aim of imag-
ining an integration into a mature adult. Rather, such a path is forged
by and for only the boy. I would argue that the apparent gender symmetry does not attempt to model a natural complementarity between male
and female as a map to potential wholeness. Nor does this parallelism
merely arrange the two terms hierarchically in order to assert the natural superiority of the male. Rather, the gendering here, underwritten by
contemporary scientific models, is ordered particularly along the lines
of a temporality that permanently embeds the female into the atavistic
origins of human development (phylogenic and ontogenic) and charges
her with its conservation.

As we saw in the passage that I quoted at the beginning of this chapter,
the girl protagonist from the first tale, Pervinca, is linked to the home
and to abundance. Furthermore, her desires are described in a way that
warns readers against greed or ambition (as Mencarani has persuasively
documented, a prevalent lesson of the post-unification period, especially
for girls) but also advocates a kind of stasis: "era sempre contenta" [she
was always content] (4). In the story, once she and her brother receive
their talismans from the woodland fairy, Pervinca immediately sets up
house, and then we as readers lose sight of her while we instead follow
the itinerary of her brother. It is Fiordiligi, her brother, who pursues his
desire, travels, hatches plots, and in fact has a story to narrate. His per-
egrinations constitute the tale: "Voglio conquistare il mondo" [I want to
conquer the world] (4) he declares before separating from his sister. The
stasis/mobility dichotomy dramatized here replicates Cesare Lombroso's
notions of sexual difference, differences that he claims are grounded in
biological facts.

Lombroso drew on the "legacy of pre-Darwinian comparative ana-
tomy" and the "phrenological tradition" and combined them within a
"strictly evolutionary perspective" in formulating his theories of the atavistic nature of criminals (Pancaldi 145). Chiara Beccalossi has pointed
out that this empiricism in the study of behavior generally, and in the
analysis of deviance, criminality, and gender differences, specifically,

was part of general strategy in the post-unification Italian psychiatric community broadly to bolster the field's scientific credibility and to wrest influence away from the Church in the "moral sphere" and in public policy (43–51). Perhaps the most radical example of this drive to biologism in terms of gender determinism appears in Lombroso's study of the female criminal. Here, he suggests that the egg's stability accounts not only for women's sedentary nature, but also for their essential "sameness" to each other and for their role in conserving the fundamental aspects of the species. The motility and energy of the sperm, conversely, inform men's adventurousness and their role in moving the species forward through their "genius" and through individual differentiation.[28] He writes,

> In her, anomalies are extremely rare when compared with man; and this phenomenon, with a few exceptions among lower animals, holds good throughout the whole zoological scale. For this reason, as Viazzi well observes (Anomalo, 1893), the *common* characters of a genus are more evident in the forms of the female. Most naturalists agree that for the type of a species also one must look to the female rather than to the male; and this remark may be applied with equal justice to the moral sphere. ... Compilers of the public statutes have also noted the conservative tendency of women in all questions of social order; a conservatism of which the primary cause is to be sought in the immobility of the ovule compared with the zoosperm. (*Female Offender* 108–109; italics in orig.)

The sociologist and criminologist Scipio Sighele (1868–1913), who builds on both Lombroso and Otto Weininger, maintains the insistence on fundamental sexual difference. In his 1910 study on the contemporary status of women, *Eva moderna* [*Modern Eve*], he vigorously supports women's right to vote, legalization of divorce, and women's education, but does so from the premise of biological difference, not from what he considers the feminists' "delusion" of sexual equality, a notion he considers "scientificamente sbagliata" [scientifically erroneous] (133). Like Lombroso, he maintains, furthermore, that psychological and moral phenomena have an organic basis: "alla base di ogni anormalità morale, c'è un'anomolia fisica" [at the root of every moral abnormality, is a physical anomaly] (90) and argues that woman's primary calling is maternity and the "conservazione della specie" [conservation of the species] (55–56). Women, who are biologically driven to maintain the species, contribute to its *progress* only indirectly in the form of providing men with their muses: "Se mi chiedesse qual forza ha più contribuito al progresso del mondo, dopo le spade dei grandi capitani e le scoperte dei genii, direi che fu la seduzione e il fascino delle donne" [If you were to ask me what force has most contributed to the world's progress, after the swords of great captains and the discoveries of geniuses, I would say that it was the seductiveness and fascination of women] (131).

Cordelia's tales dramatize the gender categories that the dominant scientific community was theorizing. Pervinca's contented domesticity bookends the first tale, serving as the point from which Fiordiligi emerges and to which he returns, after having grown, developed, learned, and changed through the plot and over time. A similar structure plays out in "Le avventure di Sassolino" ["Sassolino's Adventures"], whose plot evokes the biblical story of Joseph and the dream coat. In this tale, a poor woman has five children, the first four of whom are lazy and cruel. The boy/girl parallelism I mentioned earlier emerges here in the structure of two brothers and two sisters, all four of whom function as essentially interchangeable characters. The fifth and youngest child, thus the one who breaks the gendered symmetry, is a boy who emerges as the protagonist. Named "Sassolino" [little stone] because he comforts himself by contemplating a shiny rock, he has a good heart and a delicate constitution.[29] After the death of the mother, Sassolino becomes stronger with work but still displays a "una fisionomia gentile e delicata come quella d'una fanciulla" [a soft and delicate physiognomy, like that of a young girl] (43). His feminine golden hair and luminous eyes elicit a jealousy in his siblings that motivates their cruel behavior toward him. Indeed, the siblings' viciousness evokes the violence visited upon little Johnny Whirlwind when he inappropriately donned his sister's clothes, yet Cordelia stages this violence in a deadly seriousness, with none of Vamba's subversive humor. The tale narrates Sassolino's transformation into the manlier and mature "Splendore," making clear that his maturation is mediated and inspired by the Princess Speranza [Hope]. Sassolino's adventures include saving Speranza from wild horses, receiving the diamond talisman from the princess, being thrown into a deep well by his siblings (as an archetypal descent of the hero into the underworld), and enabling the king to purge his palace of dishonest ministers. The tale ends with the marriage of Sassolino-now-Splendore to Speranza (who in no manner has changed) and with the two assuming the throne and justly punishing his siblings. Certainly, the story advocates honesty and hard work, as these are qualities Sassolino displays,[30] but it also charts the male subject's necessary abandonment of femininity, from the death of the mother to the hardening of his body, in the process of maturation and codes this gendered maturation as simultaneously personal (as an individual he obtains a wife and punishes his siblings) and political (he assumes the throne of the kingdom which is now ruled with wisdom and justice).

In short, Sassolino must mature out of his delicate, feminine qualities to become Splendore the king. This rejection of the feminine is embodied in the figure of the doll in the penultimate tale of the collection, "La bambola del Principe Valoroso" ["Prince Valorous' Doll"]. This tale opens rather abruptly with the reported deaths of the queen and the princess, named Fior di Gaggìa [Lotus Flower]. The rest of the tale narrates the attempts to separate the prince from "Stella," the doll that belonged to his sister and that the prince now, after her death, obsessively cherishes and indeed wants to marry. Upon discovering this attachment that had been formed in grief, the king is enraged: "Sei forse una fanciulla? Lascia ad altri quei divertimenti infantili" [What are you, a little girl? Leave those childish amusements to others!] (202). As clearly articulated in the words of the father and lawgiver, this attachment to the doll renders the prince both feminine and childish and in fact implicitly links the two (the feminine *as* childishness). Furthermore, the doll functions as part of a brother-sister pair rather than the far more common mother-daughter relationship. Here too, then, we have the initial appearance of a gender parallelism or symmetry, which is then belied by the a-symmetrical temporality: unlike Valoroso, the silent sister-doll will never grow, develop, or have her own story.

Dolls and their representations in literature have been explored through a variety of lenses, perhaps most famously as a powerful figure of the uncanny in Freud's analysis. In Treves's account, the doll's function as a stand-in for the dead sister works as a fetish, as the perhaps unintentionally yet clearly erotic language suggests: the king storms into the room and "surprises" his son, who "stavo ritto in mezzo alla stanza tenendo fra le braccia una bella bambola" [was standing erect in the middle of the room holding a beautiful doll in his arms] (202). As a remedy for this unfortunate attachment, the father then urges that he "va'...a rinvigorire le membra esauste" [go... restore his exhausted limbs ("members")] (202). Thus, the tale immediately suggests the power of the manufactured doll to produce the same sexual effects as a real woman, thus making the boundaries between "woman" and "doll" fluid. At the time of the collection's publication, the association of real women and dolls would have been strengthened by the Italian production of Ibsen's *A Doll House*. Translated by Luigi Capuana as *Casa di bambola*, it ran in Milan from February 1891 through November 1892 with none other than Eleonora Duse in the role of Nora.[31] More specifically, both Cristina Mazzoni and Lindsay Myers have recently examined Italian literary uses of the doll. While, as I will show, Treves's use of the doll departs from the models analyzed by Myers and Mazzoni, such as Contessa Lara's *Il romanzo della bambola* [*The Novel of the Doll*] (1896), I would however submit that "Stella" continues to signify the kinds of anxieties that had accrued to literary dolls through earlier and contemporary texts. That is, the associations of Italian literary dolls with maternity, class difference, violence, industrialization, value, and waste—as Myers and Mazzoni show—are elicited in this figure and inform the dynamic at play in Treves's tale.

Lindsay Myers has insightfully argued that in the period of 1870–1896, dolls often appear in Italian children's books as a useful narrative device

by which the reader can be exposed to characters of many different socioeconomic classes. As wealthy girls pass their dolls "down" to poorer
children, the inanimate protagonists preserve a coherent narrative
thread while providing the reader with a lens onto a range of social
realities. Myers sees this strategy as a way to promote interclass "tol-
erance and co-operation" in post-unification Italy (*Making* 35). At the
same time, the abuse these literary dolls typically suffer at the hands of
their young owners makes them an effective way to document and de-
cry the abuse of real children.[32] Noting that the national organizations
for the protection of children had been established in Paris, London, and
eventually Rome in these very same decades, Myers perceptively points
out how dolls dramatized violent realities in a mitigated way, reflecting
and promoting growing concern for the real life victims of abuse and
exploitation.[33] Prince Valoroso's doll, however, never leaves her royal
home, and is treated throughout the fairy tale with the utmost devotion
and tenderness by the boy who adores her. Thus, the doll here functions
differently than do those in the nearly contemporary "memoir fantasy"
novels that Myers explores, but the associations with both class and violence are still at play, as I will show.

An image of the doll "Stella" greets the readers immediately. The fairy
tales opens with an illustration that depicts the Prince standing up and
holding the doll in a defensive and protective posture and with raised
eyebrows in a look of defiance. In the same image, the king has his head
extended toward his son and both palms facing upwards, and thus seems
to be imploring him to give up his companion (as evidenced in the verbal
text that follows). The doll here is dressed in a long gown, hair pulled
back in a bun, with delicate facial features. She is just a bit shorter than
the Prince himself, and thus almost life-size in relation to the 15-year-old
deceased princess. The verbal text tells us that she is made of wood and
that she was endowed with "capelli biondi e due occhi espressivi che
mandavano scintille e si muovevano come se fossero veri" [blond hair
and two expressive eyes that truly sparkled and moved as if they were
real] (202). In defending his desire to marry the doll, Valoroso insists
that she is in fact alive, pointing to her smiling mouth and soft hair as
evidence (203). As Mazzoni and Beretta point out, Italy's earliest doll
factory, Furga, was founded in 1872 by a nobleman from Mantua on his
estate outside of Milan (Mazzoni 251, Beretta 41), and the production
of luxury "*bèbè*" dolls began in Milan in 1890, feeding into a "late-
nineteenth-century doll craze" (Mazzoni 254). The Furga dolls were initially made of papier-mâché bodies and wax heads and then composed
of papier-mâché and wood with ceramic heads (Beretta 42). Thus, in
the period in which Treves wrote her tale, factory-produced dolls would
have already become familiar to her readers. "Stella" is clearly not a
widely accessible play doll, but rather a high-quality, potentially hand-
crafted luxury item. I suggest, then, that the doll reveals and attempts

to remedy certain anxieties about the ways modernization seemed to de-personalize (the emphasis on her "life-like" qualities") and devalue (the emphasis on her preciosity) human relationships. In other words, seen in the context of the kinds of dolls Treves's young female readers are likely to have had on their laps while reading this book, the precious "Stella," referred to as the prince's "tesoro" (both treasure and beloved), works as a kind of nostalgic antidote to certain forms of industrial progress and perhaps creates ideal readers who would be among those with access to the precious dolls mirrored in the tale.[34]

Stella is not the first doll to be treasured in Italian children's books. Tracing its appearances from Straparola (1550–1556) to Ziliotto (1993), Mazzoni unearths the literary doll's intimate relationship to both "treasure" and trash. In these works, the thematic links to feces and corpses reveal that, like other forms of waste, the doll represents "that which the self must expel in order to preserve its identity" (255). Drawing on psychoanalysis and, specifically, trash theory, she argues that "[r]egardless of the actual value of excrement, the process of its exchange is emotionally and socially significant" (252) because through such separation the "self" is constituted as such. Indeed, the entire plot of this fairy tale is driven by the king's attempts to force a separation between the prince and his doll, precisely so that he may become who he is – valorous, as a man and a monarch. In spite of the title, "The Doll of Prince Valorous," the subject, in all senses, is clearly the prince: in fact, the tale might be seen as the process of moving the prince from the geni-tive to the nominative by displacing the doll. While the precious "Stella" never becomes trash, the prince must repudiate her, and she is linked thematically and linguistically to other "abject" objects. As Mazzoni ex-plores the process of "casting off" in the formation of the subject's iden-tity (254), here too the doll comes close to being literally cast off in order to save the prince. As his ship hits a storm, the "useless" weight of the doll and her box are considered as a sacrifice for the safety of the vessel: "già si parlava di gettare in mare ogni carico inutile, e il principe temeva per la sua cassa" [already there was talk of tossing all useless weight into the sea, and the prince feared for his box] (208) (and we should note here the metonymic use of "box" for the doll inside it). This moment in the tale is too premature for the separation, though, as the prince con-tinues to adore the doll as if he were "una debole femminuccia" (a weak little girl] (210). The carrying case is explicitly likened to a tomb: "poi le chiese perdono di averla lasciata chiusa per tanto tempo nella cassa, come in una tomba" [then [the prince] asked her forgiveness for having left her shut up for such a long time in the box, as if in a tomb] (210); and Stella's final depiction, as she is reassociated with her first dead owner, is that of a corpse "la bambola di Fior di Gaggìa, rimase per sempre dimenticata nella cassa di velluto" [Lotus Flower's doll remained, for-gotten forever, in the velvet box] (239, the final sentence of the fairy tale).

The story narrates the adventures that will enable Valoroso to transfer his attachment to a proper female mate in order to become king—both as familial and political patriarch. In this regard, the doll serves a function similar to that of the imaginary "La Talia" in Nuccio's historical novel, that is, as an intermediary (and feminine) figure of attachment that enables the male subject's transfer to a more "correct" object of cathexis. As Italy replaces La Talia in Nuccio's tale, here a living woman (conveniently also named Stella) replaces the eponymous doll. In its function as an attachment—a "queer" attachment, in fact, given its nonhuman status— the doll works much as the pet dog in so many American "boy and his dog" stories for children, as Eric Tribunella has insightfully analyzed. Drawing on a range of texts, particularly Fred Gibson's *Old Yeller* (1956), Tribunella argues that the boy (and sometimes girl)-dog relationship must be understood as an erotic one, much as Valoroso's relationship to "Stella" is depicted in the lines I quotes above. Typically, "the dog-lover represents a transitional figure between parental and romantic attachments" (40), much as the doll mediates between the dead mother and the wife for Valoroso. Just as the dogs in so many of the classic and prized American narratives must be given up for the boys to become heterosexual, mature men, so too Stella and the queer pleasures she provides must be given up. Such narratives of "contrived traumas," Tribunella proposes, function as a "disciplinary device that involves promoting intense affectional attachments and then demanding their sacrifice as a way of (re)forming social subjects that are properly gendered and sexualized" (*Melancolia* 30). While Tribunella has unpacked the uniquely American nuances of the dog stories, in Cordelia's tale, this Italian doll, I suggest, functions fundamentally in a similar fashion as an intermediary attachment that must be relinquished to enable the boy's melancholic maturity. Crucially, the doll is neither destroyed, passed to another owner, nor thrown away as trash. Rather she is lovingly and carefully placed in a box where she is both preserved and "forgotten," the very figuration, indeed, of repression.

The doll that had replaced the sister is ultimately replaced by a living woman, but the perhaps unintentional effect of this metonymic chain of object substitutions is to cast this "real woman" as uncannily doll-like, as the fetish of a fetish.[35] The prince's ability to ascend to his father's place both as adult man and as the kingdom's monarch is effected, then, more through melancholy than though mourning: the doll *remains* both in the velvet box and in the form of the dollish Queen Stella. Early in the story, it had been Valoroso himself who, withdrawing from the world in a way typical of both mourning and melancholy, remains in a kind of velvet box: the narrator tells us that he "passava tutto il giorno chiuso nella stanza di Fior di Gaggìa" [spent all day closed up in Lotus Flower's room] (200) and in a seemingly unnecessary repetition on the very same page, his father expresses concern about what he might be doing "tutto il giorno chiuso nella camera di Fior di Gaggìa" [all day long closed up in Lotus Flower's bedroom] (200). In order not to "sentence [him]self to lie in the Thing's grave" as Kristeva puts it, the prince must undertake the melancholy narrative itinerary that will be mediated through the doll.[36] This object must be killed off yet also kept in order for the boy to emerge from the room that threatens to entomb him. The careful and loving burial of the sister-doll and her replacement by the wife-doll embodies the simultaneous abjection and introjection of the infantile and the feminine in the constitution of the mature male subject.[37]

So far, I have been tracing how Cordelia's nostalgic and politically conservative collection of fairy tales uses strategies like the generic conventions of a royal setting and the use of a talisman, clear, "naturalized" language, and the omission of a frame narrative to deploy a series of tales that seek to serve as an antidote to "progress." This "progress," gendered masculine as was typical and scientifically authorized in the period, included not only more liberal political configurations and economic development but also a destabilization of gender. Thus, the tales seek to reattach gender to biological sex and offer (problematic) images of women as agents of conservation, paradoxically both inspiring the maturation of boys and retaining what is lost in that process. In the final tale, young Belfiore, a poor fisherman, spends seven years learning science and brings back fantastic machines that revolutionize his home island and bedazzle his beloved. The last illustration shows Belfiore at the helm of a kind of speed boat, with his beloved but "confused" Marinella, with her "head spinning," at his side (300) (see Figure 3.2). They race toward the reader with the water behind them, visually bursting forth out of the circular frame and indeed out of the book itself. Next to Marinella sits her beloved pet monkey, an image that further reinforces the association of girls with the species' premodernity and the individual's infancy through its strong evolutionary connotations.[38] The water, which Marinella has claimed several times in the tale to be her "element" (and which is echoed, naturally, in her name), recedes into the background as the boy and his motor boat spirit her into the future. This final illustration of Marinella in the speed boat contrasts sharply with the cover image of Aurora with her book (see Figure 3.1). In the last picture, the faces of boy, girl, and monkey are directed outward toward the reader as the boat roars toward the future, as opposed to the profile view of Aurora's face placidly engrossed in her reading. The motion of the boat is underscored by Marinella's scarf, which flies in the wind, and by the caption that claims that the boat "se n'andò rapido come il pensiero" [moved with the rapidity of thought] (301). The cover image instead exudes a contemplative tranquility, undercut only slightly by the precarious position of the chair, although the strong rock castle wall lends it support and stability. Finally, while Aurora is figured prominently with her whole body in view as she reads, Marinella is obscured behind Belfiore, peeking out from behind his shoulder, which she grasps in an expression of trepidation.[39] Belfiore, we readers are told, has learned about "talking

LA FIGLIA DEL MARE   301

— Il tuo desiderio sarà appagato — le ri-
spose, e si avvicinarono alla riva.

Belfiore fece un fi-   Il battellino se n'andò ra-
                           pido come il pensiero....
schio. Un bel basti-   (Pag. 302).

Figure 3.2 Duilio Cambellotti, from *L'ultima fata* by Virginia Treves [Cordelia].

walls" (perhaps a futuristic image of movie screens, in the years of silent film) as well as machines that are able to move by themselves: through the water, in the air, and over land (299). Such fantastic innovations have been realized not because of magic but because of "man's intelligence" ["per opera dell'intelligenza dell'uomo" (299)]. Just six years after the founding of FIAT in Turin, and just six years before Italy would inaugurate the military use of airplanes in the Libyan War, Treves's final fairy tale registers deeply ambivalent and rigorously gendered account of progress.

Throughout the collection, girls are never narrated as having to relin-quish masculine qualities or as having to change, grow, or learn any-thing at all. Instead, Pervinca, Speranza, Stellina, Marinella, and the others remain always the same. They both inspire the development of their brothers and their suitors and provide a safe home to which their male counterparts can return. Although the fairy tales do all include a culminating moment of marriage and coronation, several of the tales, rather than coming to rest on the "happily ever after" ending we might anticipate, conclude instead with more somber images. In the first tale, the last remaining gift of the last fairy, the unused magical walnut, is safely ensconced in a museum. The adventures of Prince Valoroso begin with the announcement that his mother and sister have both died, and similarly end by telling us that his beloved doll, which had served as fetish of his deceased sister, has now been left behind "forgotten in her velvet box." The last tale, and thus the concluding moment of the collection as a whole, ends not just with the marriage of Marinella and Belfiore and with their coronation as king and queen of Progress Island, but rather with an explanation that after many years of faithful service, Marinella's pet monkey has died and that Marinella has had a memorial erected to honor his fidelity: thus a 300-page volume of seven fairy tales concludes with the image of a stone monument to a dead monkey: "e quando morì, Marinella fece erigere un monumento in riva al mare a rammentare le imprese del scimmiottino" [and when he died, Marinella had a monument built on the seashore to commemorate the deeds of the little monkey] (304).

A museum, a tomb-like box, a commemorative monument: images that bespeak ways of burying but also conserving and protecting the past, all as-sociated with the feminine and the primitive—the monkey that was taken from the island of cannibals, the doll that substituted for the sister, and the nut bequeathed by the last fairy. Indeed, girls function as the creators and curators of these repositories, of these museums and monuments and tombs. Ultimately, just as a fairy tale talisman typically lends its powers to the person who bears it, this book of tales seeks to lend its powers to its characters and readers: as the girls in the book have done, so the girls reading the book (as modeled in Aurora on the cover) *themselves* are called upon to become talismans against the perceived threats of modernity, their powers derived from their quotidian roles as repositories of the stability threatened by the motion of progress. *L'ultima fata* remains as a symptom of the fraught and ambivalent relationship to modernization being played out in books that sought to offer models for Italy's new citizens.[40]

A Shelter for Italy's Children: Carolina Invernizio

Marinella's uneasiness as she is whisked away in the speed boat takes on a more disastrous figuration in Carolina Invernizio's collection of ten short stories from 1915, entitled *Cuori dei bimbi* [*The Hearts of Kids*].[41]

The penultimate story, "Fior di Paradiso" ["Flower of Paradise"], tells the tragic but inspiring tale of young Marina Costanzi. Appropriately named for both her Marian devotion to the Madonna, and her constant unwavering faith and goodness, the 16-year-old girl spends her days happily between the convent school and her dear father's Tuscan villa, having lost her mother before the story begins. Although still a child herself, it is in the performance of the maternal task of protection that Marina is fatally wounded, thus she simultaneously encapsulates within herself the figures of child, mother, and sacrificial victim. One day, Marina, who is called "Flower of Paradise" by her companions, is taking a walk with her nurse and the two children of the estate's gardener. When she sees seven-year-old Pasqualino in the path of an on-coming car, she immediately runs to push him out of the way, taking the brunt of the impact herself.

This sudden eruption of modernity, figured by the speeding automobile, shatters Marina's tranquil, sheltered, and beatified realm. The narrative makes clear that her world functions as a chronotope of the past, associating this space with childhood, as well as with the rituals of Catholicism. In this time-place, too, even Marina's physician, an educated, adult man of science, continues to adhere to the traditional Catholic conception of the body as a temporary home for the soul (211).[42] Invernizio dramatically narrates the sudden, violent penetration of this utopia:

> Proprio in quel momento sbucava da una curva un'automobile lanciata a tutta corsa. Marina vide il pericolo. ... Fu cosa di un attimo. La fanciulla ed il bambino vennero travolti entrambi sotto l'automobile, che non ebbe tempo di scansarli, fra le grida di spavento di quelli che erano nella vettura e gli urli di disperazione di Ortensia. ... Lo *chauffeur* non aveva colpa alcuna dell'accaduto, tanto improvvisa era stata l'irruzione sulla strada del bimbo, seguito tosto dalla generosa fanciulla che si era precipitata dietro a lui per salvarlo. (200–202; italics in orig.)

> [Just at that moment an automobile hurling along at full speed came around a curve. Marina saw the danger. ... It all happened in a flash. The girl and the boy were both crushed under the automobile, which did not have enough time to avoid them, among the screams of fear of those who were in the car and Ortensia's cries of despair. ... The *chauffeur* could in no way be blamed for the event, so sudden had been the boy's appearance on the road, followed immediately by the generous girl who threw herself behind him in order to save him.]

The car that comes unforeseen careening around the curve in the road is marked by foreignness, with the French word "chauffeur" highlighted by italics, and masculinity, as the car carries two adult men. As the vehicle crashes into the group of women and children, the incident is described not only as sudden and inevitable, but also as unaccountable because the blame for it is impossible to assign:[43]

> La stessa Ortensia, benchè disperata, non poteva deporre a suo carico; soltanto disse ai due signori che se non avessero dato ordine di lanciare l'automobile a quella velocità, la disgrazia non sarebbe accaduta. –Avete ragione; – disse il medico – ma io mi recavo da un ammalato gravissimo, che forse a quest'ora è già morto, ed avrei voluto che l'automobile divorasse la via. (202)

> [Ortensia herself, although in despair, could not put down her charge (carrying the girl); all she said to the two men was that if they had not given the order to drive at that speed, the accident would not have happened. "You are right," said the doctor, "but I was on my way to an extremely ill patient, who perhaps by now has already died, and I wanted the automobile to devour the road."]

Pasqualino ran suddenly into the road, but such behavior is typical of a young boy. The chauffeur was at the wheel, but he simply could not have stopped in time no matter how skillful a driver he may have been. The doctor had urged his driver to speed, but only for the noble purpose of saving a seriously ill patient. Various individual characters are proposed and dismissed as the sources of the tragedy—that is, as the human agents of this sudden misadventure—but all are found blameless (just as the first known motorcar fatality in 1896 had been ruled an accidental death). Thus the accident becomes, like the literal meaning of "automobile" (Invernizio uses this word, rather than "macchina" to signify the car) seemingly self-propelled, as inevitable and bewildering as the experience of modernity itself.

Marina, who had already voiced a desire not to know the world but to stay forever in her sanctuaries (199), is in this sense saved by the very accident that kills her: namely, she is saved from the onslaught of modernity by its own quintessential embodiment—the very same image that F.T. Marinetti used in 1909 to herald the "birth" of Futurism.[44] The death brought on by the car, too, protects her from having to grow up and develop and from the looming sexuality already prefigured in her St. Teresa-like ecstasies (196): thus once again, we see the fusion of modernity and maturation here. For the reader, as well as for Pasqualino (who, thanks to Marina, does survive and thus can grow up), she is sacrificed: kept permanently in her maternal/child femininity, reassuringly immobilized in the past to serve as a sanctuary for her present and future readers. The story itself, in this sense, becomes a kind of *asilo* [shelter, refuge], embodying the name given both to the story and to the protagonist: "paradise" in the etymological sense of enclosed garden. The tale metadiegetically realizes Marina's last wish: before dying, she had expressed to her father the desire to have an "asilo" [here in its other sense of "nursery school"] built for the local children.[45]

Invernizio had dramatized a similar fusion of the feminine with a natural, premodern, domestic utopia in her fanciful 1909 fairy tale *I sette capelli d'oro della Fata Gusmara* [*The Seven Golden Hairs of Fairy Gusmara*]. The tale's protagonist, tiny Topolina ["little mouse"] has escaped from the torturous Elefantessa, who used the highly flexible and tiny young girl as a circus act, and has hidden herself in a tree trunk.[46] A young boy named Falco [hawk], who lives in the forest with his father, a woodcutter, discovers her. The tale is notable for the abundance of female characters: the protagonist Topolina, small, good, humble, and constant; Tea, the antagonist and object of Falco's desire, is instead vain, cruel, and rich; the eponymous good fairy, Gusmara, who bestows her favor and protection on Topolina; and the sequence of evil women who reign over the realms through which Falco must pass to earn Gusmara's golden hairs—the princesses and queens who rule the lands of "Caprice," "Wealth," "Vanity," and "Revelry." This plethora of female figures seem to overcompensate for the void left by the woman who is missing: the first page announces matter-of-factly that Falco's mother had died when he was three years old, and his father has been catatonic with grief ever since (3). The two male figures, in fact, live a nearly savage existence, barely surviving as the father has been so incapacitated that the young boy must fend for himself. Topolina's emergence, literally from the earth itself, remedies this loss. She becomes both daughter and mother to the woodcutter and ultimately becomes mother, sister, and wife to Falco. Indeed, one of her first acts in her newly established family is to make clothing for the father and son, thus she reinscribes the common cultural link between the feminine and fabric and maternally leads the men back into civilized life (7).

In spite of the prevalence of female characters, the real protagonist of the tale, in the sense of the character who has a developmental story to be narrated, is in fact Falco. The domestic utopia apparently reestablished by Topolina after the mother's death is destabilized when Falco, upon turning 14, is taken by a desire to explore and to see a "great city" (9). This stirring of dissatisfaction coincides with the appearance of Tea, who diverts his love from Topolina and instigates his heroic quest for Gusmara's hairs as the chivalric act that will win him the rich damsel. Reenacting the home-away-home structure, the tale narrates Falco's process of maturation, while Topolina, ever-steady, serves as his guide and his faithful companion. After succeeding in his quest, thanks to Topolina's wisdom and constancy, Falco encounters Tea, who demands the prize. Topolina offers herself as a sacrifice: she urges her beloved brother/son/companion to cut off her arm so that he may retrieve the enchanted bracelet, which cannot otherwise be removed, and give it to

Tea. Tea is more than willing to see her rival dismembered.[47] At this display of selfish cruelty, Falco is converted, embraces the humble, familiar domesticity embodied by Topolina, and renounces Tea's urbane vanity.

The narrative uses several of the antimodern strategies that we have seen in Cordelia's tales, including proper names that reliably reflect the characters they designate—particularly through recourse to natural imagery—and talismans gifted to the girl by donors (here the woodland creatures: a bird, a marmot, and a boar) so she may protect the boy as he journeys. Invernizio, furthermore, employs imagery that solders traditional and biologically grounded notions of gender: while Topolina travels with the small, enchanted marmot (who transforms into a grandmother figure), Falco instead earns a sword, reinforcing a range of gender binaries including soft/hard, nature/culture, and care/aggression.

In his detailed and insightful analysis of this fairy-tale novel, Spinazzola takes into account its structural, thematic, and linguistic qualities and points to how the tale intervenes in the contemporary class struggles. Topolina domesticates Falco by making him realize that true happiness is not to be found in ambition and upward mobility but in finding contentment with what he already has (167), a socially conservative message to Invernizio's working-class readers. Spinazzola further argues that "[a]gli occhi della scrittrice piemontese, il declino del patriarcato fa sì che il sesso femminile liberi tutte le sue potenzialità: positive e negative" [for Invernizio, the decline of patriarchal structures enabled the female sex to liberate all her potentials: positive and negative] (170). Taking the Madonna—daughter of her son—as the model of the superwoman *par excellence* (171), Invernizio embraces a "bold but circumscribed" feminism that affirms the dignity of women without stepping out of the bounds of her role as angel of the hearth (171), thus mirroring and condoning the views of many of her readers. I would add that the maturation of Falco here and his return to the feminine are offered as a *solution* to melancholy: at the conclusion, he realizes for the first time that "in tutto il mondo non c'era una creatura più contenta di lui" [there was not a child on earth more content than he] (181), whereas he had begun the story with "un sorriso melanconico" [a melancholy smile] (3).

Sugar and Spice and Everything Nice: Arpalice Cuman Pertile

The literary doll makes multiple appearances and plays various symbolic and narrative roles throughout the works of Arpalice Cuman Pertile (1876–1958).[48] An educator and children's writer of both pleasure reading and school texts, Cuman Pertile began writing for children at the dawn of the twentieth century. She penned most notably *Il trionfo dei piccoli* [*The Little Ones' Triumph*] (1915), *Ninetta e Tirintin* [*Ninetta and Tirintin*] (1918), and *Per i bimbi d'Italia: Poesie*

[*For Italy's Kids: Poems*] (1921). Her patriotic values were inflected through Christianity, pacifism, and a dedication to the working classes, and she articulated her pacifist agenda through a gendered lens. Speaking against intervention in 1915, she claimed that Homer and Virgil "affidano alla donna ed agli educatori il compito di preservare i giovani e i popoli dalle fallaci illusioni della guerra" [trust to women and to educators the task of protecting the youth and the people from the false illusions of war] (qtd. in Giolo 6–7).

Her collection of poems (1921, in the fourth edition by 1948) was illustrated by Adelina Ceas-Ramorino and Attilio Mussino, and the front cover sports an array of *commedia dell'arte* characters, including the well-known Harlequin and Colombina.[49] The collaboration of image and title, then, claims a specifically Italian character for the collection through recourse to one of Italy's hallmark cultural traditions. The collection, as Gianni Giolo rightly describes it, "propone ai bambini piccoli quadri di vita domestica: vi emergono le figure del nucleo familiare che comunicano i valori del lavoro, del sacrificio, della scuola, della preghiera e dell'amore" [offers young children depictions of domestic life. The image of the nuclear family emerges and communicates the values of work, sacrifice, school, prayer and love] (13). The following short poem typifies the thematic concerns and formal approach of the collection:

"Il nido e la casa"
Dice contento il piccolo uccellino:
-Ho un nido bello, morbido, carino,
di pagliuzze e di piuma fabbricato,
dalla mamma e dal babbo riscaldato.
Là, co'miei cari, dolci fratellini
Io dormo, gioco e mangio i moscerini. –
Dice contento il piccolo bambino:
-Ho anche il mio nido morbido e carino.
È la casetta, la casetta mia,
la più bella e gentile che ci sia.
Là con la mamma, il babbo, i fratellini
Io dormo, mangio e faccio ai balocchini. (16)

["The nest and the house"
Says contentedly the little baby bird: / "I have a pretty soft and dear nest / made of straw and feathers / mommy and daddy keep it warm. / There, with my sweet little brothers and sisters / I sleep, play, and eat gnats." / Says contentedly the little young boy: "I have a soft and dear nest, too / It's the little house, my little house / the prettiest and nicest that there is. / There with mom, dad, and my brothers and sisters / I sleep, eat, and play with my toys."]

Clearly evoking Pascoli's well-known poetry, which deployed the recurrent image of the nest as a metaphor for the home, Pertile's poem, through both content and structure, creates a forceful mirroring effect. The child echoes the little bird, establishing a parallelism that makes the home a mirror image of the nest, and the child a mirror image of the bird. This echoing effect makes the similarities seem inevitable and obvious. In other words, the poem naturalizes the modern nuclear family, as opposed to the multigenerational rural family, such as that depicted in Emma Perodi's frame narrative, where the Tuscan grandmother lives with more than 20 relatives. Simultaneously, it reinscribes and validates the child-as-animal *topos*: the child himself speaks, apparently constituting himself ("io, mio, mia, io") and thus seeming to affirm that his position within the home, and indeed his position as an animal, is in fact willed and chosen. Furthermore, the young boy (again recurring to a Pascolian theme) is explicitly *content* with his position, secure in the knowledge that his parents and his little house shield his vulnerability, announced by repetition of "piccolo" [little] and the heavy use of diminutives. The illustration that appears on the top of the page, in fact, shows both a nest and a house, though here the home is not actually a "casetta" but rather a sturdy two-story structure with three chimneys, ten windows, and a second-floor balcony visible, thus making clear that this young boy's home is not a ramshackle hut or a sordid urban apartment but rather a comfortable middle-class house. The image of a soft, warm, and protected space, which is articulated by the gentle voice of the young boy, seduces readers into adopting this "natural" perspective of childhood, thus imbuing the collection with all the colonizing potential that Perry Nodelman has articulated.

Within this general view of childhood, Pertile develops the gender dynamics I have been explicating. A pair of poems from the same volume, "La donnetta" ["The little woman"] and "L'ometto" ["The little man"], appears to suggest a parallelism between boys and girls, implying that each one goes through developmental stages that, while inflected differently for each sex, remain structurally homologous. Cuman Pertile had mobilized this kind of gender parallelism and complementarity in several of her previous texts. Indeed, Pertile seems to deploy boy-girl pairings with surprising frequency. I will examine three such manifestation of this gender-pairing theme before returning to the girl-boy poems from the 1921 collection.

Her 1915 *Il trionfo dei piccoli*, which openly announces its inspiration in Edmondo De Amicis's text, not only speaks to and about children who are younger than those for whom *Cuore* was written, but also replaces the male protagonist Enrico with the brother-sister twins Franco and Luisa: "Ecco. Nel *Cuore*, c'è un ragazzo che narra tante cose di sè, dei parenti, degli amici. E qui ci sono due gemelli, ometto e donnina, che parlano di sè, dei fratellini, dei cari compagni di scuola" [Here we are.

In *Cuore*, there is a boy who tells many things about himself, about his relatives, and about his friends. And here, there are two twins, a little man and a little woman, who speak about themselves, about their siblings, and about their dear schoolmates] (4–5). The fictional "editor" of the text, in the role analogous to that of Enrico's father in *Cuore*, is "Aunt Nora." As in *Cuore*, the narrator is the child-protagonist, but here rather than Enrico's single voice the chapters alternate between "Parla Luisa" and "Parla Franco" [Luisa speaks, Franco speaks], and in the place of De Amicis's famous monthly stories, didactic fables and poems are inserted. At first blush, then, Pertile's project—a *Cuore* written by a woman, with a female fictional editor and a female double for the boy protagonist—may appear to offer a feminine and even potentially feminist revision of the classic "Schoolboy's journal." The feminization of *Cuore*, I will argue here, actually achieves very conservative effects.

If certain strains of feminism in early-twentieth-century Italy were perceived as advocating gender equality, then Pertile's text certainly appears initially to seek to buttress this agenda.[50] Early in the book, various characters remark upon the twins' likeness. Luisa's voice tells us that "La mamma dice ch'eravamo proprio uguali, come due fantoccini della stessa fabbrica" [mommy says that we were exactly alike, like two little dolls from the same factory] (10). Later, in the description of the first photograph taken of the siblings, the same language returns to insist on this equality, as the photo portrays the "due bamboccini fasciati, proprio uguali" [two plump little children all bundled up, exactly alike] (19), and the phrase appears yet a third time when the grandfather meets the children for the first time three months later: "disse con gioia - Sono proprio uguali!" [he said joyfully, 'They are exactly alike!'] (55). Adelina Ceas-Ramorino's graceful and delicate cover image of the book visually underscores the resemblance so vigorously asserted by the verbal text.[51] In a circular frame, two very young children, both charmingly chubby, are shown in profile as they stand face-to-face, leaning slightly forward toward each other and meeting in a gentle kiss. Both figures have their eyes closed and elbows bent, sporting very similar short A-line frocks whose hems reach exactly the same length. The distinctions between the two are limited: the girl's hair is longer, her collar appears laced, and she has a bow at her lower back. Both figures are drawn in fine black outline with no interior coloring except the red lips. They are completely surrounded within the circular frame by a green field populated by flowers, butterflies, and lambs. The strong mirroring effect created by their similarity and position (if one were to fold the circle at the vertical diameter, the two figures would exactly overlap) confirms the verbal text's insistence on both "likeness" and "equality" [*ugualanza*] of twins. The surrounding field of green with its floral and animal imagery further naturalizes this early, undifferentiated state, setting it in a pristine and Edenic *locus amoenus*. Finally, the viewer's eye is drawn to the bright red lips on the vertical diameter, almost at the circle's center and the point of contact between the two figures. The eroticism conjured by the passionate bright red is almost immediately dispelled by all the signs of innocence that surround it (little lambs, chubby legs), but not before fixing our attention on the contact itself: the boy and girl do not just co-exist in a utopian state of natural equality, but are crucially *connected*. This core theme of connection will be taken up in *Ninetta e Tirintin* by the motif of the single thread of yarn that links the dolls and must not be broken at any cost.

The two ways in which Pertile here revises *Cuore*, namely adding a girl twin and writing for younger readers, are causally linked. The equivalency of the twins in spite of their gender difference obtains only because the book is set earlier in the characters' lifespan. The text, we learn, was created specifically to appease the desire of the younger twins (age six at the story's genesis) who wanted to have a book of their own like *Cuore* but appropriate for their younger age. The descriptions of the twins' older siblings, Mario and Nerina, already presage the differentiation that will develop over time. Mario, for example, is described early in the story as the "protector" of the baby twins, and specifically of Luisa, as he valiantly defends her from the uncle who pretends to want to steal her away. Similarly, when the grandfather visits he brings gifts to all four children. To both Franco and Luisa, he gives Pulcinella puppets: the twins who are alike—and who were at their birth compared to "dolls" by their mother—each appropriately gets the same doll gift. Mario and Nerina, however, can no longer be treated with such equality: he receives a self-playing organ, and she gets a "marvelous" doll in a silver bed (57). In other words, after a few years, Mario has grown out of his "doll" state, while Nerina remains in hers. In the text that celebrates all the "triumphs" of the "little ones"—their first words, first photographs, first teeth, first steps, and so forth—the sexual symmetry of brother and sister remains safely ensconced in the utopian period of early childhood. The very developmental steps forward that constitute the children's celebrated "triumphs" are precisely the ones that will lead them out of their utopian sameness. Indeed, the last pages of *Trionfo* celebrate the "miracle" of school: "E la scuola compì proprio il miracolo! La bambina imparò a leggere, a scrivere, a lavorare, a voler tanto bene alla sua mamma e a tutti, si corresse dei suoi capricci" [And the school truly did accomplish miracles! The girl learned to read, to write, to work, to truly love her mom and everyone, and she corrected her caprices] (237). Since we know that Mario and Nerina are reading *Cuore*, we can presume that the twins, too, will march out of this infantile space of equality and into De Amicis's classroom, subjected to and by its rigid gender differentiations.

The utopian period of the boy-girl connection will, however, reemerge, as promised by one of the tales inserted in the text. In the story of Munini the kitten, the young readers learn that after a period of mischievousness, little Munini has become "un giovanotto serio e garbato" [a serious and well-mannered young man] thanks to "i miracoli dell'educazione" [the miracles of education] (44). The matured Munini soon meets and falls in love with "una gattina bianca che somigliava tutta alla sua mamma" [a little white girl cat that looked just like his mom] (44). They marry, and their image appears at the culmination of the tale (45). Here, Ceas-Ramorino's illustration of the cat Munini and his new cat-wife visually echoes the cover image of Franco and Luisa. This male-female pair, too, are depicted in a circular frame and surrounded by flowers. They too face each other and appear to the viewer mostly in profile, positioned centrally with the vertical diameter running exactly between them. The parallelisms between the two images suggest that the latter carries through and reincarnates the former: the married couple reestablishes the natural male-female pairing of the young brother and sister.[52] The strategy clearly promotes a heterosexual and pro-marriage paradigm, where the chaste kiss between the siblings can now be transformed to fulfill its reproductive role (as suggested, too, by the various uses of dolls in the text that prepare girls for their mothering function).[53] The pairing of male and female as husband and wife seems to find its validating precursor in the sexually "innocent" pairing of brothers and sisters and is further naturalized by its displacement onto the animal world. In this way, Pertile does not replace, challenge, or "update" De Amicis so much as she prepares her readers for him. She offers the vision of a momentary infantile *ugualanza* between the sexes, but to the effect of naturalizing the itinerary in which the paths of the boys and girls will inevitably bifurcate, in order for their fundamental connection to reemerge in a different key in marriage.

The vision of the male-female pair as a harmoniously balanced difference rather than as a mirrored identity emerges forcefully in Pertile's most esteemed tale, the 1918 novel *Ninetta e Tirintin*. The author takes up and literalizes the simile she used in *Trionfo*: here, the two protagonists actually *are* two dolls. The maneuver, again recalling Myers' analysis, allows Ninetta and Tirintin to go where real children cannot and to pass through multiple hands, providing the reader with multiple perspectives. Attilio Mussino's cover image from the second edition (1923) visually underscores this aspect of the verbal text. It shows the two dolls connected by a common thread of yarn and standing side by side in perfect mirror symmetry, with the girl-doll's skirt as the only difference between them. Pertile's texts vigorously underscore the mutually fulfilling roles that the different sexes play for each other, as I will indicate. The notion of "balance" is visually enacted on Mussino's cover for the third edition: the yarn dolls, literally hanging by a thread, provide stabilizing counter weights to each other.

Whereas Pertile conjures the model of De Amicis in the preface to *Trionfo*, in *Ninetta e Tirintin*, she evokes the figure of Collodi as her initiating gesture: "Una volta babbo Geppetto fabbricò Pinocchio e il burattino se n'andò allegro per il mondo" [Once upon a time daddy Geppetto made Pinocchio the puppet, and he went out happily into the world] (9). While Geppetto at least had some strong wood, the poor mother of Pertile's story, we learn, has only some threads of wool from which to fashion a tiny doll for her daughter, Rita. Just as Franco and Luisa had bifurcated the role of *Cuore's* Enrico, so here Pinocchio's role is split into the girl-boy pair Ninetta and Tirintin (and so too, apparently, Pertile herself sought to balance out, if not replace, both De Amicis and Collodi). The mother fashions Ninetta first, but the priority of the girl only becomes an occasion to underscore her deficiencies (too tender, all sentiment, given to crying) and thus her need for the male companion to balance and complete her: "la donnina troppo tenera, tutta sentimento; l'omino invece fiero e ragionatore: insieme staranno bene, soli no!" [the little woman was too tender, all sentiment; the little man, instead, proud and rational: together they will get on well; alone, they will not] (10–11). Such mutual dependence is the aggressively repeated and overt message of the book. It is figured in the image of the seesaw, and rendered in plot and characterization: Ninetta is too hot after she is left outside under the sun, Tirintin is too cold after he suffers from a scorpion's pincers; she is too "sensitive," he too "serious" for either possibly to manage in the world without the other. The vigorously asserted complementarity of the dolls based on their natural sexual difference is the lesson that is repeatedly reinforced both to the dolls themselves and to the readers through a series of adventures, as, too, is the urgent mandate never to sever the thread that unites them.

While the two dolls experience a series of adventures that reinforce this moral, their itinerary follows the home-away-home paradigm that I have explored in the previous chapter. Here, this plot structure takes on a spe-cifically gendered manifestation that links, not surprisingly, home with the feminine and away with the masculine. The dolls begin their "lives" with Rita, the daughter of the woman who sewed them. Eventually, Rita sends them as a gift to her brother, Gianni, who is recovering from war wounds in a hospital. Once returned to action, Gianni lends the dolls as a "good luck charms" to various (male) companions, enabling Ninetta and Tirintin to fly in an airplane, travel in a submarine, and undertake other dramatic adventures. Finally, when the war concludes and brings a glorious victory to Italy, the dolls return to Rita. Back at home, they are treated to a beautiful allegorical fairy tale narrated by the mother and advocating world peace. The tale uses the same conceit that had hitherto been limited to the personal but now seeks to extend to the political: "tutti i paesi del mondo sono legati da tanti fili" [all the countries of the world are united by so many threads] (119).

The narrative maps a set of correlated concepts onto this feminine/ home (Rita and the mother)—masculine/away (Gianni and the soldiers)—feminine/home trajectory. These correlated concepts include but also go beyond the private sphere/public sphere dichotomy vigorously advocated by much political and scientific rhetoric of the period. The novel overtly links the feminine/home space both to nature and to the fairy tale genre. While the dolls are in Rita's care, they wander through the garden and encounter bugs, butterflies, snakes, reeds, pools of water, mice, and other elements of the natural world. Rita in fact fashions them a bed out of flower petals. In addition, Rita and her mother narrate fairy tales to the twins, prompting the reasonable Tirintin to wonder if such tales are "true" (34).[54] In these opening chapters, other than the inference that we are in a post-Pinocchio world, no historically specific time or geographically specific place can be gleaned from the text to situate the narrative. Instead, the novel, like the fairy tales embedded in it, seems to take place in a timeless realm, and in fact the dolls, having heard Rita's fairy tales, interpret the actual animals they encounter as goblins and fairies. For example, one creature must explain to Ninetta "Non sono la fata dalle ali d'oro, no: mi chamo 'io' e sono una farfalla" [I am not the fairy of the golden wings, no. My name is "I" and I'm a butterfly] (60). Here, even the butterfly's name "io" bespeaks a kind of self-enclosed time-space ("I call myself I") detached from historical contingency. Gianni's appearance triggers the intrusion of history into this "natural" fairy-tale world. When the dolls are carried by Rita's mother on the train to the military hospital and meet Gianni, the reader is finally given information that grounds the story. We learn that the family's last name is "Pellegrini" (81) and that the Spanish flu is afflicting the soldiers (86). Trieste, a "magnificent city," is named (102), and the dolls hear Garibaldi's hymn being sung (100). Technological progress in the form of trains, planes, and submarines enable the dolls to experience new perspectives, and concrete geographical differences are signaled by a southern soldier's use of his local dialect.[55]

The return home is highlighted by mother's narration of an allegorical fairy tale, which features "Ninetta" and "Tirintin" as the heroic protagonists who successfully tie together the golden thread and thus open the hope for permanent world peace. The conclusion, then, seeks on a narrative level to fuse the feminine timeless fairy tale and the masculine historical novel, mobilizing "feminine" ideals to launch a political intervention through this children's book. Having relegated the feminine to the immobilized world of timeless nature, however, the book itself reveals the limits of its utopian project: Tirintin poignantly remarks, in regard to the recently concluded Great War, "speriamo che sia l'ultima" [let us hope that this may be the last one] (102), while Ninetta, also using the nebulous subjunctive mood, exclaims "Io vorrei che questa bella fiaba fosse vera!" [I wish this beautiful fairy tale were true] (120).

Returning now to the 1921 poetry collection, and through a closer examination of the "Little woman" and "Little man" poems, I suggest that the gendering at play works on a level that actually severs complementarity and balance:

"La donnetta"
Il prim'anno nelle fasce:
il secondo cosa nasce?
La piccina ha la gonnella
e contenta trotterella.
Poi nel terzo ride e parla,
e nel quarto ciarla ciarla ...
È nel quinto già mammina
d'una bella bambolina.
A sei anni è una donnetta
prende i libri, la calzetta,
ed a scuola se ne va:
tante cose imparerà! (28, ellipsis in org.)

[The first year in her swaddling clothes: / the second, what is born? / The little girl has a little skirt / and toddles along contentedly. / Then in the third she laughs and talks, / and in the fourth she prattles away... / In the fifth year she is already the little mommy / of a pretty little doll. / At six years old she is a young lady / the little squirt takes her books / and off to school she goes: / so many things she will learn!]

"L'ometto"
Il primo anno balbettava,
il secondo camminava,
poi nel terzo saltellava,
le scarpette consumava.
A quattr'anni con gli amici
trascorreva i dì felici.
Era a cinque un birichino,
ma il sest'anno fu un omino:
prese i libri, e a scuola andò,
buono e bravo diventò. (29)

[The first year he was stammering, / the second he was walking, / then in the third he was hopping along, / wearing out his little shoes. / At four years old, with his friends, / he was spending happy days. / At five he used to be a little rascal, / but at six he was a young man: / He took his books, and went to school, / he became good and capable.]

In each case, the poem acts as a chronicle, marking the child's yearly growth verse by verse. The lack of proper names that might individualize the subjects, as well as the use of the definite article ("the" rather than "a") suggest that the poems offer a universal model for boys and girls as they mature along a path that leads from the home to school. Both poems deploy a heavy use of diminutive suffixes in the titles and throughout (-*etto*, -*ino*, -*ella*), forcefully generating an effect of endearing smallness. Both compositions employ the *ottonario piano* (eight-syllable line with accent on the penultimate syllable of the last word of the verses) and the *rima baciata* ("kissed rhyme" or couplet). Thus, the two compositions appear strictly parallel in meter, rhyme scheme, lexicon, and theme.

The fact that Pertile composed two poems rather than one (hypothetically, "The little person") immediately announces that assumed essential differences would make such a single model "child" inappropriate or impossible. The specific content of each reveals the stereotypical gender differences that each poem repeats and celebrates. The girl's poem depicts mostly verbal activity (*ridere, parlare, ciarlare*; laughing, talking, chatting) in contrast with the boy's physical activity (*camminare, saltellare, consumare*; walking, hopping, wearing out), thus reinscribing the Italian proverb that "le parole son femmine e i fatti sono maschi" [words are feminine, deeds are masculine]. Furthermore, the boy's freedom of movement contrasts with the clothing that binds the girl's body, from the *fasce* [swaddling bands] to the *gonnella* [little skirt]. Even the term *calzetta*, denoting the girl herself, literally means a small sock. Finally, the boy moves in the public sphere with his friends, while the girl remains within the familial and domestic realm, becoming already at five years old a "little mother" to her "little doll."[56] The poems emphasize the boy's vigorous motion while the girl, wrapped up in her skirts and mirrored in her own doll, already seems trapped in a repetitive cycle of reproduction. Thus, the content begins to imply that only the boy matures and develops. Indeed, the concluding lines tell us that the boy "becomes" (actively developing and transforming), while the girl "learns" (receiving information).

Beyond the content, however, the most powerful (yet subtle) way in which the poems convey the difference between masculine progress and feminine immobility is through the verbal forms. I have already noted the difference in the semantic value of the verbs: those related to the girl denoting linguistic activity and the boy's showing physical action. It is, however, the verb *tenses* that register the most significant gender differences. In "The little woman," there is no verb at all in the first verse. The very existence of the girl is simply implied by the elliptically absent verb "is" among the nouns and adjectives that describe the infant wrapped up in her swaddling clothes: linguistically her *essere* [being] disappears much as she herself does, swallowed up in her fabric bundle (and much as the illustration does not show us her face). Once she emerges from that bundle, all the verbs in the verses that follow, regardless of meaning, are in the present indicative: *nasce, ha, trotterella, ride, parla, ciarla, è, prende, va.* By contrast, the boy's story is narrated through verbs in the imperfect and the remote past: narrative tenses used to recount historical actions. We read about the things he used to do or did habitually (imperfect) or things that he accomplished within a delimited time frame or only once (remote past).[57] The boy's poem, then, is actually a story: he has experienced a childhood and has become a man over time and within history. The girl, however, is conjured in a permanent and unchanging present. Always a child and "already" a mother, her roles as *piccina/mammina/donnetta* [little girl, little mommy, little lady] exist simultaneously in a static and eternal moment.[58]

Only one verb, the last one, is in the future tense: she will learn. What exactly she will learn, however, remains vague and undefined: "so many things." This future tense verb seems to catapult the female child out of the eternal present of the domestic space into the historical realm of the public sphere, represented by the school and the books. Pertile in fact dedicated her career as both teacher and author of school books to promote scholastic instruction for girls, as well as for the working class. Already in 1898, she was teaching Italian to military daughters in Turin.[59] However, the vagueness of the phrase *tante cose*, and the circularity of the *piccina-bambolina-mammina* [little girl-little doll-little mommy] cycle that already makes the girl perfectly "content" suggests that what "she will learn" may already be modeled by the poem itself and by the book in which she (and we) reads it. The boy has instead become *buono* [morally good] and *bravo* [capable, competent]: his developmental itinerary, carried by the verbs, is narrated through time as a historical march into maturity.

Whether in texts that bemoaned the ills of progress, in those that promoted modernization, or in those that critiqued particular effects of modernity, the imaginative work of making Italians in the post-unification period was predicated on an image of the girl as essentially (and paradoxically) immobilized yet mobilizing. While boys were offered developmental models that wrote their personal maturation onto Italy's modernization, girls instead remained embedded in the past, both as individuals and as ciphers of national development.

Notes

1   On the economic connotations of the home as a feminine space, see Lucia Re on post-unification gender politics in light of the exigencies of modernization: "Essentially an agrarian and mercantile society until the 1880s, Italy lacked the resources generated elsewhere in Europe by industrial capitalism and the exploitation of colonies. In the complex network of ideological apparatuses through which the Italian moderate leadership gradually sought to consolidate its hegemony and to improve the state's economy, the exploitation of women and the idea of 'the home' as a productive space thus took on particular relevance" (163). Katherine Mitchell has analyzed the nuances

of gendered space as represented in the very popular "domestic fictions" of the late nineteenth century in Italy. Drawing on fictional works by Matilde Serao, Neera, and La Marchesa Colombi, as well as on conduct manuals of the period, Mitchell demonstrates how, particularly for middle-class families, men and women were expected to behave differently both in private and in public spaces. She examines domestic spaces such as the kitchen, the window, and the *salotto*, as well as public spaces such as the piazza and the street (59–93). Looking specifically at an 1890 novel by Neera, but drawing generally on a wide range of both fictional and nonfictional texts, Mitchell argues that "[t]he home is indeed presented as a metaphor for motherhood, and it is a place where wives are expected to provide their husbands and children with protection, shelter, and stability" (65).

2 For a compelling and richly documented account of how children's literature in the immediate post-unification decades (1860–1890) constructed the ideal "literary" girl, see Mencarani, esp. 164–220. A wide range of the most popular texts of that period depict the feminine sphere as limited to the family (165). The "woman"—whether daughter, sister, wife, or mother—conforms to very fixed stereotypes (165), and such depictions often result in characters who are stiff and lifeless. Girls must often "dimenticare di essere bambine" [forget that they are children] (183), so overburdened are they with the demand of being self-abnegating future mothers.

3 The book was first published in 55 installments between 1907 and 1908 in *Il giornalino della Domenica* [*The Little Sunday Paper*] and, with some modifications, as a volume in 1912 by Bemporad (Florence). It was in its 87th reprinting by 1967. The Feltrinelli edition from which I cite reproduces the text of the original journal series, with the volume's changes in the notes.

4 In her *Pinocchio Effect*, Stewart-Steinberg summarizes Asor Rosa's analysis of Collodi's *Le avventure di Pinocchio*. Collodi, he claims, "is able to recuperate popular inventive energies in such a way as to articulate and map them in the form of a double passage: on the one hand, the passage from popular traditions to the ideology of the dominant classes, and on the other hand, from the naïve and primitive stage of infancy to the relative maturity of adolescence. Modernization and growing up become homologous processes" (58). Stewart-Steinberg questions this neat trajectory posited by Asor Rosa's reading, arguing instead that Collodi's novel actually *resists* any sort of passage, progression, or development. Rather, the narrative, like a perpetual motion machine, enacts a series of repetitions until it just stops (as opposed to concluding). She claims that "[t]his influencing machine...creates its own meanings and pleasures that can never be completely anchored to the symbolic order in ways that would make stable meanings possible" (61). I would argue that Vamba's Gianni reincarnates this particular aspect of Collodi's masterpiece: he does not undertake a developmental passage but rather enacts episodic repetitions.

5 See Chapter 1 for a more detailed discussion of this book specifically in regard to its use of heroism generally and Garibaldi specifically, and Chapter 2 for its use of mapping.

6 Antonio Faeti underscores how, in *Cuore*, the academic calendar replaces the liturgical year, with commemorations of Cavour, Mazzini, Garibaldi, and Victor Emmanuel in the place of saints' feast days. This "libro unificante e assoluto" [unifying and absolute book] offers an itinerary for the protagonist that is "più laico che religioso" [more secular than religious] ("Il crepuscolo" xxv–xxvii). This strategy, I suggest, not only performs an effective secularizing mission, positing the public school rather than the

Church as the instrument of subject formation, but also promotes the progress and development implicit in the academic calendar (as each child learns and moves forward from grade to grade) over the cyclical nature of the liturgical year, with its unchanging rituals. *Cuore*, in other words, deploys the diary structure to advocate a temporality of maturity and modernization.

7 In this regard, see especially Zipes' reading of Pinocchio ("Carlo Collodi's *Pinocchio* as Tragic-Comic Fairy Tale"). Zipes asserts that one aspect of this complex novel is its celebration of "the successful rise of a ne'er-do-well" (144). Boero and De Luca point out that Emma Perodi advocates a "far da sè" optimism in her 1892 children's book *Cuore del popolo* (74). Also indicative of this ideology is the success of Michele Lessona's *Volere è potere* [*Where There Is a Will There Is a Way*] (1869), modeled on Samuel Smile's *Self-help* (1859, Italian translation 1865) which sold 20,000 copies between 1869 and 1883 (Pancaldi 158. See also Myers, *Making* 59–61). Lessona participated in the Turin conference on wine, where he would have met Lombroso and De Amicis (see my Introduction). See also Mencarini, who examines how scores of children's books from 1860 through 1890 vigorously promoted hard work and industriousness. At the same time, she rightly points out, these books profited from Catholicism's teachings on suffering, patience, and the sin of greed to serve the labor needs of a still proto-industrial capitalist economy and to reign in the possibilities of potentially destabilizing worker agitation (375–76).

8 Roberto Freak Antoni asserts, "[i] suoi contenuti, infatti, esprimono posizioni/intuizioni decisamente, radicalmente, lucidamente contro il conformismo sociale (le ipocrisie degli adulti piccolo borghesi)" [its content, in fact, decisively, radically, and lucidly expresses positions and intuitions against social conformism (the hypocrisy of petite-bourgeoisie adults)] (xi). Antonio Faeti has observed how Vamba effectively adopts the child's point of view to give voice to those who are typically denied one. In *Gian Burrasca*, this point of view opens the possibility of poltical critique: "Gian Burrasca è un vivente e futuribile progetto politico rivolto, dal suo autore, simbolicamente a un paese in cui Vamba vuole che i giovani spazzino via un'eredità vecchia e penosa" [Gian Burrasca is a living and future-oriented political project. Vamba symbolically aims his character at a nation in the hope that the youth of this nation might clear away its old and pitiful legacy] (*Letteratura* 161).

9 And a failure to do so, it should be noted, elicits a violent reaction.

10 For information on these journals and their directors, see Boero and De Luca 29, 357, Nacci 12, and the *Letteratura dimenticata* [*Forgotten Literature*] website: http://www.letteraturadimenticata.it/index.html. On Baccini, Lombroso, Mancini, Invernizio, and Vivanti, see Panizzi and Wood 282–337. Restieaux Hawkes offers summary sketches of many of these authors in Chapter Five of her study, devoted to "Women Writers of Children's Books" (121–44). More recent scholarly biographies and other information in English about several of these authors are available at the University of Chicago's *Italian Women Writers* website: http://www.lib.uchicago.edu/efts/IWW/

11 See Lucia Re for details on how certain policies strove to direct what were considered feminine qualities toward appropriate pedagogical aims: "The new Italy, under the leadership of one of the most influential of its moderate intellectuals, Francesco De Sanctis ...dealt with the problem of women's education by creating effectively a two-tiered system. Basic literacy was culturally acceptable and even desirable for women. ... the few women who were able to continue their studies were channeled toward schools designed just

for them—the so-called 'normal schools' and institutes for the training of nursery and elementary-school teachers....True to their name, these schools for women were supposed to normalize and discipline women's instinctive and emotional nature by containing any tendency toward the unruly or the passionate and nurturing a healthy desire for the maternal and for a mothering kind of pedagogy" (160).

12 Rembadi-Mongiardini takes a similar approach to teaching marine biology in her *Il segreto di Pinocchio* (1894) [*Pinocchio's Secret*]. Here, the Dolphin magically empowers the puppet to breath under water so he may see the many wonders of the sea firsthand: "quello che vedrai sotto il mare, te lo assicuro, non è opera di nessuna magia ... esistono realmente in natura" [what you will see under the water, I assure you, is not the work of any kind of magic ... they really exisit in nature] (40). Pinocchio's ignorance, like Maria's, becomes a prompt both to comically enliven and to repeat the science lessons meant to override superstition. When the puppet tries to recall the name of a shell, for example, he reconstructs the term phonetically as "Tre dadi vanno alla pesca" [literally, "three dice go fishing"], to be corrected with the proper "Tridacna gigantesca" (75).

13 See later in this chapter my discussion of Pertile's ellipsis (in the form of the missing but implied verb "to be") in her poem "La donnetta." Also, in this regard, see Barbara Spackman's essay on Sibilla Aleramo's *Una donna* [*A Woman*], where she analyses Aleramo's frequent use of ellipses throughout as a strategy of rendering the clichéd discourse of maternity, and of disclosing that discourse as cliché. For Aleramo, and I suggest for Baccini, these textual blanks ("...") become abysses absorbing women's speech, but also sites that make that silencing visible.

14 "hanno cura di farsi circondare da un cerchio di schiavi neri" [they take care to surround themselves with a circle of black slaves] (52).

15 Virginia's husband, Giuseppe Treves, was the brother of Emilio Treves, who founded the Milanese press that bore the family name. This was the same house that had published De Amicis's *Cuore*. In many ways, Treves's *Piccoli eroi* is deeply indebted to that model text, as it imitates De Amicis's strategy of inserting short tales of young heroes within the novel and rehearses many of his themes and lessons. See Chapter 1 for a discussion of this novel.

16 Cambellotti was born in Rome in 1876 and was known for his Art Nouveau work in drawing as well as stained glass and lamps. In addition to Treves's collection, he illustrated the Italian edition of *Le mille e una notte* [*The Thousand and One Nights*] issued in the Biblioteca dei ragazzi series by the Milanese Istituto editoriale italiano (volumes XIII and XIV) in 1913. Cambellotti also created the general design used for this series. See Faeti, *Guardare* 2011, 230–32.

17 See Kidd 3–4.

18 As I quoted in the first chapter, children's literature scholars Pino Boero and Carmine DeLuca rightly note that "Cordelia teme l'interclassismo, prova paura all'idea della perdita di privilegi e potere da parte della sua classe di appartenenza, perciò mette in opera tutte le possibili strategie per 'blindare' commozioni e pietà all'interno di gerarchie ben definite" [Cordelia fears the mixing of classes, and is afraid of the idea that her own class may lose its privileges and power. Thus, she deploys every possible strategy to mobilize sympathy and compassion for the established hierarchies] (73).

19 I thank my colleague Sarah Salter for this phrasing.

20 Guido Gozzano in fact entitles one of his tales "I tre talismani" ["The Three Talismans"]. In his version, the agents are a worn-out purse, a wrinkled tablecloth, and a cape, each with magical powers.

21 Canepa examines how the progression and imagery of the frame tale work to reflect on the process of storytelling itself and to announce Basile's innovative literary project: from the opening proverb that warns against apish imitation, to the fountains that suggest sources of creativity, to the hag narrators whose epithets parody the contemporary academies, to the "game of games" that echoes the "tale of tales" itself. Ultimately, the frame advocates "the necessity of reading social or ideological content into what might seem to be even the most frivolous or ludic of pastimes" (92).

22 Vamba refers to his narratees as "piccoli e amati miei persecutori" [little beloved persecutors of mine] and describes them as demanding a sequel to *Ciondolino* (his novel of 1896). "Vamba" tries to convince them to be content with his translations of the French tales. The staging of the scene of reading works to ingratiate the readers by bringing them into the text and giving them a voice.

23 *Novelle*, published in five volumes in Rome as part of Perino's *Biblioteca fantastica* series, includes 45 tales narrated by the Marcucci family grandmother, Regina (whose name means "queen" and who is the eldest of a 26-member clan). The frame narrative is set on a contemporary small Tuscan farm, while the tales themselves take place in medieval Casentino (Tuscany). Several of the tales make reference to dantesque characters and places. In "Il crepuscolo dell'orco pedagogico" ["The Twilight of the Educational Ogre"], Antonio Faeti argues that Perodi's collection combines elements of the *lunario* (Farmers' almanac) and the *abbecedario* (literacy instruction text). He suggests that the frame narrative seeks to rein in the subversive, popular forces at play in the tales. Often, the discussion that follows or precedes the tales elucidates lessons applicable to contemporary life from the story and also dismisses or discounts the story's magical, demonic (and thus potentially threatening) elements. The relationship between modern frame and premodern tales becomes, in other words, a kind of power struggle. Advertisements for Perodi's text from the back pages of Carolina Invernizio's children's books of 1912 and 1915 indicate that book marketers, at least, awarded the victory to the domesticating frame. Noting that the author has spun a little domestic novel around the fantastic tales ("ha intrecciato alle sue novelle una specie di romanzetto per la gioventù, la storia della famiglia della Regina"), the advertisement highlights especially the "purity" of the dear and beautiful Tuscan language spoken by the good old woman ("dalla bocca della buona vecchietta toscana escono le frasi della nostra bella lingua parlata, nella loro purezza che tanto ci è cara"). Describing this "pure" language as "ours" and "dear to us" both nationalizes this dialect and implies that other dialects are contaminants. Finally, we learn that the "sweet voice" of this good old lady "condanna il vizio e vanta le virtù" [condemns vice and extols virtue] in her narration of the tales. In short, the summary offered in the advertisement gives a reading of the text in which virtue unambiguously triumphs over vice; pure, sweet Tuscan silences contaminating voices; and the modern domestic frame novel contains the fantastic tales "dei vecchi tempi" [of olden times].

24 Gina Miele points out that the definitive 1889 version of *C'era una volta* was more "tuscanized" than the 1882 edition (307), but also that Capuana's use of free indirect discourse allowed for the inclusion of "Sicilian idioms and terminology" (309).

25 Recall here the statistics on female literacy in the unified Italy discussed in the Introduction.

26 In his *Letteratura per l'infanzia*, Faeti argues that many modern appropriations of the fairy tale tradition are impoverished narratives that merely string

together bits and pieces of the fairy tale heritage. Writers such as Invernizio, Prosperi, and Palau, he asserts, seem to have drawn from the storehouse of Propp's functions only to create horizontal sequences of episodes—formulaic stories emptied out of the depth, richness, and "thickness" of the popular tales (157–58). My earlier discussion of Prosperi serves, I think, to illustrate Faeti's point. The spatial metaphors Faeti uses to distinguish the popular tradition, which he imagines as vertical "thickness" [spessore], from modern retellings, described as horizontal thinness [orizzontalmente in sequenze], seeks visually to represent the differences between the rich liberating potential of the folk tradition and the shallow didacticism of the modern versions. Faeti's formulation, I think, might be usefully applied to Treves as a way to see how her linguistic "flatness" (in which all meaning is meant to appear clearly on the surface) aims to evacuate the potentially subversive "depths" from the genre she rewrites.

27 In the final tale of Treves's collection, the protagonist Marinella is overwhelmed by the technological wonders brought to her island by her beloved: "Marinella era confusa, le girava il capo vedendo queste novità" [Marinella was confused, her head spun upon seeing all these novelties] (300).

28 In her study of Lombroso, Nancy Harrowitz has asserted that "[j]ust as women were emerging as a force to be reckoned with, the shifting parameters of gender suggesting that much of what constituted 'femininity' was in fact socially determined, 'science' began an all-out campaign to ground all difference firmly in biology. Its goal was to demonstrate the genetic inferiority of 'real' women and the 'deviant' character of so-called masculine women" (165). The influence of Lombroso's ideas reached beyond the scientific community. One explicit example is a short story collection from 1899 prefaced by Sofia Bisi Albini, a major children's writer of the period and school inspector in Milan (Boero and De Luca 72–73). Author Mara Antelling creates a narrator who looks into the face of a Sicilian and immediately perceives his brutish and bestial nature. Learning he has been convicted of premeditated murder, the narrator reflects on the "new humanitarian theories" of "our criminologists" that have replaced biblical notions of justice: "così che i nostri criminalisti ne trassero da essi nuove teorie umanitari e con queste annullarono il biblico: 'Chi di spade ferisce di spade perisce'" [so our criminologists have drawn from them (i.e., the terrifying eyes of murderers) new humanitarian theories and with these have annulled the biblical "he who lives by the sword dies by the sword"] (10).

29 Bettelheim suggests that the youngest child in fairy tales is often the "simpleton" of the family and thus serves as the figure with whom the child reader identifies (102–11).

30 The didactic nature of the stories is announced, too, through the suggestion that the talisman can serve as a kind of magic lantern: "vedeva pure passare come figure d'una lantern magica le più belle visioni" [he even saw the most beautiful visions going by as if they were figures from a magic lantern] (54). The magic lantern had for almost two decades been nearly ubiquitous in education, as John Welle points out in his analysis of Carlo Collodi's 1890 *La laterna magica di Giannettino* (175).

31 National Library of Norway. As feminist scholars have noted, Capuana asked Ibsen permission to revise the ending, essentially in order to keep Nora more doll-like (Kroha 172). This is the same Luigi Capuana who authored the fairy tale collections and the novel *Scurpiddu* that I have discussed.

32 In this regard, see also Lino Ferriani's impassioned calls for reform as summarized in Chapter 1.

33 Robin Bernstein has examined the collaboration of children's books, dolls, and readers in nineteenth-century America, examining in particular how "play" included white children burning, hanging, and performing other violence on black dolls. Bernstein argues that by examining the intersections of literature, material culture, and play, we are compelled to rethink Jacqueline Rose's formulation: children are not merely "reflectors" and "receivers" of culture (and here specifically racist culture) but also its "coproducers" (167).

34 Until the First World War, Italian toy manufacture in general tended to be a small-scale, often family-run operation that was dwarfed by the industrial capacities of France and Germany. In fact, Furga initially imported their doll heads from Germany. Thus, Treves's depiction of "Stella" may also be a nationalist endorsement of "old fashioned" (i.e., Italian) production methods (Cimorelli 34–36, Beretta 42).

35 I would suggest that in a similar fashion, the transfer of the Sicilian boys' devotion in Nuccio's text unwittingly discloses that "Italy" is as imaginary as was "La Talia."

36 *Black Sun* 158–59. Kristeva here discusses Gèrard de Nerval's poem "The Disinherited." Kristeva's formulation of the "archaic Thing," which she describes as "previous to the detectable 'object'... necessarily lost so that this 'subject'... might become a speaking being" (145), suggests that the sister herself, rather than the true or original lost object, is already a substitute, as indeed also is the other woman who dies before her: the prince's mother. We are told bluntly, "[l]a buona regina era morta, e la principessa ... l'aveva seguita nella tomba" [the good queen had died, and the princess... had followed her into the tomb] (199). Without even naming the mother, and using the trapassato (pluperfect) to mark her death as the prehistory of the narrative, the plot establishes a sequence [seguire] of women falling into the tomb: mother, sister, doll. The plot suggests this series of losses enables the prince's development. Treves's tale, in other words, materializes the "archaic Thing" of Kristeva's theory, identifying a series of lost "detectable objects," all of which are feminine. The fact that a *series* of losses is dramatized suggests that a single experience of separation is somehow not sufficient. The metonymic sequence, I suggest, reveals that all these "detectable objects" insufficiently stand in for an imaginary loss.

37 In Pertile's *Trionfo dei piccoli*, which I will discuss below, the boy also declares himself a man on the basis of not having a doll. Young Franco distinguishes himself from his sisters by claiming, "[m]a io sono un uomo, e non ho la bambola" [but I am a man, and I do not have a doll] (49). While the obvious point is that boys don't play with feminine toys (toys clearly meant to inculcate maternal practices), it is also important, I think, to note that the constitution of the masculine subject (and the inclusion of the grammatically unnecessary subject pronoun "io" emphasizes this) here is articulated as a lack: *non ho*. For Valoroso and for Franco, being a man means being without or giving up the feminine. Pertile's use of the conjunction "e" [and] renders safely ambiguous the causal relationship between the two statements: that is, her formulation leaves undecidable whether Franco's masculinity is the cause or the effect of his not having a doll.

38 Carlo Collodi's use of the monkey in *Il viaggio per l'Italia di Giannettino* and *Pipì o lo scimmiottino color di rosa,* which I explored in Chapter 2, illustrates this connection.

39 The image, with its depiction of a woman sporting a flowing scarf while perched in a racing vehicle, seems prescient of Tamara de Lempicka's Art Deco 1925 painting "Self-portrait in the Green Bugatti" and of Isadora

Duncan's actual fate in 1927. While I do not suggest any direct philological connections between these images, they each may register the ambivalence (exhilaration and fear) around the intersection of traditional images of femininity in modern contexts of speed and technology. Sofia Bisi Albini had in fact already suggested the potential incompatibility of feminine fabric and masculine motion in her extremely popular 1887 *Una nidiata* [*A Brood*], first published in installments in *Cordelia* in 1881. Here, the protagonist Silvio tells his bored sister Sandra, "Ah, tu vorresti buttarti nel mondo? Slanciarti anche tu in questa corrente che si chiama progresso? Oppure in quella che si chiama piacere? Bada, sia nell'una che nell'altra la gonnella imbroglia, e tira nel fondo" [Ah, so you would like to throw yourself into the real world? You, too, want to dive into this current called progress? Or into the one called pleasure? Take care, lest in either one your get caught up in your skirt and pulled to the bottom] (58). Thanks to Sherry Roush and Mary Barnard for the connections with the Lempicka and Duncan.

40 Later, under the fascist regime, Treves would join writers such as Annie Vivanti and Laura Orvieto on the list of over 900 Jewish authors "non graditi in Italia" [not welcome in Italy]. Between 1939 and 1940, their books were taken out of circulation, and public libraries were instructed to stamp them as "excluded from reading" and to store them in separate designated repositories (Boero and De Luca 169, 174).

41 As suggested by the title, Invernizio's 1915 collection recalls Edmondo De Amicis's 1886 novel. Like the "monthly stories" in *Cuore*, the ten tales here offer young protagonists—often orphaned or abandoned—who display uncommon heroism and goodness. Echoing the regional scope in De Amicis's tales, Invernizio's ten stories take place in Messina (Sicily), Rome (Lazio), Florence (Tuscany), and Lombardy. Whereas *Cuore*'s tales all take place within the new Italy's borders, as part of the novel's post-unification nationalist project, Invernizio widens the geographic lens to include stories set in the United States after the Lincoln assassination, in France during the time of Napoleon Bonaparte (with an inserted discussion of the 1870–1871 Franco-Prussian War), and in Libya during the 1911–1912 war. In this way, the collection generates a Romantic sense of the universality of childhood goodness and innocence. At the same time, the geographic scope, the inclusion of wartime settings, and the extremely nationalist rhetoric of the final tale, "La piccola araba" ["The Little Arab Girl"], express an anxiety about Italy's place within the contemporary international conflict. Invernizio, who penned over 100 novels, was an extremely popular writer of the "romanzo d'appendice" [*feuilleton*], usually in a gothic mode, and enjoyed a wide readership among women and the working classes. On Invernizio, see Lepschy and Zaccaria.

42 Examining Marina after the accident, the doctor remarks, "[p]are che lo spirito cerchi di spezzare i legami che lo tengono avvinto al corpo, per volare al Cielo" [it seems that her spirit is trying to cut the ties that bind it to her body, so it may fly up to Heaven] (211).

43 In this regard, Invernizio's narration echoes the actual reports following the first known motorcar fatality. Bridget Driscoll, a 44-year-old mother, was killed after being struck by a car in London on August 17, 1896. Witnesses emphasized the shocking speed of the vehicle (four miles per hour) and noted that Driscoll seemed "bewildered" as the car approached. The death was ruled "accidental" (McFarlane). Eric Tribunella has recently analyzed Kenneth Grahame's 1908 novel *The Wind in the Willows*, particularly the role of Mr. Toad, in light of the way in which the image of the motorcar

triggered both "ominous and exciting" affects, eliciting both exhilaration and fear, in the wake of the 1896 accident. Tribunella notes that in the British press children were represented as being especially vulnerable to the modern dangers posed by automobiles (Tribunella "The Wind").

44 Marinetti famously narrates the car crash into a muddy ditch, from which he emerges with the inspiration for his avant-garde movement, in the founding manifesto of Futurism, which was first published in the French journal *Le Figaro*. Invernizio had in fact explored the image of the car accident in her 1905 novel, *Un assassinio in automobile* [*Murder in a car*].

45 On the *asilo* movement in post-unification Italy, see Ipsen 168–72. The first *asilo* in Italy was founded by a Catholic priest in 1830 (168). After unification, the attempt to provide protection to "inadequately cared for" children aged two to six received support from the "emerging bourgeois Liberal elite," especially as female labor increased in the cities (169). Ipsen argues that the *asilo* movement was part of a strategy to "to assimilate the popular masses just as those masses began to assert themselves politically." Administration of the growing number of *asili* remained mostly private, local, and often religious, and it was not until Mussolini took power that a national law regulating them was passed in 1923 (170). Thus, the protagonist's desire to have a nursery school built for the local children inscribes the tale historically into this social movement, a movement that responded to and sought to remedy the effects of modernization.

46 The exploitation of children for profit by adults in traveling circus-like street performances was not an uncommon theme in Italian children's literature. Invernizio herself returns to and develops this topic in one of the ten tales from her 1915 *Cuori*; Ida Baccini penned *Una famiglia di saltimbanchi* [*A Family of Acrobats*] in 1901; and, most famously, Edmondo De Amicis made such an exploited boy his hero in "Il piccolo patriotta padovano" ["The Little Patriot of Padua"] as one of the monthly stories in *Cuore*. Legislation prohibiting the employment of children under the age of 16 in "wandering professions" such as tight-rope walkers, acrobats, street musicians, or fortune tellers had been passed in Italy in 1872, but remained "disattesa" [ignored] (Tamburini 31). Silvana Andretta examines the representation of abandoned and abused children in a range of late-nineteenth-century Italian literary genres and suggests that this motif was often deployed to elicit strong emotional responses in the reader and also to justify bourgeois condescension toward the lower classes whose suffering is depicted as being deserved (among other effects). Such effects are certainly cultivated by Baccini's sentimental tale, which concludes with the narrator's affirmation that the poor performing children, rescued by a rich Signora, have earned their new happiness through their honesty (75).

47 Spinazzola rightly notes the "pedagogy of cruelty" at play in this often violent, indeed "sadistic" tale (160–61).

48 On Pertile, see Boero and De Luca 193–94. They identify *Ninetta e Tirintin* as worthy of more critical attention.

49 *Commedia dell'arte* characters figure frequently in Pertile's opus. The twins Franco and Luisa receive a Pulcinella doll as their first gift (*Trionfo* 57), and Ninetta and Tirintin, themselves puppet-like dolls, attend a marionette show featuring the Venetian mask Facanapa (*Ninetta* 77). Pertile had written her thesis on Carlo Goldoni and thus would have been well versed in this Italian theatrical tradition. In her work, then, the literary doll as a device for gendered subject formation and as a cipher for class distinctions takes on a specifically Italian nuance.

50 Scipio Sighele ridicules what he terms "quel desiderio assurdo di perfetta
    egualanza fra i due sessi che è nel programma del feminismo" [that absurd
    desire for perfect equality between the sexes that one finds in the feminist
    agenda] (11). He criticizes advocates both of free love and of chastity, claim-
    ing that such programs, while noble in their goals of trying to ameliorate
    the plight of modern women, refuse to acknowledge the irreducible bio-
    logical differences between men and women, especially in regard to sex
    drive. More generally, Stewart-Steinberg notes that "[t]he years between
    1904 and 1908 were the most active and impressive years of the Italian
    feminist movement," with the First National Congress of Italian Women
    being held in 1908 (313).

51 For an account of Ceas-Ramonino (d. 1967), see Faeti, *Guardare* 2011,
    262–63. Faeti notes that she moved in internationally elite circles, collabo-
    rated primarily with the Bemporad Press, and drew with a "stile elegante e
    colto" [elegant and cultivated style] (262).

52 Sighele's text evaluates the various ways in which marriage was being re-
    considered in the first decades of the twentieth century, with proposals for
    legalizing divorce, for delaying marriage until both men and women had
    enjoyed a long period of multiple partners, for free love, and for chastity
    all being debated in light of economic, spiritual, biological, psychological,
    and even aesthetic factors. See also Chapter 1 for a synthesis of the divorce
    debates in Italy in this period. Marinetti would take up the issue through a
    Futurist perspective with *Contro il matrimonio* [*Against marriage*] in 1919.
    We can note along these lines that "Franco" and "Luisa," the sibling twins
    in Pertile's text, are the names of the protagonists in Antonio Fogazzaro's
    highly popular 1895 novel *Piccolo mondo antico*, where the two characters
    are in fact lovers who eventually marry.

53 In the inserted tale of Rina and Piccetti (71–73), the eponymous children
    are convalescing in a hospital and develop a strong bond. Piccetti (the boy)
    recovers first, but when his mother arrives to take him home, he refuses to
    leave until Rina, too, gets better. This friendship between unrelated children
    works to model an intermediary phase of male-female connection, between
    the sibling pair and the husband-wife pair.

54 "io vorrei sapere se le fiabe sono vere" [I would like to know whether or not
    these fairy tales are true].

55 This soldier "esclamò nel linguaggio del suo paese – Ah chillu filu, chillu
    filu!" [exclaimed in the dialect of his town – Ah, chillu filu, chillu filu!] (96).
    The standard Italian of the soldier's words would be "quel filo quel filo!"
    [that thread, that thread!].

56 The accompanying illustration shows the girl with her doll: the viewer is
    positioned behind and slightly above the blond young girl who is donning a
    skirt and standing calmly with her small rag doll in her right hand.

57 The name of this tense (*passato remoto*) may be misleading: it can but does
    not have to convey actions that took place in the "remote" past (a very long
    time ago). It is used with great frequency in Italian writing, and, varying by
    region, in spoken Italian, to convey completed action in the past regardless
    of how long ago that past period may be.

58 In his analysis of Invernizio's *I sette capelli d'oro della Fata Gusmara*,
    Spinazzola astutely notes that the happy ending of this novelized fairy tale
    is recounted in the present tense rather than the more typical *passato re-
    moto*: "vivono nella foresta ... ove si sentono amati e protetti" rather than
    the standard "vissero sempre felici e contenti" ["they live in the forest ...
    where they feel loved and protected," as opposed to "they lived happily

ever after"] (165). Spinazzola persuasively suggests that the present tense, which appears once the narrative is over, "proietta con qualche efficacia su un orrizonte di permanenza la quiete d'un raccoglimento vissuto nel grembo materno della natura" [projects rather effectively the family's serenity, lived within nature's maternal womb, onto a horizon of permanency] (165). Here, too, the present tense, when linked to the feminine, connotes stasis rather than historical (or narrative) development.

59 See Gianni Giolo's biography of Pertile.

Conclusion
The Heart of the Matter

Running as a kind of *fil rouge* through the previous chapter is the link between girls and clothing. Young Gianni, we recall, is physically rebuked for wearing his sister's outfit (Vamba); Silvia is warned by her brother that her skirts may drag her down (Bisi Albini); Marinella appears with her scarf flying dramatically behind her as her beloved spirits her away in his speed boat (Treves); Topolina maternally weaves clothing for her adopted rustic family (Invernizio); a patient mother sews the dolls Ninetta and Tirintin for her daughter, and insists that the thread that links them must never be severed (Pertile).

Lombroso himself had speculated on the connections between women and clothing, and indeed for Lombroso, women's propensity to "make themselves up" with adornments and fabrics is symptomatic of the same fundamental female need to attract men as is their other strategy of seduction: the natural female tendency to "make up" and to fabricate, that is, to lie (*Criminal Woman* 77–79). In fact, once again recurring to the causal facticity of the body, Lombroso demonstrates women's tendency to lie ("habitual and almost physiological") (77) by pointing to the western legal tradition of regarding only men as capable of providing testimony, noting that "in many langagues the words *oath* [*giuramento*] and *testimony* [*testimonianza*] have the same root as *testicle* [*testicolo*]" (77; italics in orig.).[1] A similar opposition at play throughout the children's books that I have reviewed appears as a variant of Lombroso's gendered dichotomy between feminine fabrication and virile veracity. Namely, these texts stage a consistent tension between what is merely external clothing and what is truly "in the heart."

It is not, I think, by chance that the image of the "heart" was adopted as the title of one of the most influential books of the period, then to be echoed in the titles of many books that followed: Emma Perodi's *Cuore del popolo*, Collodi Nipote's *Il cuore di Pinocchio*, Carolina Invernizio's *Cuori dei bimbi*, and Haydée's (Iva Finzi) *Il cuore delle bimbe* to name a few, as well as in the title of a children's journal that ran from October 1921 through December 1923. The Milanese weekly *Cuore*, aimed particularly at the children of the working class, overtly proclaimed its indebtedness to De Amicis's humanitarian ethos and held up the good Garrone in particular as a model for its readers (Boero and De Luca 166–67). The place to begin to articulate how the image of the heart was leveraged in children's books of the period is of course in "the" book *Cuore*.

The image given the privileged position of title reappears frequently throughout the book: in Ernico's diary entries, in the monthly stories, and in the letters from Enrico's parents. The school year opens with the paternal teacher enjoining his new pupils to show him that they are "ragazzi di cuore" [boys of heart] (29). As the year progresses, it becomes clear that Carlo Nobis, who embraces the arrogant pride of his station but not the social obligations of his class, may indeed be "un ragazzo senza cuore" [a boy without heart] (106). We can note that this most grievous of accusations—to be without heart—appears in the February diary entry entitled "Superbia" [Pride], precisely the deadly sin that Dante had identified as the most serious and fundamental; thus, De Amicis again translates familiar religious concepts into a modern, secular key. Wealth in and of itself is not condemned, however: another well-off student, Votini, is susceptible to vanity, but we are assured that "non ha mica cattivo cuore" [he does not really have a bad heart] (64). By contrast, Marco, the protagonist of the longest monthly story "Dagli Appennini alle Ande" ["From the Apennines to the Andes"], proves that he is "pieno di cuore" [full of heart] (201) through his heroic journey: he travels alone by ship, barge, train, cart, and foot from Genoa to Argentina in search of his emigrant mother. In short, uses of the word abound throughout the novel, forming a unifying theme among the multiple stories and the ensemble cast.

This recurrent image draws some of its power from the connotations derived from its literal, anatomical meaning: an organ inside the body that is necessary to life and common to all people. Indeed, its role as an underlying unifier is emphasized when Marco is called "un *bagai* pieno di cuore" [a boy full of heart] (201; italics in orig.). Here, an Italian immigrant in Argentina is using a Lombard dialect word for "boy" rather than the standard Italian *ragazzo* as he persuades his comrades to give Marco a hand. The "heart," in a sense, overcomes this regional linguistic difference to make Marco's goodness legible to all the immigrants in the text and all the readers of the text. More fundamentally, though, De Amicis deploys the heart's common association in western culture with sentimentality, emphasizing its fraternal potentials and repressing any erotic connotations. Boero and De Luca have pointed out how De Amicis's sentimentality influenced not only the pleasure reading for Italian children that followed *Cuore* but also the texts used in Italian primary schools through the early twentieth century (84).

In his trenchant account of De Amicis's novel, Vittorio Spinazzola has insightfully described this image's role in the book's secularizing, community-building project. He writes,

> Il titolo del libro ne sintetizza il senso; e ne pervade le pagine, in suono di *verità prelogica*. Ma il termine "cuore" ha una pregnanza singolare: non indica solo una capacità di sentire che accomuna tutti

gli esseri umani, esprime anche una disposizione d'animo che quanto
più patisce la sofferenza tanto più vi reagisce operativamente. Le la-
grime che l'individuo dotato di cuore versa ... inducono un rilancio
di vitalità espansiva fra gli altri, per gli altri. (99; italics added)

[The book's title encompasses its meaning; it pervades its pages with
the ring of prelogical truth. But the term "heart" is singularly preg-
nant with meaning: not only does it designate that capacity to feel
which unites all human beings, it also expresses a spiritual disposition through which the more suffering one endures, the more effectively and concretely one reacts to that suffering. The tears shed by a
person with heart... prompt a springing forth of exuberant warmth
among others, for others.]

Ideally, the capacity to experience pathos symbolized by the "heart,"
then, grounds the individual's ability to form bonds with his peers and
contribute to his community. Heart enables the transition from narcissism to altruism. It is the task of texts like De Amicis's to call forth this
capacity and gently guide it in the right direction.

While the "heart" functions on the one hand as a marker of
unity-within-difference—both a poor Garrone and a well-to-do Derossi
can be boys of heart, as can both able-bodied and disabled boys—it does
at the same time establish a gendered difference. Spinazzola, who does
not take a gender-informed approach to his discussion of *Cuore* nor even
remark much on gender issues at all, does note that the kind of sentimentality so forcefully at work in De Amicis's text can be effective only in
a culture that does not despise tenderness or disdain pity, one in which
"il pianto non sia considerato melensaggine da femminucce ma mani-
festazione di interezza umana" [crying is not considered to be a marker
of little-girl silliness but rather the sign of being fully human] (104).
Sentimentality, then, is rescued from the merely feminine to designate
instead the fully human, and thus the heart seems to transcend gender
differences as well as those of class and ability. However, this apparent
transcendence plays out in a text in which the only characters of heart
are male. Sentimentality is rescued as a marker of the fully human by
defeminizing it. The "interezza umana," I would suggest, does not so
much include the feminine as abject it.

In the quotation cited above, Spinazzola tellingly describes the "heart"
in De Amicis's text as a "disposizione," and he later goes on to use it as
a synonym for that which is innate: "insite nella natura, cioè nel cuore
di ognuno" [intrinsic in the nature, that is, the heart, of each person]
(115–16). I would recall here Judith Butler's critique of how Freud uses
the term "disposition." As I summarized in my Introduction, Butler analyses how Freud, who, she points out, "avows his own confusion" on the
question (77), must assume that masculine and feminine "dispositions"

are a given. He uses the "dispositions" as a ground on which to construct his argument and as a natural tendency from which human sexuality develops. For Butler, these alleged "dispositions" must themselves be accounted for. She asks "how do we identify a 'feminine' or a 'masculine' disposition at the outset?" (77), and her critique seeks to dismantle this "false foundationalism" (81). She goes on to argue that "the dispositions that Freud assumes to be primary or constitutive facts of sexual life are effects of a law which, internalized, produces and regulates discreet gender identity and heterosexuality" (82). Linking conceptually (if not substantially) the "prelogical truth" of the deamician "heart" with the prediscursive given of the Freudian dispositions, I explore in these concluding pages the manifestations and stakes of this analogous aporia in Italian children's literature: of the heart as the proclaimed precondition and, simultaneously, as the produced effect of these books. Specifically, I look at key moments in which hearts and clothing are put in opposition, often along a gendered axis and with reference not only to the individual's heart but also to Italy's.

Various connotations of "heart" can be discerned in the range of texts I have explored in the previous chapters. In Invernizio's *I sette capelli d'oro della Fata Gusmara* (1909) [*The Seven Golden Hairs of Fairy Gusmara*], little Topolina can see right away that she need not fear the wood cutter "perchè hai cuore, e non vorrai farmi del male" [because you have heart, and you won't want to hurt me] (6). Here, the use of "heart" without adjectives means in itself a "good" or "pure" heart. Gianelli dedicated his nostalgic *Storia di Pipino* to the two children he rescued from the Messina earthquake, calling them "due cuori nel mio cuore" [two hearts in my heart] (no pg.). This image reappears in the title to the first chapter, which assures us (with gentle humor) that the pipe whose heat enlivens the statue that becomes Pipino is "Una pipa di buon cuore" [A pipe with a good heart] (1). In both the dedication and the chapter title, the "heart" serves as the source of origin: for the tale itself, and for the life of the protagonist. Ubertis Gray, in her stirring *Piccoli eroi della grande guerra* (1915) [*Little Heroes of the Great War*], includes the inspiring story of young Teofilo Jagout, who chooses to serenely face death by firing squad rather than betray the French soldiers hiding in his house. Offering this martyr figure as a model of patriotism for Italian children, the author entitles this section "Un cuore fedele" ["A Faithful Heart"] (9). The insistence on the notion of the interiority, goodness, truth, and originating force of the "heart," as established by De Amicis, echoes throughout this corpus of texts.

Carlo Collodi mobilizes these associations and deploys them on a national plane. He underscores the incompatibility between feminine frilliness and modest manliness in his portraits of both Victor Emanuel and Garibaldi in the final chapter of *La lanterna magica di Giannettino* (1890) [*Giannettino's Magic Lantern*]. In narrating the life of the man who would become Italy's first monarch, Giannettino (who, we recall, uses the magic lantern to teach the younger boys about Italy's great men of the past) highlights in particular the speech that Victor Emanuel made in 1870 upon the taking of Rome. Claiming that at last the promise he had made to his father Charles Albert had been fulfilled, Victor Emanuel is quoted as proclaiming, "[i]l mio cuore di Re e di figlio prova una gioia solenne nel salutare qui raccolti per la prima volta tutti i rappresentanti della nostra patria diletta. L'Italia è libera e una. Ora non dipende che da noi il farla grande e felice" [my heart, both as a King and as a son, feels a solemn joy in greeting, assembled here for the first time, all the representatives of our beloved fatherland. Italy is free and united. Now it depends entirely on us to make her great and happy] (187). The "heart" here works metonymically to stand for "I," that is, Victor Emanuel himself who greets those assembled. The rhetorical figure he deploys not only effectively conveys the emotional weight of the moment—a solemn joy, both deep and serious—but also links the celebration of fulfillment back to an earlier moment when unity was still merely a dream. Giannettino had previously recounted the events of the battle of Novara (1849) and had described "la fede e la speranza nel cuore" [the faith and the hope in the heart] of Charles Albert's son even in that moment of defeat (187). What was a hope and a promise then at Novara has been realized now in Rome. The heart in this passage, too, is gendered as masculine: the heart of a king and a son celebrating the fatherland. All these connotations—seriousness, fulfillment, and masculinity—coalesce to ground the sentences that declare Italy's unity (literally "Italy is one"). The cadence, structure, and significance of these two sentences seem to conjure and simultaneously refute the perhaps more cynical adage of D'Azeglio: "Italy is one, now we must make her great" replaces "Italy is made, now we must make Italians." Essence trumps fabrication. This gesture of mobilizing the "heart" as a sign of (masculine) essence is implicitly buttressed by the rather detailed discussion of Victor Emanuel's taste in clothing that follows soon after the passage recounting his speech in Rome. Giannettino, speaking, we recall, to a classroom full of boys, describes at some length the first king's attire. He notes first of all that his "*guardaroba*" was "*molto modesta*" [wardrobe was very modest] (191). The monarch disdained capes and greatcoats and simply could not stand top hats. Even wearing gloves was as much of a nuisance to him as getting smoke in his eyes (191). The description implies not just certain preferences for one style over another, but a sense that the king experienced items of clothing as cumbersome, excessive, and fussy. It is in fact precisely with this celebration of the king's sartorial simplicity rather than with discussions of his military or political accomplishments that Giannettino concludes the monarch's biography. This otherwise apparently odd choice seems to make sense in the context of opposing the interior, masculine truth of the "heart" with the external frivolity of vestments and deploying that opposition to ground the nation-making project.

The opposition, with the same effects, carries forward into the next and final biography of Collodi's book, that of Garibaldi himself. Giannettino makes clear to his pupils that the hero not only had but indeed was a "cuore nobile e generoso" [noble and generous heart] (193), again using "heart" metonymically for the man. I would suggest, too, that coming as the final biography in a sequence of stories about great men of Italy's past, as if a litany of lay saints, this exposition of Garibaldi and his generous heart via the magic lantern becomes a secularized enactment of devotion to the Sacred Heart. The same metonymic maneuver (heart for the man) applies here as that which operates theologically in the devotion to Jesus's heart: "This is not, however, because the two are synonymous but when the word heart is used to designate the person, it is because such a person is considered in whatsoever related to his emotional and moral life. Thus, when we designate Jesus as the Sacred Heart, we mean Jesus manifesting His Heart, Jesus all loving and amiable" (Bainvel no pg.). This gesture of offering the Generous Heart of Garibaldi as a secular analog to or, perhaps better, displacement of the Sacred Heart of Jesus may have been more palpable to the readers of Collodi's 1890 text, since it was only one year before (in 1889) that the Church had elevated the feast of the Sacred Heart to "the double rite of first class" (Bainvel no pg.).[2] This displacement exemplifies De Amicis's secularizing strategies as part of his national project.

Once again, the narrative seems to take an odd turn from these solemn heights into the apparently trivial question of attire. Giannettino goes on to insist that the famous "red shirts," which the General had adopted as a uniform for his volunteers, were chosen for strategic rather than aesthetic purposes, the red serving as the best camouflage against the particular hues of the surrounding landscape (195).[3] More broadly, the Hero simply could not tolerate any sort of "luxurious" clothing, but always insisted upon simplicity (195).[4] Eschewing showiness, excess, and vanity, Garibaldi, like the king, opts for modesty and functionality: coming as close to the "naked truth" as possible without causing a scandal. The heart of Italy's new secular Christ must be essential, not a mere accessory.

Ida Baccini's *I piccoli viaggiatori: Viaggio in China* (1878) [*The Little Travelers: Trip to China*] puts the matter bluntly and yet already problematizes the very binary that the heart/clothing opposition seeks to assert. Signor Tebaldi, one of the fatherly figures in the journey narrative, exclaims to the children, "non è il vestito che fa l'italiano e l'inglese, è il cuore! E domani potrei benissimo vestirmi da turco, senza cessar d'essere, per questo, un figlio amoroso della nostra dolcissima Italia" [it is not the clothes that make the Italian or the Englishman. It is the heart! And tomorrow I could very well dress myself up as a Turk, without ceasing to be, for all that, a loving son of our sweet Italy] (169). A rhetoric of anti-rhetoric, a construction of the natural: his exclamation here unequivocally claims that Italian identity is interior, natural, and given (that is, heart), vehemently denying that it is external, fabricated, or made (that is, clothes). But the text makes this claim in the very moment in which it is doing the fabrication. The phrase itself "weaves" Italian identity together with Englishness (that is, northern and civilized, as the rest of the novel had established it) while disentangling it from Turkishness (i.e., barbarism, again according to the text's constructions). At the same time, the claim offers a metaphor of Italy as mother and of Italians as her children, and thus here too, as in its use of "heart," rhetorically leverages images of biology.

Not only in titles but also in key passages throughout the children's books of the period, the image of the "heart" as "Italian core" emerges with frequency. In his *Da Quarto al Volturno*, we recall, Abba claims that the *picciotti* as they marched north into Calabria "found their hearts" at the very moment in which they also became Italian: "ma marciando per la Calabria trovarono i loro cuori" (219). More problematic is Carolina Invernizio's "La piccola araba" ["The Little Arab Girl"] from the *Cuori dei bimbi* (1915) [*Kids' Hearts*] collection, set during the Libyan war. Ziba, the 12-year-old child referenced in the title, proudly proclaims "[i]l mio cuore è italiano" [my heart is Italian] (227). She is soon after killed by an Italian soldier who does not recognize her Italophile heart and sees only the threat of her Arab identity. I would suggest that the narrative elimates Ziba not just for dramatic effect but also in order to foreclose the crisis rendered by the irreconcilable rhetorical split opened between the heart as a natural given and the heart as a learned behavior (Ziba had been educated by Italian nuns and developed her Italian affiliation from that experience).

I suggest that high frequency of the use of the "heart" image in this corpus of texts functions according to the same mechanism that Freud identified in his reading of the Medusa: the repetition of the figure seeks to compensate for what is actually perceived to be missing. Working according to the logic of the fetish, the proliferation of hearts in these texts simultaneously announces and covers the anxiety generated by their very project: the highly visible dramatization that one must be taught what one should already know, must become what one should already be, must put on as clothing what should be a natural disposition in the heart. In these cases, what "should be there" but indeed must be taught, envisioned as the "heart," is the essence of Italianness. Italy's heart, as these books attest, must be fabricated: narrated as the story of losses, woven, to quote the author of the book *Cuore*, as the poetry of sad things.

Notes

1 On Lombroso, fabric, and the spirit world, see Stewart-Steinberg, 109.
2 See Bainvel for a rigorous discussion of the literal, metaphorical, and symbolic meanings of the "heart" as well as the history of the devotion to the Sacred Heart in the Catholic Church.
3 "egli era persuaso che da lontano il color rosso si fondesse meglio colle tinte generali del paese" [he was convinced that from a distance the color red blended in best with the dominant hues of the landscape] (195).
4 "In quanto poi al vestire. ... [n]on poteva patire il lusso, ma intorno a sè voleva la nettezza" [Regarding attire, he could not stand luxury, but instead wanted to be surrounded by simplicity] (195). "Nettezza" has connotations of "clarity" and "purity."

Bibliography

Primary Sources

Abba, Giuseppe Cesare. *The Diary of One of Garibaldi's Thousand.* Trans E.R. Vincent. London: Oxford UP, 1962.

———. *Da Quarto al Volturno: Noterelle di uno dei Mille.* 1891. Bologna: Zanichelli, 1961.

———. *Edizione nazionale delle opere di Giuseppe Cesare Abba. Scritti garibaldini.* Ed. Luigi Cattanei, Enrico Elli, and Claudio Scarpati. Vol. 1. Brescia: Morcelliana, 1983.

———. *Storia dei Mille.* Florence: Bemporad, 1904.

Albini, Sofia Bisi. *Donnina forte.* 1879. Florence: Bemporad, 1903.

———. *Una nidiata.* 1887. Florence: Bemoprad, 1902.

———. Preface. *La poesia delle cose.* By Mara Antelling. Milan: Giacomo Agnelli, 1899.

Antelling, Mara. *La poesia delle cose.* Milan: Giacomo Agnelli, 1899.

Baccini, Ida. *Una famiglia di saltimbanchi.* 1901. Florence: Marzocco, 1948.

———. *Libro moderno, ossia nuove letture per la gioventù.* Turin: Paravia, 1887.

———. *Memorie di un pulcino.* 1875. Ed. Laura Nacci. Milan: Greco & Greco, 2000.

———. *I piccoli viaggiatori: Viaggio in China.* 1878. Illus. C. Sarri. Florence: Bemporad, 1910.

Bertelli, Luigi [Vamba]. *Ciondolino.* 1895. Milan: Mursia, 1996.

———, ed. *Il giornalino della Domenica.* 2.27. Florence: July 7, 1907.

———. *Il giornalino di Gian Burrasca.* 1907–08; 1912. Milan: Feltrinelli, 2002.

———. *O patria mia.* 1911. Ed. Ettore Allodoli. Florence: Bemporad, 1932.

Capuana, Luigi. *Scurpiddu, Cardello, Nel paese della Zàgara, Gli americani di Ràbbato.* Ed. Attilio Inturrisi. Messina: G. D'Anna, 1972.

———. *Scurpiddu.* 1898. Lexington, 2014.

———. *Tutte le fiabe.* Ed. Maurizio Vitta. 2 vols. Milan: Mondadori, 1983.

Catani, Tomaso. *Pinocchio nella luna.* Florence: Nerbini, 1911.

Checchi, Eugenio. *Garibaldi: Vita narrata ai giovani.* 1907. Milan: Treves, 1910.

Cherubini, Eugenio. *Impresa Granchio, Bullettino e compagni.* Illus. Carlo Chiostri. Florence: Bemporad, 1910.

———. *Pinocchio in Affrica.* Illus. Giuseppe Garibaldi Bruno. Florence: Bemporad, 1903.

————. *Pinocchio in Africa*. 1911. Trans. Angelo Patri. Whitefish: Kessinger Publishing, 2004.

Collodi, Carlo. *The Adventures of Pinocchio/Le avventure di Pinocchio*. Trans. and Introd. Nicolas J. Perella. Berkeley: U of California P, 1986.

————. *La lanterna magica di Giannettino. Libro per i giovanetti*. Illus. Enrico Mazzanti. Florence: Bemporad, 1890.

————. *Pipi o lo scimmiottino color di rosa*. Ed. Vittorio Orsenigo. Milan: Greco & Greco, 1993.

————. *Un romanzo in vapore: Da Firenze a Livorno: Guida storico-umoristica*. Ed. Roberto Randacchio. Collodi (Pistoia): Fondazione Nazionale Carlo Collodi; Florence: Giunti, 2010.

————. *Il viaggio per l'Italia di Giannettino: Italia Superiore*. Florence: Bemporad, 1894.

————. *Il viaggio per l'Italia di Giannettino*. Florence: Bemporad, 1931.

DeAmicis, Edmondo. *Cuore*. 1886. Milan: Mondadori, 1984.

————. *Heart: A School-Boy's Journal*. 1901. Trans. Isabel Hapgood. Amsterdam: Fredonia Books, 2003.

Errico, Giuseppe. *Mily e Michele: Storielle per fanciulli*. Naples: F. Bideri, 1890.

Fumagalli, Giuseppe. *Vita di Giuseppe Garibaldi narrata ai giovinetti*. Milan: Libreria di educazione e di istruzione, 1892.

Ferriani, Lino. *Un piccolo eroe*. Florence: Bemporad, 1905.

Gianelli, Giulio. *Storia di Pipino nato vecchio e morto bambino*. 1910/1911. Turin: Soc. Ed. Internazionale, 1942.

Invernizio, Carolina. *Cuori dei bimbi*. Florence: Salani, 1915.

————. *I sette capelli d'oro della Fata Gusmara*. 1909. Milan: Moizzi, 1975.

————. *Spazzacamino*. Illus. Adriano Minardi. Florence: Salani, 1912.

Lorenzini, Paolo [Collodi Nipote]. *Il cuore di Pinocchio*. 1917. Illus. Carlo Chiostro. Florence: Bemporad 1923.

————. *Sussi e Biribissi: Storia di un viaggio verso il centro della terra*. Illus. Carlo Chiostri. Florence: Adriano Salani, 1902.

Novelli, Enrico [Yambo]. *Le avventure di Ciuffettino*. 1902. Florence: Vallecchi, 1924.

Nuccio, Giuseppe Ernesto. *Picciotti e garibaldini: Romanzo storico sulla rivoluzione del 1859–60*. Illus. Alberto Della Valle. Florence: Marzocco, 1956.

Perodi, Emma. *Fiabe fantastiche. Le novelle della nonna*. 1892. Ed. Antonio Faeti. Turin: Einaudi, 1974.

Pertile, Arpalice Cuman. *Ninetta e Tirintin*. 1918. Florence: Giunti, 1967.

————. *Per i bimbi d'Italia: Poesie*. Florence: Bemporad, 1921.

————. *Il trionfo dei piccoli*. 1915. Illus. A. Ceas-Ramorino. Florence: Bemporad, 1929.

Prosperi, Carola. *Tre fiabe di Carola Prosperi*. Turin: L'uinione dei maestri elementari d'Italia, 1910.

Rembadi-Mongiardini, Gemma. *Il segreto di Pinocchio: Viaggio ignorato del célèbre burattino di Collodi*. 1894. Florence: Bemporad, 1922.

Ricciardi, Michele. Preface. *Mily e Michele: Storielle per fanciulli*. By Giuseppe Errico. Naples: F. Bideri, 1890.

Salgari, Emilio. *I drammi della schiavitù*. 1896. Turin: Andrea Viglongo, 1992.

Stoppani, Antonio. *Il bel paese: Conversazioni sulle bellezze naturali; La Geologia e la geografia fisica d'Italia*. 1873. Milan: L.F. Cogliati, 1915.

Treves, Virginia [Cordelia]. *Piccoli eroi*. Milan: Fratelli Treves, 1892. Progetto Iperteca. Electronic edition: March 4, 2007.

———. *L'ultima fata: Fiabe di Cordelia*. 1905. Illus. Duilio Cambellotti. Florence: Bemporad, 1909.

Ubertis Gray, Corinna Teresa [Térésah]. *Piccoli eroi della grande guerra*. Florence: Bemporad, 1915.

Vecchi, Augusto Vittorio [Jack La Bolina]. *Al lago degli elefanti: Avventure di un italiano in Africa*. 1897. Turin: G.B. Paravia, 1922.

Vivanti, Annie. *Sua Altezza! (Favola candida)*. Florence: Bemporad, 1923.

Zucca, Giuseppe. *Vincere, vincere, vincere: Liriche di guerra*. Florence: Bemporad, 1918.

Secondary Sources

Alcorn, John. "Sicilian Fasci." *Europe 1789–1914: Encyclopedia of the Age of Industry and Empire*. Ed. John Merriman and Jay Winter. Vol. 4. Charles Scribner's Sons, 2006. 2173–2175. *Gale Virtual Reference Library*, ezaccess. libraries.psu.edu/login?url=http://go.galegroup.com/ps/i.do?p=GVRL&sw= w u=psucic&v=2.1&id=GALE%7CCCX3446900772&it=r&asid=7bc1ef895 ea6d2d51736ea161a8130e. Accessed 4 Dec. 2016.

Amosu, Tundonu. *The Land of Adventure: The Representation of Africa in Emilio Salgari*. Milan: Istituto Italiano di Cultura, 1988.

Anderson, Benedict. *Imagined Communities*, Revised Edition. London: Verso, 2006.

Anderson, J.K. "Xenophon." *Reference Guide to World Literature*. Ed. Sara Pendergast and Tom Pendergast. 3rd ed. Vol. 1: Authors. Detroit: St. James Press, 2003. 1103–1104. *Gale Virtual Reference Library*. Web. 6 Jan. 2014.

Antonelli, Quinto. *Giannetto, Polissena e gli altri. Mostra di libri italiani per ragazzi (Otto e Novecento)*. Trent: La Provincia, Servizio attività culturali, 1996.

Antoni, Roberto Freak. Preface. *Il giornalino di Gian Burrasca*. By Luigi Bertelli [Vamba]. Milan: Feltrinelli, 2002. vii–xix.

Ascoli, Albert Russell, and Krystyna von Henneberg, eds. *Making and Remaking Italy: The Cultivation of National Identity around the Risorgimento*. New York: Berg, 2001.

Bainvel, Jean. "Devotion to the Sacred Heart of Jesus." *The Catholic Encyclopedia*. Vol. 7. New York: Robert Appleton Company, 1910. 30 Oct. 2016 www. newadvent.org/cathen/07163a.htm.

Battistelli, Vincenzina. *La letteratura infantile moderna: Guida bibliografica*. Florence: Vallecchi, 1923.

Beccalossi, Chiara. *Female Sexual Inversion: Same-Sex Desires in Italian and British Sexology, c. 1870 1920*. New York: Palgrave, 2012.

Bencivenni, Marcella. *Italian Immigrant Radical Culture: The Idealism of the Sovversivi in the United States, 1890–1940*. New York: New York UP, 2011.

Beretta, Paola. "Cent'anni di storia (e oltre) della bambola italiana: la Furga." *Pinocchi, bambole, balocchi: Un percorso tra giocattoli del '900*. Ed. Patrizia Bonato and Marco Tosa. Venice: Silvana, 2000. 41–55.

Bernstein, Robin. "Children's Books, Dolls, and the Performance of Race; or, The Possibility of Children's Literature." *PMLA* 126 (Jan 2011): 160–169.

Bettelheim, Bruno. *The Uses of Enchantment: The Meaning and Importance of Fairy Tales*. 1975. New York: Vintage, 2010.

Bhroin, Ciara Ni. "Recovery of Origins: Identity and Ideology in the Work of O.R. Melling." *Politics and Ideology in Children's Literature*. Ed. Marian Thérèse Keyes and Áine McGillicuddy. Dublin, Ireland: Four Courts Press, 2014. 83–94.

Boero, Pino. *La scrittura della morte: Intellettuali, produzione letteraria, cultura dell'infanzia*. Turin: A. Meynier, 1987.

Boero, Pino, and Carmine De Luca. *La letteratura per l'infanzia*. Rome: Laterza, 2009.

Boylan, Amy. "Carving a National Identity: Collodi, *Pinocchio* and Post-Unification Italy." *Approaches to Teaching Collodi's Pinocchio and Its Adaptations*. Ed. Michael Sherberg. New York: MLA, 2006. 16–20.

Brooks, Peter. *Reading for the Plot*. New York: Alfred A. Knopf, 1984.

Butler, Judith. *Gender Trouble: Feminism and the Subversion of Identity*. New York: Routledge, 1999.

Canepa, Nancy. *From Court to Forest: Giambattista Basile's Lo cunto de li cunti and the Birth of the Literary Fairy Tale*. Detroit: Wayne State UP, 1999.

———. "Capuana, Luigi." *Greenwood Encyclopedia of Folktales and Fairy Tales*. Ed. Donald Haase. Vol. 1. Westport: Greenwood, 2008. 160–61.

Cappelletti, Maurizia Alippi. "Giglioli, Enrico Hillyer." *Dizionario Biografico degli italiani*. Vol.54. Treccani, 2000. www.treccani.it/enciclopedia/enrico-hillyer giglioli_%28Dizionario_Biografico%29/. Accessed September 12, 2015.

Cappelli, Lucia, and Marta Zangheri. "Salgari e altro." *Biblioteche oggi* (October 1999): 64–67.

Capuana, Luigi. *Gli 'ismi' contemporanei*. Ed. Giorgio Loti. Milan: Fabbri, 1973.

Carbognin, Maria, Anna Levi, and Lia Madorsky, eds. "Onorato Fava e la società napoletana di fine Ottocento." www.letteraturadimenticata.it/Fava.htm. Jan. 6, 2013.

Castellino, Onorato. Presentation. *Storia di Pipino nato vecchio e morto bambino*. By Giulio Gianelli. Turin: Soc. Ed. Internazionale, 1942.

Central Intelligence Agency. *The World Factbook*. Accessed July 19, 2016. www.cia.gov/library/publications/the-world-factbook/geos/us.html. www.cia.gov/library/publications/the-world-factbook/geos/it.html.

Champagne, John. *Aesthetic Modernism and Masculinity in Fascist Italy*. New York: Routledge, 2013.

Cimorelli, Dario. "Il giocattolo in Italie e le industrie nazionali." *Pinocchi, bambole, balocchi: Un percorso tra giocattoli del '900*. Ed. Patrizia Bonato and Marco Tosa. Venice: Silvana, 2000. 29–39.

Coats, Karen. *Looking Glasses and Neverlands: Lacan, Desire and Subjectivity in Children's Literature*. Iowa City: U of Iowa P, 2004.

Coda, Elena. "Trieste è una donna: Woman and Urban Space in Svevo's *Senilità*." *Quaderni d'italianistica* 26.2 (2005): 75–103.

Colin, Mariella. "Children's Literature in France and Italy in the Nineteenth Century: Influences and Exchanges." *Aspects and Issues in the History of Children's Literature*. Ed. Maria Nikolajeva. Westport: Greenwood, 1995. 77–87.

Clark, Martin. *Modern Italy: 1871–1982*. London: Longman, 1984.

De Amicis, Edmondo. *Gli effetti psicologici del vino*. Turin: Loescher, 1881.

———. *Il vino*. Milan: Treves, 1890.

Della Coletta, Cristina. *World's Fairs Italian Style: The Great Exhibitions in Turin and Their Narratives, 1860–1915*. Toronto: U of Toronto P, 2006.

Detti, Ermanno. "Introduction." *The Lion and the Unicorn: A Critical Journal of Children's Literature* (April 2002): 143–49.

De Maeyer, Jan, ed. *Religion, Children's Literature and Modernity in Western Europe*. Belgium: Leuven UP, 2005.

Dickie, John. "The Notion of Italy." *The Cambridge Companion to Modern Italian Culture*. Ed. Zygmunt G. Baransky and Rebecca J. West. Cambridge: Cambridge UP, 2001. 17–33.

Donato, Giulia. "Collodi scrittore di fiabe." *Fabbrica del libro: Lavori in corso*. Milan: Mondadori. http://docplayer.it/12349404-Ifratelli-paggi-proprietari-della-libreria-editrice fiorentina-di-via-del-proconsolo.html 2005 13–18. 2006.

Doonan, Jane. *Looking at Pictures in Picture Books*. Stroud, England: Thimble P, 1993.

Doumanis, Nicholas. *Inventing the Nation: Italy*. New York: Oxford UP, 2001.

Eco, Umberto. *Diario minimo*. Milan: Mondadori, 1963.

———. *La misteriosa fiamma della Regina Loana*. Milan: Bompiani, 2004.

———. *The Open Work*. Trans. Anna Cancogni. Cambridge: Harvard UP, 1989.

Fava, Sabina. *Percorsi critici di letteratura per l'infanzia tra le due guerre*. Milan: Vita e pensiero, 2004.

Farinelli, Giuseppe. Introduction and Afterword. *Tutte le poesie di Giulio Gianelli*. By Giulio Gianelli. Ed. Farinelli. Milan: Istituto di Propaganda Libraria, 1973. 17–61, 149–84.

Faeti, Antonio. "Il crepuscolo dell'orco pedagogico." Introduction. *Fiabe Fantastiche: Le Novelle Della Nonna*. By Emma Perodi. Turin: Einaudi, 1993. vii–lxi.

———. *Guardare le figure: Gli illustratori italiani dei libri per l'infanzia*. 1st ed. Turin: Einaudi, 1972.

———. *Guardare le figure: Gli illustratori italiani dei libri per l'infanzia*. 2nd ed. Rome: Donzelli, 2011.

———. *Letteratura per l'infanzia*. Florence: La Nuova Italia, 1977.

Ferriani, Lino. *I drammi dei fanciulli*. Como: Vittorio Omarini, 1902.

Frau, Ombretta, and Cristina Gragnani. *Sottoboschi letterari: Sei Case Studies fra Otto e Novecento*. Florence: Firenze UP, 2011.

Freud, Sigmund. *The Ego and the Id*. Trans. Joan Riviere. Ed. James Strachey. New York: Norton, 1960.

———. "Mourning and Melancholia." (1917) *The Standard Edition of the Complete Psychological Works of Sigmund Freud*. Vol. 14. Trans. James Strachey. London: Hogarth Press, 1957.

Galli Mastrodonato, Paola I. "Il 'caso' Salgari e gli studi paraletterari in Italia." *Belphégor: Littérature populaire et culture médiatique* 1:1 (2001): n.p. http://etc.dal.ca/belphegor/

Gambarota, Paola. *Irresistible Signs: The Genius of Language and Italian National Identity*. Toronto: Toronto UP, 2011.

Giacobbe, Olindo. *Letteratura infantile*. Turin: Paravia, 1925.

——. *Letteratura infantile*. 4th ed. Turin: Paravia, 1937.

——. *Note di letteratura infantile*. 2nd ed. Rome: Giorgio Berlutti, 1923.

Giacosa, Piero. "Un postulato meno avvertito della dottrina dell'evoluzione." *R. Accad. d. sci. Atti* [Reale Accademia di Scienze di Torino] 48 (1913): 385–92.

Giolo, Gianni. "Arpalice Cuman Pertile, educatrice, poetessa e scrittrice per l'infanzia." 2012. 17 pages. www.giannigiolo.it/?Scheda_bibliografica%26nbsp%3B: Saggi:Arpalice_Cuman. Accessed 3 January 2016.

Guagnini, Elvio. Introduction. *Un romanzo in vapore: Da Firenze a Livorno: Guida storico-umoristica*. By Carlo Lorenzini. Ed. Roberto Randacchio. Collodi (Pistoia): Fondazione Nazionale Carlo Collodi; Florence: Giunti, 2010. 23–41.

Haeckel, Ernst. *The Evolution of Man: A Popular Exposition of the Principal Points of Human Ontogeny and Phylogeny*. 2 vols. New York: Appleton, 1898.

Hazard, Paul. *Books, Children and Men*. Trans. Marguerite Mitchell. Boston: Horn, 1983.

Harrowitz, Nancy. *Anti-Semitism, Misogyny and the Logic of Cultural Difference: Cesare Lombroso and Matilde Serao*. Lincoln: U of Nebraska P, 1994.

Hiller, Jonathan. "*Bodies that tell*": *Physiognomy, criminology, race and gender in late nineteenth-and early twentieth-century Italian literature and opera*. University of California, Los Angeles, ProQuest Dissertations Publishing, 2009. 3363906.

Ipsen, Carl. *Italy in the Age of Pinocchio: Children and Danger in the Liberal Era*. New York: Palgrave, 2006.

"Italian Americans." *Worldmark Encyclopedia of Cultures and Daily Life*. Ed. Timothy L. Gall and Jeneen Hobby. 2nd ed. Vol. 2: Americas. Detroit: Gale, 2009. 310–313. *Gale Virtual Reference Library*. Web. 6 Jan. 2014.

Kertzer, David I. and Marzio Barbagli, eds. *Family Life in the Long Nineteenth Century, 1789–1913*. Vol. 2, *The History of the European Family*. New Haven: Yale UP, 2002.

Kidd, Kenneth. *Freud in Oz: At the Intersections of Psychoanalysis and Children's Literature*. Minneapolis: U of Minnesota P, 2011.

"Klemens von Metternich." *Encyclopedia of World Biography*. 2nd ed. Vol. 10. Detroit: Gale, 2004. 533–536. *Gale Virtual Reference Library*. Web. 5 Sept. 2015.

Kristeva, Julia. *Black Sun: Depression and Melancholia*. Trans. Leon S. Roudiez. New York: Columbia UP, 1989.

——. *New Maladies of the Soul*. Trans. Ross Guberman. New York: Columbia UP, 1995.

Kroha, Lucienne. "The Novel, 1879–1920." *A History of Women's Writing in Italy*. Ed. Letizia Panizza and Sharon Wood. Cambridge: Cambridge UP, 2000. 164–176.

LaCapra, Dominick. *Writing History, Writing Trauma*. Baltimore: Johns Hopkins UP, 2001.

LaValva, Rosamaria. *The Eternal Child: The Poetry and Poetics of Giovanni Pascoli*. Chapel Hill: Annali d'italianistica, 1999.

Lepschy, Anna Laura. "The Popular Novel: 1850–1920." *A History of Women's Writing in Italy*. Ed. Letizia Panizza and Sharon Wood. Cambridge: Cambridge UP, 2000. 177–189.

Lewis, David. *Reading Contemporary Picturebooks*. London: Routledge Falmer, 2001.

Lollo, Renata. "Catholic Children's Literature in Italy in the 19th and 20th Centuries." *Religion, Children's Literature and Modernity in Western Europe, 1750–2000*. Ed. Jan de Maeyer. Leuven: Leuven UP, 2005. 195–213.

Lombroso, Cesare, and Guglielmo Ferrero. *Criminal Woman, the Prositute and the Normal Woman*. Trans. Nicole Hahn Rafter and Mary Gibson. Durham: Duke UP, 2004.

———. *La donna delinquente, la prostituta, e la donna normale*. Turin: Roux, 1893.

———. *The Female Offender*. New York: Philosophical Library, 1958.

Lucas, Ann Lawson. "The Archetypal Adventures of Emilio Salgari." *New Companion: A Journal of Comparative and General Literary Studies* 20 (Autumn 1995): n.p.

———. Ed. *Gunpowder and Sealing-Wax: Nationhood in Children's Literature*. Market Harborough, UK: Troubador, 1977.

———. "Salgari, the Atlas and the Microscope." *Literature and Travel*. Ed. Michael Hume. Atlanta: Rodopi, 1992. 79–91.

Lyttelton, Adrian. "Politics and Society 1870–1915." *The Oxford Illustrated History of Italy*. Ed. George Holmes. Oxford: Oxford UP, 2001. 235–63.

Manson, Michel. "Children's Literature, Religion and Modernity in the Latin Countries (France, Italy, Spain). *Religion, Children's Literature and Modernity in Western Europe, 1750–2000*. Ed. Jan de Maeyer. Leuven: Leuven UP, 2005. 175–194.

Mazzoni, Cristina. "Treasure to Trash, Trash to Treasure: Dolls and Waste in Italian Children's Literature." *Children's Literature Association Quarterly* 37.3 (Fall 2012): 250–65.

McFarlane, Andrew. "How the UK's First Fatal Car Accident Unfolded." *BBC News Magazine*. 17 August 2010. www.bbc.com/news/magazine-10987606. Accessed 2 January 2016.

Mencarani, Patrizia. *Piccoli italiani leggono: La letteratura per l'infanzia tra il 1860 e il 1890*. Rome: Cromografica Roma, 2013. Self-published.

Merger, Michèle. Preface. *Un romanzo in vapore: Da Firenze a Livorno: Guida storico-umoristica*. By Carlo Lorenzini. Ed. Roberto Randacchio. Collodi (Pistoia): Fondazione Nazionale Carlo Collodi; Florence: Giunti, 2010. 14–19.

Miele, Gina. "Luigi Capuana: Unlikely Spinner of Fairy Tales?" *Marvels & Tales* 23.2 (2009): 300–324.

Mitchell, Katherine. *Italian Women Writers: Gender and Everyday Life in Fiction and Journalism 1870–1910*. Toronto: U of Toronto P, 2014.

Muñiz Muñiz, Maria de las Nieves. "Tecniche di Capuana novelliere (Per una rilettura di *Scurpiddu*)." *Problemi: Periodico Quadrimestrale di Cultura* 92 (1991): 285–95.

Murray, Peter, and Linda Murray, eds. *Dictionary of Christian Art*. Oxford: Oxford UP, 2004.

Myers, Lindsay. "'Flying the Flag': Arturo Rossato's Fantasy Novel, *L'aeroplano di Girandolino*." *Children's Literature and Culture of the First World War*. Ed. Lissa Paul, Rosemary Ross Johnston, and Emma Short. New York: Routledge, 2016. 30–47.

———. *Making the Italians: Poetics and Politics of Italian Children's Fantasy*. Bern: Peter Lang, 2012.

National Library of Norway. "All about Henrik Ibsen." Oslo, Norway. http://
ibsen.nb.no/id/11166494.0. Accessed 23 December 2015.

Niceforo, Alfredo. *L'Italia barbara contemporanea.* Milan: Remo Sandron,
1898.

Nikolajeva, Maria. "Children's Literature as a Cultural Code; A Semiotic Approach to History." *Aspects and Issues in the History of Children's Literature.* Ed. Maria Nikolajeva. Westport: Greenwood, 1995. 39–48.

Nodelman, Perry. "Decoding the Images: How Picture Books Work." *Understanding Children's Literature.*2nd ed. Ed. Peter Hunt. New York: Routledge,
2005. 128–139.

———. "Former Editor's Comments: Or, The Possibility of Growing Wiser."
Children's Literature Association Quarterly 35 (Fall 2010): 230–42.

———. "The Other: Orientalism, Colonialism, and Children's Literature."
Children's Literature Quarterly 17 (Spring 1992–Winter 1993): 29–35.

———. "Pleasure and Genre: Speculations on the Characteristics of Children's
Fiction." *Children's Literature* 28 (2000): 1–14.

Orestano, Francesca. "On the Italian Front: Salvator Gotta's *Piccolo Alpino*
(1926)." *Children's Literature and Culture of the First World War.* Ed. Lissa
Paul, Rosemary Ross Johnston, and Emma Short. New York: Routledge,
2016. 48–59.

O'Sullivan, Emer."Comparative Children's Literature." *PMLA* 126 (Jan. 2011):
189–196.

———. "Does Pinocchio have an Italian Passport? What is Specifically National
and What is International about Classics of Children's Literature." *The
Translation of Children's Literature: A Reader.* Ed. Gillian Lathey. Clevedon:
Multilingual Matters, 2006: 146–162.

———. "Imagology Meets Children's Literature." *International Research in
Children's Literature* 4.1 (2011): 1–14.

Pallottino, Paola, ed. *L'occhio della tigre: Alberto Della Valle fotografo e
illustratore salgariano.* Palermo: Sellerio, 2000.

Palumbo, Patrizia, ed. *A Place in the Sun: Africa in Italian Colonial Culture
from Post Unification to the Present.* Berkeley: U of California P, 2003.

Pancaldi, Giuliano. *Darwin in Italy: Science across Cultural Frontiers.* Trans.
Ruey Brodine Morelli. Bloomington: Indiana UP, 1991.

Panizza, Letizia, and Sharon Wood, eds. *A History of Women's Writing in
Italy.* Cambridge: Cambridge UP, 2000.

Pascoli, Giovanni. *Il fanciullino.* Ed. Giorgio Agamben. Milan: Feltrinelli, 1996.

Pavlik, Anthony. "'A Special Kind of Reading Game': Maps in Children's Literature." *International Research in Children's Literature* 3.1 (July 2010): 28–43.

Perella, Nicolas J. "Brief Remarks on the Illustrations." *The Adventures of
Pinocchio/Le avventure di Pinocchio.* By Carlo Collodi. Trans. and Introd.
Perella. Berkeley: U of California P, 1986. 76–79.

Pitrè, Giuseppe. *The Collected Sicilian Folk and Fairy Tales of Giuseppe Pitrè.*
Ed. Jack Zipes and Joseph Russo. New York: Routledge, 2009.

Pius X. *On the Doctrines of the Modernists (Pascendi Dominici Gregis) and
Syllabus Condemning the Errors of the Modernists (Lamentabili Sane).*
Boston: Daughters of St. Paul, n.d.

Pizzi, Katia. "Building a Nation: The National Question in Vamba's *Giornalino
della Domenica,* First Series (1906–1911). *Children's Literature Association
Quarterly* 28 (Winter 2003): 203–209.

Pozzo, Felice. "Il sorriso di Seghira, la zattera della Medusa e la sete di Re Bango." Introduction. *I drammi della schiavitù*. By Emilio Salgari. Turin: Viglongo, 1992. xix–xxxii.

Propp, Vladimir. *Morphology of the Folktale*. Trans. Laurence Scott. Austin: U of Texas P, 1984.

Rank, Otto. *The Myth of the Birth of the Hero and Other Writings*. Trans. F. Robbins and Smith Ely Jelliffe. New York: Vintage, 1964.

Re, Lucia. "Passion and Sexual Difference: The Risorgimento and the Gendering of Writing in Nineteenth-Century Italian Culture." *Making and Remaking Italy: The Cultivation of National Identity around the Risorgimento*. Ed. Albert Russell Ascoli and Krystyna von Henneberg. New York: Berg, 2001. 155–202.

Restieaux Hawkes, Louise. *Before and After Pinocchio: A Study of Italian Children's Books*. Paris: The Puppet Press, 1933.

Richardson, Brian. "Questions of Language." *The Combridge Companion to Modern Italian Culture*. Ed. Zygmunt G. Baranski and Rebecca J. West. Cambridge: Cambridge UP, 2001. 63–79.

Rose, Jacqueline. *The Case of Peter Pan, or, the Impossibility of Children's Fiction*. London: Macmillan Press, 1984.

Sarti, Vittorio. *Bibliografia salgariana*. 1st ed. Milan: Libreria Malavasi, 1990.

———. *Nuova bibliografia salgariana*. 2nd ed. Turin: S. Pignatone, 1994.

Seward, Desmond. *Metternich: The First European*. New York: Viking, 1991.

Seymour, Mark. *Debating Divorce in Italy: Marriage and the Making of Modern Italians, 1860–1974*. New York: Palgrave Macmillan, 2006.

Sighele, Scipio. *Eva moderna*. Milan: Treves, 1910.

Sinibaldi, Caterini. "Pinocchio, a Political Puppet: The Fascist Advetnures of Collodi's Novel." *Italian Studies* 66.3 (November 2011): 333–52.

Somigli, Luca, and Mario Moroni. "Modernism in Italy: An Introduction." *Italian Modernism: Italian Culture between Decadentism and Avant-Garde*. Ed. Luca Somigli and Mario Moroni. Toronto: U of Toronto P, 2004. 3–31.

Spackman, Barbara. "*Puntini, Puntini, Puntini*: Motherliness as Masquerade in Sibilla Aleramo's *Una donna*." *MLN* 124 Supplement (2009): S210–S223.

Spinazzola, Vittorio. *Pinocchio & C.: La grande narrativa italiana per ragazzi*. Milan: Il saggiatore, 1997.

Stephens, John. "Analyzing Texts: Linguistics and Stylistics." *Understanding Children's Literature* 2nd ed. Ed. Peter Hunt. New York: Routledge, 2005.73–85.

———. "Representation of Place in Australian Children's Picture Books." *Voices from Far Away: Current Trends in International Children's Literature Research*. Ed. Maria Nikolajeva. Stockholm, 1995. 97–118.

Stewart-Steinberg, Suzanne. *The Pinocchio Effect: On Making Italians, 1860–1920*. Chicago: U of Chicago P, 2008.

Sòrgoni, Barbara. "Italian Anthropology and the Africans: The Early Colonial Period." *A Place in the Sun: Africa in Italian Colonial Culture from Post-Unification to the Present*. Ed. Patrizia Palumbo. Berkeley: U of California P, 2003. 62–80.

Tamburini, Luciano, ed. *Cuore*. By Edmondo De Amicis. Turin: Einaudi, 1974.

Tribunella, Eric L. *Melancholia and Maturation: The Use of Trauma in American Children's Literature*. Knoxville: U of Tennessee P, 2010.

———. "*The Wind in the Willow* as Horror: Kenneth Grahame and the Motorcar." *42nd Annual Children's Literature Association Conference.* Richmond, VA. June 19, 2015.

Truglio, Maria. "African Plots in Italian Children's Literature: Cherubini's *Pinocchio in Affrica.*" *MLN Italian Issue* 126:1 (Jan. 2011): 114–136.

———. "Annie in Wonderland: Vivanti's *Sua Altezza!* and Italian Children's Literature During Fascism." *Quaderni d'italianista* 25 (2004): 121–142.

———. "Dino Buzzati's *La famosa invasione degli orsi in Sicilia* and the Possibilites of Children's Literature." *California Italian Studies* 2.2 (2011). http://escholarship.org/item/1963d93x.

———. "Garibaldi's Shadows: Heroism and Melancholia in Italian Children's Literature." *Children's Literature* 43 (2015): 51–83.

———. "Wise Gnomes, Nervous Astronauts and a Very Bad General: The Children's Books of Umberto Eco and Eugenio Carmi." *Children's Literature* 36 (2008): 115–144.

Welle, John P. "The Magic Lantern, the Illustrated book, and the Beginnings of the Culture Industry: Intermediality in Carlo Collodi's *La laterna magica di Giannettino.*" *The Printed Media in Fin de-siècle Italy: Publishers, Writers, and Readers.* Ed. Ann Hallamore Caesar, Gabriella Romani, and Jennifer Burns. London: Modern Humanities Research Association and Maney, 2011.

Wunderlich, Richard, and Thomas J. Morrissey. *Pinocchio Goes Postmodern: Perils of a Puppet in the United States.* New York: Routledge, 2002.

Zaccaria, Giuseppe. "Invernizio, Carolina." *Dizionario biografico degli italiani.* Vol. 62. Treccani, 2004. Accessed 1 January 2016. www.treccani.it/enciclopedia/carolinainvernizio_%28Dizionario_Biografico%29/.

Zipes, Jack. *Breaking the Magic Spell: Radical Theories of Folk and Fairy Tales.* Revised ed. Lexington: UP of Kentucky, 2002.

———, ed. *The Great Fairy Tale Tradition from Straparola and Basile to the Brothers Grimm.* New York: Norton, 2001.

———, ed. *The Oxford Companion to Fairy Tales.* 2nd ed. Oxford: Oxford UP, 2015.

———. *When Dreams Came True: Classical Fairy Tales and Their Tradition.* New York: Routledge, 1999.

Index